Making Strategy and Organization Compatible

Originally published as *Strategie et Sociologie de l'Entreprise* by Village Mondial/Pearson Education

Making Strategy and Organization Compatible

Claude Michaud

Jean-Claude Thoenig

Translated by Malcolm Stewart

© Village Mondial/Pearson Education, Paris 2001
Translation copyright © Malcolm Stewart 2003

First published 2003 by
PALGRAVE MACMILLAN
Houndmills, Basingstoke, Hampshire RG21 6XS and
175 Fifth Avenue, New York, N.Y. 10010
Companies and representatives throughout the world

PALGRAVE MACMILLAN is the global academic imprint of the Palgrave Macmillan division of St. Martin's Press, LLC and of Palgrave Macmillan Ltd. Macmillan® is a registered trademark in the United States, United Kingdom and other countries. Palgrave is a registered trademark in the European Union and other countries.

ISBN 1–4039–1123–1 hardback

This book is printed on paper suitable for recycling and made from fully managed and sustained forest sources.

A catalogue record for this book is available from the British Library.

A catalog record for this book is available from the Library of Congress.

Editing and origination by
Curran Publishing Services, Norwich

10 9 8 7 6 5 4 3 2 1
12 11 10 09 08 07 06 05 04 03

Printed and bound in Great Britain by
Creative Print & Design (Wales),
Ebbw Vale

CONTENTS

Contents

LIST OF FIGURES

LIST OF TABLES

This book reflects the relatively long experience in lecturing and research consultancy that the authors have been privileged to amass through direct, often daily, contact with large organizations, their executives and their staff.

Firms tend to follow the same mould and favour the same profile. They differ little one from the other. Their reports seem indistinguishable. Any attempt to point up differences or specific traits is a bold step that may incur penalties.

Firms also may quite often dismiss or forget the fact that they are moral communities. Top executives may for instance over-emphasize the idea that people are basically driven by financial opportunism and short-term self-interest. They pay little attention to the fact that, as members of a social and human organization, employees and managers are also driven by feelings such as sharing a common identity or belonging to a long-term collective venture, and by common values and norms. To speak of shared destiny and internal culture sounds somewhat anachronistic when short termism and performance hold sway with the force of law. Wrongly, moreover, the community dimension of the firm as a human and social organization conjures up a management style consisting of moral manipulation and out-moded humanism.

We believe that in fact the problem is deeper, more diffuse and rarely identified. Does the firm not have something more to offer in order to mobilize its membership? What really differentiates it from other social groups and thus brings about a sense of collective constructiveness at its heart? In other words, would being employed in this firm or elsewhere be the same for individuals: simply the opportunity to have a job or practise a trade? The firm as such would have disappeared to become no more than an extension of the labour market.

The very justification of the firm rings hollow. The customers and the owners are usually considered as the two sacred benchmarks for its existence. The firm must create value for both. The observed facts look different, however. They do not necessarily chime with the stated objectives in every case.

On the one hand, shareholder value, so often cited as an unbearable constraint imposed from outside, in fact becomes a cloak for a less explicit purpose: allowing the executive suite of the company to gain a level of autonomy that frees it from any third party control. CEOs may use the stock markets as levers to finance the takeovers of competitors, using high-rated stock in preference to cash. The influence and pressure of shareholders on the conduct of affairs are none the stronger for that. By inflating their size and diluting share ownership, company executives become *de facto* accountable to nobody.

On the other hand, nobody listens properly to the customer. It is accepted that marketing has won and is legitimized everywhere. But it has also become a tool of the occult in relation to customers. Because it remains stuck in its category analysis, responding only to quantitative variation, it is rarely able to anticipate new demands or potential. What is more, it devalues intuition, sensitivity to faint messages from the marketplace, and the qualitative. Innovation itself becomes a risk against which marketing serves as a protection.

The firm is threatened by the temptation to retreat into itself and by the phenomenon of self-sufficiency at the very moment when it is becoming global. To be precise, two types of disconnection, the obvious and the consequential, are at work.

First, the firm is at risk of cutting itself off from external reality. It rationalizes about the market while it ignores its customers. It measures big numbers and is blind to emerging trends. It follows along behind the course of events while the competition is increasing speed.

Second, it also risks cutting itself off from its internal reality. A gulf appears between executives and staff, between head office and business units. The top does not take account of the messages from below. Those at the lower levels do not understand the intentions of those who act above. The company does not benefit from the varied appraisals of the core aspects that are essential to it. A single hierarchical mindset becomes established. Instead of being viewed as a potential source of enrichment, any alternative becomes a threat that must be repressed.

Such a situation has serious consequences. General management finds it difficult to hear or accept information that is both credible and appropriate. The growing recourse to so-called internal communications (house journals, video circuits, seminars, company sessions with the CEO and the like) is a poor substitute. The messages are out of tune, stereotyped or quite simply empty. They do not mobilize. They do not encourage a lasting capacity to act collectively to build a shared future.

This weakness in communication poses the question of management's competence. In fact, the inability to construct messages reveals a problem with the originator. If the message sent out by head office is not clear or believable, it means that the actions of head office are also not comprehensible or trustworthy.

At present there is a relative crisis in head offices. Almost all find it difficult to mobilize their operational units. The stated strategies do not match up with daily behaviour. Head office isolation grows, while operator frustration, even cynicism, becomes entrenched.

The remedies that are adopted usually make the sickness worse rather than cure it. Such is the case with the accelerated rotation of managerial executives, the adoption of bipolar organization models (head office and business units), recourse to virtual market mechanisms to manage the relationships between the various functions at the core of the company, or even the veneer of 'best practice'. Everything is thrown in and everything is provisional. Where interpretation of an action needs to be reinforced in a community, such remedies end up by further destroying the cognitive matrix without which there can be no categories of shared thought or reserves of trust (Courpasson, 1999).

The firm that survives cannot be likened to a kit or a Lego game, some one-size-fits-all made up of commonplace components that anyone could assemble to produce the expected outcome immediately. At a time when competitive positions are more than ever fragile and short lived, the economic battle demands a specific answer, not some mass-produced product that can be exchanged for an identical one like a Kleenex, and one that cannot be copied by a third party, which means by competitors. In fact, the capacity to act together develops through time, through shared history and internal socialization. Such phenomena are important, but do many executives consider them as part of their daily concern and as manageable?

We are convinced that the function of general management contains the answer to these difficulties to a large extent. We also know that few CEOs are successful in handling them. Our aim is to facilitate better formalization and conceptualization of the stakes, the problems and the solutions of cognitive fine-tuning, improvization or trial and error – in short, a kind of creative tinkering – as a major way to make strategy and organization compatible.

The book is based on research projects that have been financed jointly by CEDEP (European Centre for Permanent Education, Fontainebleau), INSEAD (Fontainebleau) and CNRS (Group for the analysis of public policy and the Cachan École normale supérieure). We are grateful to the companies of CEDEP and to their directors who have agreed to be studied and who have never fobbed us off with platitudes.

CHAPTER 1

In Praise of Complexity

Apparently, common sense has finally won in the field of management. In our present day world, those firms that win are necessarily the ones whose organization is simple and whose strategy is univocal.

The organizational model essential for daily operation is a source of costs and problems. All the more reason to reduce them in the first place. No top-heavy bureaucracies, no organizational charts that look like plant pipe-work. The task is to slim down, decentralize and empower. A good model is by nature easily readable, quickly understood, stable, transparent to all its members and to outsiders. Simplifying is the key to economic success. The clear economic model goes with the simple organizational model.

1.1 How to Make Things Simple in a World That is Not Simple

The managers of firms see themselves surrounded by all kinds of publicity and slogans that hammer home the same message. Financial analysts give preference to clear structures and univocal strategies. Boards of directors detest functional services and praise the systematic subcontracting of skills considered to be secondary. Experts laud the value of a management based on the military model of platoons of soldiers or guerrillas: that is, small mobile units, operating in the front line and led by an officer who enjoys great operational autonomy. What CEO would dare to publicly state the contrary?

The conduct of firms is thus reduced to an art and to techniques that make use of a few simple truths that claim universal validity and tolerate no ambiguity.

The international consultant sells the best practices, devised and distributed like standard products, necessary for everyone and easily consumed. The chief executive thinks about the organization of the 165,000 people that he manages as though it was internally like a virtual market in which the 658 subsidiary companies it consists of are made to compete with one another.

Simplifying is considered as a requirement for internal communication: to be understood by the lowest levels of the hierarchy a message has to avoid any nuance and has to be unidimensional. It is also considered as a requirement for external communication: to charm financial analysts and media, formal structures and policy statements have to be politically correct, which means clear cut and transparent. Simplifying is perceived to be possible thanks both to the qualities that the new information technologies are supposed to bring – direct, unequivocal and transparent communication that is understood by everyone identically – and to the fact that managers share a common training, chiefly through the MBA mould. In short, simplifying is the approved solution to the management of firms that have become unwieldy, as if its leaders could succeed as global players by ignoring the importance of local specificities and instead considering the world as a single, homogenous economic space that can be managed in some single, universally applicable 'best way'.

It is often assumed that the right solution for a company headquarters implies that its main functions are brought down to three and to three only. It lays down a strategic aim, it formulates a financial/economic criterion for evaluating the performance of all managers, and it appraises quarterly quantitative indicators on economic and financial performances provided by controllers and auditors. In fact, there is little to differentiate it from a financial holding or conglomerate head office characteristic of the 1960s.

Such a firm externalizes 92 per cent of its operations, keeping to itself only those skills deemed to be key, the ideal being that these are restricted to one or two at most. Examples include marketing in the clothing industry and design and development in the advanced technological industries.

Mergers between giant firms of different nationality frighten no one. Some certainly turn out to be spectacular failures. Daimler suffers from absorbing Chrysler. But the setbacks are seen as exceptions, put down to special circumstances: the personality of the chief executive, cultural shock, clumsiness or bad luck. Meanwhile, faith in the economies of scale remains strong, feeding the belief that the size and globalization of an organization are compatible with simplicity.

Does a firm recognize difficulties? Its management dismisses one or two top people and seeks solutions outside. To correct an unsatisfactory profit level the magic solution of the condottiere is adopted. In order to make operations at the bottom less opaque to head office, a specialist consultancy in organizational re-engineering is engaged; its consultants spend several weeks in the firm and promise immediate profitability in return for full authority.

The above judgement may appear severe. The aim is certainly not to caricature the daily facts of life of firms or pass judgement on the intelligence of individual managers. The pursuit of simplicity certainly expresses a practice; it represents above all an acceptable method of reasoning, if not a kind of ideal in a world where firms see their benchmarks fading, in which productivity no longer has much meaning, people and organizations are becoming mere numbers and local connections are drifting apart. The contrast is striking when we see them having recourse to network systems in the very name of simplicity, whereas these networks are much more intangible and delicate to manage than pyramids.

1.2 Strengths and Weaknesses of Organizational Simplicity

We need to reconsider common sense. It is certainly true that in practice it is not easy to simplify. One has only to look at the manager's daily routine. The problem is much more serious however. The simple firm is fragile and vulnerable to threats at short notice.

Organizational complexity is not by nature a cost or a problem. It is an investment, a weapon or an essential asset in a world traversed by the dynamics of hypercompetition.

In the immediate and short term, simplification produces valuable effects. It helps achieve economies of scale. It allows redundancy and double employment to be done away with. It makes for greater clarity of tasks and their performance. It gives shareholders the comfortable feeling that they understand the firm.

In the medium and long term, on the other hand, simplification has destructive effects. It leads to regression. A firm where the organizational management is too basic and the internal relational set-up too homogenous – that is, too impoverished – is predisposed to lower profitability and inexorable economic decline. In fact, the utopia of simplicity is eaten away by time. Sooner or later, the firm will have to react and adapt to the turbulence that will disturb its area of activity. Simple organizations struggle with the instability and discontinuity of their time horizon (Dupuy and Thoenig, 1986).

Suppose profitability targets give priority to immediate goals. The solution is obvious. What is required is the simplest possible organization, containing only those functions that create added value and a flow of benefits that the market absorbs immediately. This stance is typical of a positioning that is referred to as an exploitation strategy.

The firm milks the cow. It takes maximum advantage of what it knows best how to do and produce, and as quickly as possible. It is thus called upon to adopt a strongly decentralized management style. This is based on homogenized procedures. It focuses solely on quantifiable data. It gives preference to multipurpose, interchangeable units. It has recourse to external mercenaries who are taken on to use what they know and have learnt elsewhere. Adoption of the combat platoon model of the US Marine Corps becomes a must for companies wishing to be nominated as the best run (Peters and Waterman, 1982). The commando approach certainly achieves rapid results in strategic contexts where the firm can rely on skills acquired in the past for guidance in the present. Even so, in the medium term all the income operators will die from the depletion of their resources.

Suppose now that the medium term is uncertain, unstable and turbulent. Tomorrow may well not be like today, whether in terms of consumer behaviour, available technology or the nature of the competition. In this case, the firm needs the capacity and potential that allow for anticipation, innovation and flexibility. It needs to be able to prepare today the new answers that are likely, but not certain, to bring it income or advantages tomorrow, and what is more using methods and products that do not yet exist.

The organizational demands required for this are the opposite of, and incompatible with, a logic of simplicity. Management for the medium term in fact requires at least four types of collective skills and capacities:

- The firm effectively explores different avenues from its current routines; it identifies and learns new ways of doing things more quickly than its competitors.
- It gives preference to permanent systems of internal cross-fertilization that allow different and almost spontaneous recombinations of skills and approach to emerge.
- Its members demonstrate strong loyalty to it at all levels through the fact that their decisional behaviour follows the strategic targets outlined by top management.
- They feel and share a common destiny.

Organizations that are oversimplified suffer from congenital deficiencies where the medium term is concerned. In fact, the consequences of extreme simplification are a range of difficulties:

- too marked a disconnection between strategic ambitions and organizational actions, between the policies and operation of the organization
- a persistent inability to react quickly enough to the unexpected, the key weapon in military campaigns as in the economic arena
- a chronic weakness in managing heterogeneous environments and specific regional markets
- handling dynamic situations using simple static structures
- inability to manage different horizons concurrently.

This last point is fundamental for one reason at least. On the one hand, in the medium term the operators eventually die out owing to the extinction of their income; on the other hand, in the short term, it is often the innovators who die from a lack of tangible economic profitability. Knowing how to manage both the short term and the long term, that is, securing an income while at the same time preparing for innovation, implies that the firm should develop a complex organizational model at its core.

1.3 Why do Hybrid Models Offer an Advantage?

Competition demands that firms respond at the same time to two requirements that are mutually contradictory: short-term security and medium-term development. They must be profitable and they must also regenerate. In other words, they are forced to be both simple and complex. This is what we mean by organizational complexity.

Those firms that survive in the economic battle are the ones that know how to reconcile the logic of exploitation and that of regeneration by using hybrid organizational set-ups routinely or constantly. General management that demonstrates the ability to manage, build or improvise organizational complexity creates a competitive advantage for the firm as a whole; it becomes a decisive hidden asset that competitors find hard to copy. For it is a fact that the economics of hypercompetition is distinguished from normal competitive situations by the fact that it compels firms to face two simultaneous challenges. First, the time horizon linked to an income becomes short and uncertain. Second, regeneration must operate at its core in an endogenous way. The dynamic of hypercompetition classifies the organizational model that a firm adopts along with the two or three key activities to ensure its survival.

One misunderstanding should be cleared up immediately. Complex does not mean the same thing as complicated, if by the latter one understands designing an organization that is confused, cumbersome, erratically driven and burdened unnecessarily with details and props that have no justification. The bogey of bureaucracy is sometimes an easy foil that comes close to demagogy and electioneering. While it may allow the gurus to sell their consultation services, it blurs the essential distinction that must be established between complication and complexity. For complexity as such reflects the necessity for a firm at any instant to find organizational solutions that also satisfy the requirements arising from different performance demands of various kinds, the consequences of which may ultimately be mutually contradictory or antinomic. Complexity reflects real life, with its muddles, opaque relationships and causality systems that are clearly or badly defined.

In other words, managers find themselves deprived of two soft options: stability and unanimity. The solution required tomorrow morning will no longer be the one used today, which itself is based on principles or criteria different from those used yesterday. Moreover, there is no pure ideal type, no universal standard for an unambiguous organizational model. Managing therefore becomes an art and a skill in constructing and implementing hybrid organizations and fragile compromises. The trend towards management rationalization through procedures and structures ceases to be necessarily desirable and efficient when the survival of firms takes priority through their ability to improvise in so far as systems of action are concerned.

How can one enable a logic of the market and a logic of the non-market to coexist at the centre of a firm? How does one mobilize the same services and people in an exploitation strategy and a withdrawal strategy at the same time? There are two ways of handling this need, neither of which is very satisfactory from experience.

One approach is for the firm to separate into watertight compartments those activities dedicated to innovation and those that manage the existing firm. There are some well-known examples. At the beginning of the 1980s IBM took up the challenge from Apple by creating at its core a secret parallel organization. The idea was to keep the development of this innovation from the rest of the firm, which still bathed in the glory of its success and reacted sceptically to anything that went against its way of thinking.

The other, more widespread approach is often adopted by a firm that wishes to secure a niche market or to regenerate to acquire start-up companies. It seeks out sources of regeneration that it does not itself possess, and cherishes the hope of being able to inject the innovation thus acquired, at the right time, into its own portfolio (rather than the teams who conceived it); this potential is, of course, something that it has not had to finance, give birth to or see through its early stages of life. There are numerous examples of what often seems to be a game of free-riders or contemporary plunder. Through raiding the market, the firm hopes to assimilate an exogenous contribution.

Now, in many cases, the innovation does not emerge, and may even be rejected by the purchasing company. This is because there is scarcely ever a match between the two totally different worlds: size, management style, performance criteria, and the like. In addition, processes have to exist and be constructed that allow the innovation to be absorbed, an operation that has to be shared by everyone in their existing jobs, with the corollary that the success of the existing firm should not be put at risk. Any innovation, however material or technical it may be, carries with it and reflects an interpretation of the world, the marketplace and the client. It is therefore also a cognitive phenomenon. Failure is assured if a firm that imports the innovation neglects this dimension, whether owing to oversight or through incompatibility between its own knowledge and that carried by the exogenous innovation.

We propose to examine an approach less attractive to the mathematical mind, but more efficient from the point of view of the principles of reality. Hybrid methods of organizational operation, which do not come from a pure, univocal and ad hoc model but are improvised on contact with space–time circumstances, may arise from a logic of action that is perfectly rational (Powell, 1987). What does organizational improvisation in actions mean? Who ensures that it can exist in the firm? What exactly does the management of organizational complexity look like? Why does knowledge that is shared through the language of action give the key to the reconciliation between exploitation and renewal?

1.4 Managing Complexity

Three ideas sometimes taken as established truths do not withstand the test of action/experience:

- Believing that the firm will guarantee its own survival in the medium term by employing the best experts, the most creative and innovative brains, and allocating the most money if not importance to innovation.
- Maintaining a strict division of work by confining innovation and non-market activity within the R&D department, while making exploitation and the market exclusively the remit of the sales staff.
- Hoping that all that is needed is to convince staff morally and intellectually of the benefits of and need for renewal.

Management is an empirical activity, not a problem for general discussion or a subject of intellectual speculation. When all is said and done, the crucial factors are the behaviour and choices made by managers from day to day, not their beliefs or opinions, bearing in mind that – human organizations being what they are – words do not necessarily reflect actions and vice versa.

We need to demystify once and for all the connotations of the term complexity in relation to organizations. The word is intimidating in itself, since it relates to science and modern mathematics. It is sometimes regarded as a lesser evil, either in relation to a Cartesian ideal of the business world, or in relation to a vision that likens economic activity to a mechanical universe. Even if, for a small number of managers, complexity is a weapon that they often use with skill and success, it really only amounts to some sort of second-rate cuisine, which unfortunately has to be undertaken, but which is not the stuff of heroic leaders or the trademark of minds that see themselves as knowledge experts.

In fact, however, managing complexity is the essence of management. The problem underpins and ultimately sanctions the function of voluntary management within the firm.

Organizational complexity is built or destroyed proactively. It is not something natural or spontaneous. From this point of view, head office or general management has a fundamental, even irreplaceable, role. In other words, this responsibility cannot be delegated to a third party, such as a consultancy or service department. It presupposes a vigilance and alertness at all times on the part of central management, at a level as high if not higher than all the other tasks that it has to deal with. It has also at the same time to be transmitted step by step throughout the firm, both vertically and horizontally. It does not exhaust itself in structures and analysis, but mobilizes emotion and intuition.

Management of organizational complexity stems from a very special quality: dynamic do-it-yourself. In contrast to the ready-for-use/plug-and-play, this kind of do-it-yourself management presupposes an intimate knowledge and awareness of the particular context of the manager's intervention, in the activities of the organization and the environment in which the firm operates. No solution that may be valid at one given moment or in one given context will necessarily ever be valid for other moments or in other contexts. Put another way, it is the cognitive and relational skills of the managers that ensure the qualities of intuition, understanding, flexibility and cooperation, without which the collective body that constitutes the firm cannot deal with environments that have apparently conflicting demands.

It is certainly not a bad thing to recall that the firm is an economic war machine whose efficiency depends largely on the people who staff it, that they must be motivated, and that the organization must know how to listen to its customers (Dupuy, 1999). But that is not the end of the story. If complexity is a prerequisite without which there would be no regeneration, it demands much more. It is the duty of its general managers to build and to develop a language space linking top and bottom, upstream and downstream in the firm. In other terms, organizational management has to be performed in terms of cognitive ability. Mutually compatible decision references have to flow across its various parts and members. They also have to be translated so that each part of the organization is able to internalize them and adapt them. In other words, a community has to be built that shares common references for action and interpretation grids.

Organizational complexity requires a shared intelligence among the units and staff that make up the firm. It brings a dimension into play that is too often neglected by the management sciences: cognitive mechanisms. A firm offers strong potential for complexity – that is, compromise management that possesses the essential property of being durably and truly sustainable – when knowledge or language is shared at its core and where both common choice criteria for action and mutual trust in the execution of such collective choice are available. The way in which the organization's members carry out their activities, while taking into account what others do, ensures cooperation in situations fraught with uncertainty.

Such a collective patrimony is built and maintained from day to day. In other words, it is not a once and for all thing. It even has a propensity to self-destruct very quickly, in less time than it takes to emerge. The ability to decentralize and use common benchmarks to manage thousands of mutually compatible behaviours within a company is a measure of its ability to gear up to the everyday.

1.5 Shared Organizational Action Languages

The central argument presented and described in this book concerns the decisive position occupied by the languages of action.

To be more exact, it will be shown that, in any firm, there are systems of interpretation, cognitive beacons, ways of representing the world and action in that world. These languages form the basis of the choices made by the members of the organization. They guide their behaviour and their daily decisions. They are theories in use.

A peculiarity that complicates daily management lies in the fact that these languages are not generally explicit. The players assume that the criteria of choice and theories of action they embrace can be taken as read.

Another difficulty arises from the fact that these languages may be either shared by all the players (more precisely continuity is established between them) or, on the contrary, the various occupations, hierarchical levels and services have entirely different benchmarks, and cognitive discontinuities criss-cross the social fabric of the firm.

To respond to the necessary imperative of organizational complexity required by the hypercompetitive economy, it is not enough to apply the classic additives of procedures and structures, or to hope to replace them with the single vector of financial and symbolic remuneration. The function of integration between occupations, levels and different services is fuelled by the fact that common benchmarks are mobilized in the decisions these groups take in a context that is in other respects decentralized. In other words, foresight and compatibility flow first and foremost from the fact that cognitive networks link together people, occupations and services. This cognitive cohesion will be all the stronger where the firm and its management create conditions that allow the organization to generate its own language of action by itself.

The need for constant attention to be paid to cognitive processes is the main thesis of this book. They can be either a resource or a constraint for the success of the firm. In the context of hypercompetition, the competitive advantage gained by recourse to endogenous processes provides the prescription developed in the book.

We shall examine three questions in turn.

- Why is the question of the cognitive dimensions of action crucial for the success of firms? The following two chapters will show that the so-called hypercompetitive economies demand that firms simultaneously satisfy the imperatives of renewal in the medium term and the imperatives of exploitation in the short term. Reconciling these presents real problems. This can be assured and achieved through endogenically generated language.
- What is a language of action? Chapter 4 sets out a definition and presents the characteristics and properties for organizational action. Chapter 5 shows how, in a real multinational company, the phenomenon of languages appears and what consequences its content has for the conduct of business. A more technical appendix outlines the approaches for identifying their content and for gathering information in a firm.
- How does one act voluntarily on languages of action? The interpretation systems that the players in an organization call upon are neither inescapable nor unchangeable. On the contrary, to a certain extent, it is possible to remodel the type of knowledge that drives the firm. The final chapters re-establish the function of top management in a firm. Work at the top consists of three main tasks: spelling out the strategies of the firm and its organizational model, applying organizational complexity to meet the contradictory demands faced by the firm, and influencing the type of knowledge or language that permeates the firm.

CHAPTER 2

Building Bridges Between Management and Strategy

Firms pursue their ambitions. These are expressed more or less explicitly, sometimes in the form of general objectives (becoming and remaining the benchmark for the sector), sometimes as strategic positioning (achieving 30 per cent of a market sector in a given country within five years). However they are expressed, and whatever form they take, these ambitions come down to positioning and aims relating to profitability, the market, image, and so on.

Furthermore, firms are organizations: that is, social groups of people whose various parts are linked together through coordination and cooperation. Such control processes vary according to projects prescribed by the leaders of the firm which are used as means to fulfil economic ends.

2.1 Strategic Visions are Not Easily Put Into Practice

Basic common sense dictates that one's daily decision making should conform to one's stated objectives. In fact, it often happens that behaviours are not in line with preferences. Even the chief executive officer makes choices that contradict the policies he or she favours. Continuity between ambitions and actions does not occur by itself within firms. The firm has a medium-term horizon that its daily tasks prevent it from reaching. General management sets out objectives that the operational units do not share in their actions, even though the people involved are intellectually in sympathy. Implementation remains the Achilles' heel of most multinationals.

There is an important and well-known reason that is currently given to explain this shortcoming. The strategy imposed by top management may not necessarily be compatible with the systems of organizational operation at the centre, which influence the daily decision making of the operational units.

General management's mission is to articulate the strategic positioning of the firm that establishes its market profile, and the organizational model that controls its internal universe. Observance of the facts of daily life reveals a variety of examples and situations that suggest that this mission is far from apparent to, or given personal and lasting attention by, management. There are three important aspects to this.

- Priority is given to defining strategic aims and, as a consequence, day-to-day actions are neglected. Head office concentrates on the market and the competition, on the medium-term view, on formulating general targets. It steps back, if necessary cutting itself off voluntarily from the main body of the firm. It behaves like a prescriber of a desirable future, using its own discretion to impose its views (if not its orders) on the operational units, which find themselves responsible only for carrying them out mechanically.
- There is a dissociation between the formulation of strategic aims and the definition of organizational principles. The manager's right hand as it were does not know what the left hand is doing. Managers become prisoners of the pressure of events and act in a kind of neurotic rush that upsets the coherence of their actions. Head office may also be the victim of its own compartmentalization. The head of strategy and the head of management services avoid each other and do not coordinate their individual viewpoints.
- One or even both functions may be subcontracted to third parties. Internal or external consultants are called upon to help. They import their specific domains of expertise: this one scenarios of general politics, that one procedures for organizational change. Head office copes with this more or less effectively. It becomes its task to somehow reconcile the two. The worst scenario is when a complete system copying the best practice followed by competitors is delivered and sold to the top manager. Head office then becomes totally dependent on this, since it is supposed to be applying the recipes for success in an orthodox way.

It is true that management practice deserves some indulgence. Formulating one's aims and ambitions confers prestige in the scale of values and representations. In comparison, busying oneself with organizational matters is much less prestigious. The wide-open spaces of competition and the market are more attractive and loftier than menial work servicing the nuts and bolts at the centre of the firm. The former appeal to the analytical mind and to intuition. The latter seems banal and commonplace, conferring much less prestige among top management and their peers.

The days are long past when management books would praise the merits of a top manager who concentrated exclusively on two roles: that of the prophet, the Moses dictating the strategic plan, and that of the supreme management controller, the ultimate receiver of all operational data that revealed the extent to which the remainder of the firm conformed to the strategic plan. Yet if Harold Geneen, chief executive of ITT in the 1960s and 1970s, no longer appears as a contemporary heroic example, this ideal still retains its intellectual appeal. It stipulates that in a world said to be normal, the choice of strategy comes first and the choice of organizational model follows from it. In other words, the organizational configuration is the means by which the strategic objective is brought into play. In practice, one first needs to know where one wants to or can go; only then can one design an internal organization in line with this external ambition.

Of course, managers are not completely fooled by what may appear to be a pleasant illusion. Nevertheless, not everyone is ready to put it into perspective. One only has to teach on programmes of continuing education for management to be aware of this. Given that organizations are generally much more difficult, costly and slow to develop than strategies, it is ultimately just as realistic to choose strategic platforms that can be adopted by organizations in their present form. However, such a statement often leaves the public disappointed. Such realism with regard to resources is not the stuff of dreams or the ambition of MBA students.

Another obstacle is the organizational management.

The time has also definitely passed when the actual form of the organization was dismissed as a specific phenomenon, reducing management at best to universal principles (the illusion of the 'one best way' as reflected in Taylorian thinking) and to re-engineering through formal procedures (the illusion of the organization chart and profiling as being sufficient reasons for virtuous behaviour). Everyone will admit, intellectually at least, that it is unfortunately not sufficient to select the best personal profiles for there to be immediately good coordination, cooperation and communication: the illusion of alchemy through the elective affinities of the personalities.

The sociology of organizations that emphasizes the decisive importance of the power dynamics between the diverse parts of social systems still leaves many managers somewhat confused. On the one hand, with each environment possessing distinct characteristics compared with others, the message that one has to understand and pay attention to the internal environment before acting upon it suggests an approach that, albeit wrongly, the manager finds it hard to adopt there and then. On the other hand, and not without good reason, he or she is at a loss to find ways to integrate the particular behaviours appropriate for the different parts of this system into a final collective pattern. The manager is ready to admit intellectually that the firm makes up a pluralist system driven by power games and obeying a political dynamic. For him or her, reintroducing the rationality of economic aims into individual acts in the course of everyday activity remains quite a different matter, one that he or she must take pains to resolve.

2.2 When the Gap Between Ambition and Action Becomes Deadly

The discontinuity between ambitions and actions does not necessarily entail irreparably drastic or even fatal consequences. Reconciling politics and the organization is after all a classical and recurrent problem. What is more, many firms have gone through the twentieth century without much damage. The discrepancies caused by wide gaps were often offset or masked. There were virtual monopolies. Dominant market shares were accepted by the public authorities. Cartels allowed the weakest competitors to survive. Access to national markets was made difficult through technical regulations that acted as entry barriers. The national supply of goods and services was not developed so that it could immediately satisfy prime equipment needs.

Now everything points to this no longer being the case. In other words, the discrepancy or wide gap between ambition and action has become a key problem for firms. In real life, protection against competition has been reduced. Time horizons have shortened. The economic battlefield has changed radically. Financial death is now more sudden and more certain for anyone who does not know how to state and restate strategies and actions, a daily position and a future.

The essence of this assertion relates back to reasons that may be summarized in three statements that form the core of this book, the problem that justifies its existence.

- In order to survive, firms need simultaneously to exploit their competitive advantages in the short term and regenerate them in the medium term.
- They therefore oversimplify their method of organizational operation. They adopt models that are too weak, to the extent of destroying the complexity and hybridization without which there can be no internal renewal.
- By impoverishing their own cognitive capacity, they defeat their own goals in the medium term. They deprive themselves of the common languages that can unify the disparate interests of a group and hold together its contradictory demands.

Hence the paradox that victory of the short term, so often ascribed only to the influence of the gnomes of the financial and stock markets, is in fact relayed and amplified by the way that the managements of firms emasculate their own organization. The medium term goes by the board even though it is publicly proclaimed as an ambition.

Of course this phenomenon is not new in itself. But it has been exacerbated since the end of the twentieth century through the emergence of what is known as a hypercompetitive economy (Nelson and Winter, 1982). Fickle customers, the reduction in barriers to competition, innovation that has become the trivialized weapon of success, short-term pressures, all amount to factors that have profoundly and lastingly weakened the control of income for firms.

2.3 Immediate Monopolistic Rents and Future Monopolistic Rents

The term 'rent' here refers to a secure source of income derived from the control of an asset that is in some way unique or that allocates a quasi-monopolistic advantage (Schumpeter, 1967). Such an asset may be material (oil fields, weather conditions, technological innovations, etc.) or immaterial (know how etc.).

Setting a firm the task of pursuing competitive advantage is both the privilege and responsibility of general management. Business schools define competitive advantage as being based on numerous factors. The most common examples are the reduction of costs, provision of consistent quality, short time to market and the creation of various barriers to make it difficult for third parties to compete.

Such advantages are not absolute, but relative. They show a difference compared with third parties in a given area. They are not permanent or even very durable. Time regulates the economic order of the competitors.

Competitive advantages in fact constitute the visible or emergent part of physical or cultural characteristics that generate rent at a given moment and in a given context. Any advantage is competitive if and when it ensures a rent. A strategic ambition therefore appears as a search for rents. There is rent when a given characteristic of a firm provides it with temporary protection from competition and enables it to gain a surplus.

A rent comes from various sources. It may be the consequence of a gift from nature. It may be the legacy of past inventiveness. It may reflect a culture, a production method, a sense of tenacity, a climate of confidence and solidarity among the group. It may result from a protection provided by public law in the guise of a monopoly or customs duty. It is sometimes linked with risk-taking at a given moment, sometimes with experience gained over a long period of time.

A rent is the source of profits. It allows surpluses to be produced, which a particular firm takes advantage of and which separate it out from the other firms that operate in its sector or market niche. What to do with surpluses is a key question. Should they be distributed and used up immediately or hoarded for future use, reinvested in the activity that generated them or spent on other projects? Deciding on the place, the moment and the end use is a crucial act in establishing the aims of the firm. The general management in fact shapes the strategy through the use it makes of the products from the rents that the firm generates.

A head office may choose to focus comfortably on the short term. The long term is therefore not seen as an appropriate challenge. It thus acts out of either cynical opportunism or sheer negligence. Its directors may convince themselves that tomorrow will turn out to be the same as today, or they may even gamble on the ability of the firm to respond to events.

Nowadays, all rents dry up sooner or later. In particular, they can be qualified by the limited window of opportunity that they offer the firm in which to exploit them. Tomorrow's rent comes from work done well in advance, except when it is obtained by takeover or other external acquisition (public bid or acquiring a technical start-up company). Rents presuppose investment. They are characterized by uncertainty, and are therefore themselves subject to a time horizon.

Hypercompetition is defined as a context where the exploitation time is shorter than the time for rent preparation. Protection for the here and now is diluted, even though that for tomorrow is not guaranteed. The pharmaceutical industry is a recognized example of an activity in which the legally recognized rent on average covers the cost of only half the time required for the development of a new molecule.

The rent made available by the competitive nature of an advantage may be either immediate or deferred. A strategic aim conceals a positioning in time, a period. Every rent has its life cycle. Its base is undermined and even destroyed through several factors. Consumers' tastes in the marketplace change. New competitors who are better placed or better financed appear on the scene. Technologies emerge that offer more effective or more attractive alternatives that the holders of the rent did not know about or want to take on. States of complacency and sclerosis affect firms that are used to easy profits and organizations that have become too set in their ways. Firms lose their vigour when a long history in which they have been over-protected from threats has provided no spur to renewal or to a fighting spirit.

General management is invested with the duty of vigilance with regard to the rent that it benefits from at any given time. If the surpluses that arise from the short term are not invested in order to create new sources of profit for the medium term, the firm will have little hope of survival in the long run. Conversely, if the firm becomes over-preoccupied with creating sources of rent for the medium term, it will have little hope of extracting the profit and surplus from the current trading that it could count on and which would allow it to finance the future through regeneration.

A firm's ability to create new rents represents a major asset for its lasting economic success, and studies show that not all players are equal in this respect. From this perspective, being able to create new rents itself becomes a rent.

At the same time, it is not sufficient to create new rents by investing for the future. The here and now needs to be exploited to extract the maximum immediate surplus out of rents. It must exploit while it regenerates. The firm has to give the same level of attention and to allocate the same quality of expertise to both sides of its strategic agenda. This shows up when work on preparing for the future is relegated to the end of the day's tasks, if not put off to another day. Or again when it is forgotten that the future is uncertain and that progress must be speeded up in order to regenerate the firm.

The strategic aims of a firm are therefore by nature complex. The subject is not academic. In practice, it can be assumed that contradictory demands must be satisfied at the same time. What share of resources is to be allocated to the creation of short-term value that will support regeneration in the medium term? What expenditure to build future income will be compatible with an acceptable level of economic exploitation? Central management must outline an approach or policy that allows for both dimensions: exploiting current income (competitive advantages), and preparing for future income (competitive advantages). The solution will by nature be a hybrid scheme, a compromise, the fruit of intuitive judgement and implicit vision as well as explicit reasoning and empirically based demonstration. Running the firm will require quick adjustments to external events. The establishment of strategic aims therefore arises from complexity. It is an art or a skill, not a science.

To be precise, two approaches are important. One is to allow both dimensions to receive their due share of attention. The other is to develop systems that ensure mutual compatibility. The firm uses the current income (competitive advantages) while at the same time making preparations for the day that income will dry up, against a background of great uncertainty as to when this might occur and about the exact level of future income. It uses up what provides the immediate prosperity while not knowing what tomorrow will bring.

Top management is thus faced with a responsibility that represents the essence of its function and obligation. It ensures short-term exploitation while preparing medium-term regeneration, with the strong probability that the income (monopolistic rent) and competitive advantage that underpins it will not be identical and even tomorrow may well be different from what it is today.

This strategic complexity adds competitive advantage to a firm that knows how to build and maintain it. For the firm it becomes a source of meta-income (meta-monopolistic rent). Its competitors are unable to imitate it because the firm has a rare ability, namely the art of managing contradictions.

2.4 The Need for Regeneration

How does regeneration occur? There are two very different strategic answers, which are usually perceived as being mutually incompatible. Firms choose to regenerate themselves according to either endogenous logic and processes, or exogenous logic and processes.

An exogenous regeneration process is one where the source of a new income (competitive advantage or monopolistic rent) comes from outside the firm. To be precise, its origin is developed outside its social and organizational body. There comes a time when, it being judged that the

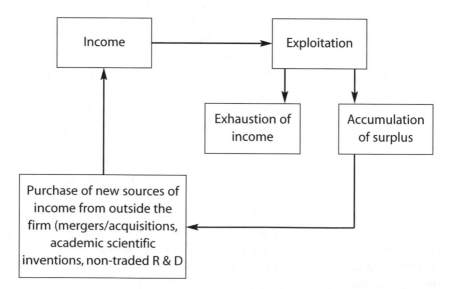

Figure 2.1 The exogenous regeneration process

moment is more or less right for income to flow, the new income (rent) source is brought within the firm.

The exogenous approach allows greater, even radical separation of the activities of exploitation and regeneration. The same units are not responsible for both. The approach follows the principle of specialization and segmentation. The innovation is pursued outside the walls of the firm: in autonomous subsidiaries that operate independently, in third party firms, in various creative and innovative centres. It is foreign and is artificially implanted into the organization.

On the other hand, as an organization the firm does not support functions that lie outside the market. In fact, its future rent is largely the fruit of acquisitions that it makes in the outside market or 'hatcheries' that it plunders if the need arises, such as by buying start-ups. The range of practices is vast. At one extreme lie modifications of the internal management: borrowing the best practice of third party firms, recruiting new staff and skills from the workplace. At the other extreme are the vectors of strategic renewal such as mergers and acquisitions of technological start-up companies. Despite their differences, all of these practices closely resemble one another in the sense that the sources of future rent are foreign to the firm that adopts them in the phase when they become mature. There is a close similarity between best practice as an internal management logic and start-up merger/acquisition as the vector for strategic renewal.

In contrast to the exogenous logic, regeneration is also possible via the endogenous route.

In the endogenous case, the firm installs and manages functions or activities that arise from both the market and non-market sectors. Furthermore, the regeneration potential that top management brings to bear is fuelled and maintained by observing the development of rivalry pursued by different parts of the firm. This observation relates to the expectations of consumers, the new weapons that competitors develop or bring into play, the potential offered by the emerging technologies, and so on. It occurs and is given attention if a precondition is satisfied at the centre of the firm. The exploitation of these factors is not the exclusive responsibility of operational units, or indeed of general management. The top management's observation will reveal both opportunities and threats for the firm; it is in no way an aesthetic armchair exercise. The strategic interpretation of the competitive environment that is thus transmitted to the social body of the firm as a whole then creates the potential for regeneration. The resources provided by exploitation of the existing situation allow that potential to be transformed into new income through the process of regeneration.

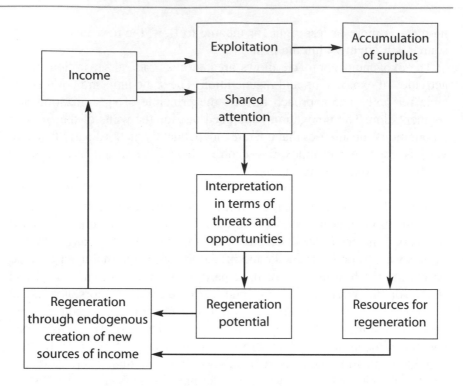

Figure 2.2 The endogenous regeneration process

2.5 When Hybrid Solutions and Complex Models of Organization are Needed

How can the demands of exploitation and those of regeneration be reconciled? The choice of the regeneration process is paramount for the firm.

Once again, the simplest approach, at least at first sight, is to entrust the regeneration to an exogenous agency. In such a scenario, the firm can focus exclusively on the short term. What is more, it calls for repetitive methods of action and an organizational and operational model that is completely simple and basic, and therefore impoverished.

The exogenous route adapts perfectly to simple management models. It does not experience or face up to any need for shared cognition, tacit or explicit dissemination of knowledge or the capacity for learning. Complexity in fact becomes a handicap for it. Similarly, the existence of community identities proves to be a source of useless dysfunction.

This is clearly the case when top management's ambition is restricted to producing a maximum surplus in the short term, thus fuelling the purely financial resources that enable the purchase or acquisition in the marketplace of new income sources. A self-sustaining cycle is set up. The firm faces a challenge in milking old rents to the limit and using the cash to buy outside new rent sources that are more or less already developed and usable for action. In fact the new rents will almost immediately be put under a strong pressure by the firm so that they generate cash as quickly as possible. They will be intensively exploited and will not last for long, and will be dropped as soon as they shall have delivered the cash, so that the firm can buy a third generation of rents. Rents are treated like lemons. Once they have been squeezed, they are thrown away. The life cycle of incomes (competitive advantages) is thus very short; the centre of power quickly burns its boats and exerts pitiless pressure on exploitation. This exploitation is like a rapid and brutal commando attack that justifies a combat platoon approach to organizational principles. The war carried out by the exogenous process does not involve holding ground for a long period. The firm behaves like a free-rider in the economy and the community. Thus, occupying the territory does not require any sophisticated organizational logistics. The approach is to eliminate deliberately and methodically any internal overlapping and redundancy between the operational units, the products, and the old and new sources of rent.

Implementation of this exogenous approach nonetheless implies several concomitants. It requires an unfailing high level of finance, and therefore favours the rich. In addition, it assumes that the new generation of rent, even if it is only exploited for a short period, will undoubtedly bring quick returns, and thus that the future is not in doubt. In short, it implies a recurring and brutal destruction of the human system, while the organizational model is characterized internally by a high degree of rigidity that facilitates codification.

In contrast, the endogenous route involves practices and set-ups that are much more complex to the extent that they do not correspond to the same criteria as would satisfy exploitation. The counterpart of such compromises is based on the fact that a firm capable of complexity has the advantage of a meta-rent and operational skill that competitors find difficult to copy.

Normally, although the reconciliation between exploitation and regeneration and between the market and the non-market may take various different forms, it is ultimately a kind of common education and socialization, that is, processes of sharing references and declining interdependent cognitions. When the two worlds of exploitation and regeneration are connected, the firm and its general management are able to discard an organizational model that runs the risk of quickly becoming ludicrous and problematic. In fact, it focuses on a single dimension for lack of a common language. The consequences are obvious and unavoidable. Either an exclusive concentration on exploitation will lead to inexorable decline in the longer term, or conversely failure will be inevitable in the short term owing to an obsession with breaking all links to the past in order to regenerate.

Complexity and hybridization provide a strategic positioning that combines endogenous exploitation and regeneration. The same resources are employed at the same time on the two horizons of the short term and the long term, and the non-market and the market. This reconciliation arises from enabling the coexistence of contradictory logics that have mixed interpretations in terms of action. One cannot learn when under pressure, just as one cannot innovate if there is no income to provide the cash. As Figure 2.3 shows, there must be an overlap between the two spheres.

This organizational and strategic complexity has a concomitant. It is affected by a cost, namely the surrender of maximum income in the short term, to the extent that the firm – both the centre and the periphery – accepts a trial and error approach to finding alternatives, along with some imprecision. Without this, endogenous regeneration cannot occur.

On the other hand, this approach offers the major economic benefit of allowing the building of new rents and regeneration systems that are protected by their intangibility or, to be precise, by their complexity. There is a good chance that social benefits will also follow, especially in terms of preserving communal integrity in the medium term.

Endogenous regeneration, coupled with exploitation, certainly deserves much more sustained attention. In the following discussion we shall focus exclusively on these and their linking together. There are two reasons for this. First, they are not easy to conduct from day to day. Second, they enable our communities to take on the aspect of something rather different from an arena where economic exploitation is the preferred activity.

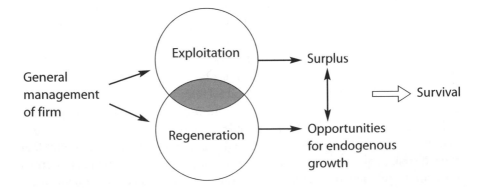

Figure 2.3 Endogenous regeneration linked to exploitation

There are some who argue that the avoidance of complexity, the refusal to take responsibility for change in the medium term and the lack of attention to human communities as shown by firms should be seen as indicators of civilization and provide the keys to success. This argument is difficult to sustain morally. We do not think that firms are like paper tissues to be used once and then thrown away. The tangible and intangible capital that they acquire contributes greatly to the extraordinary level of material well-being that our economy generates.

CHAPTER 3

The Organizational System

There is a viable response to the increasing hybridization and complexity that the conduct of firms is subjected to. It is cognitive. The more the firm resorts to organizational models that encourage the emergence of cognitive conventions between its staff and its operations, which enrich rather than impoverish its cognitive system, the more continuity is assured between its strategic positioning and its methods of operation and between its external ambitions and its internal organization.

This chapter is intended to give status to the place of knowledge, especially where two strategic demands must be followed at the same time: exploiting competitive advantage, regenerating for future income. They require firms to reconcile diverse or even contradictory demands. Hence the need for a complex and hybrid method of management. In such cases, recourse to the cognitive becomes a distinct advantage.

3.1 Sharing Common Knowledge as a Coordination Mechanism

Why was it that so many clockmakers in the Swiss Jura disappeared in the 1970s and 1980s? Because they were faced with serious cognitive deficiencies. Many of the small and medium-sized firms did not know their ultimate customers. They relied on larger firms that maintained close contact with the world market and kept up with technological developments. These large firms had played an important role in their region in disseminating knowledge, integration and transfer of information, thanks to the community of language that they shared with the smaller firms.

However, as a result of technological changes – the invention of the quartz watch – and the emergence of aggressive Japanese and American competition, many of the medium-sized and large firms disappeared, being taken over by groups whose strategic operations were often located outside the Jura region.

No longer benefiting, or at least much less than before, from the information provided by their national contacts, many managers of local workshops faced a crippling lack of knowledge about what to do. From that point they had great difficulty in obtaining flows of concrete information about their own value added chain, the new requirements of the market, and even the new forms of competition in the global market. Some did not know, at each value added stage, who their competitors were, what they did, what their advantages were and what threats they presented.

The consequence of these cognitive uncertainties was the progressive weakening of these firms, which ultimately closed or were swallowed up by international groups not located in the region. The watch-making industry was lost to the Jura through the breakdown of the mechanisms that had allowed knowledge to be accumulated and shared between its economic agents (Michaud, 1994).

Another observation may be made concerning the location of firms. Let us take an ordinary town where there were two industrial areas with similar physical characteristics (such as distance from the centre of town, road and rail services). These areas were designed to keep the centre free from congestion and attract firms from outside the region. One area was heavily oversubscribed, with very high rental rates and very strong demand. In contrast, in the other area where prices were much lower, premises remained empty owing to lack of demand.

The explanation for such differences lies largely in the rejection of cognitive uncertainty and the need for concrete information when firms take decisions. They want to be able to anticipate events.

The small firms wanted reliable, concrete information they could understand and use. In fact, these firms had neither the means nor the capacity to gather – or indeed sort and evaluate – sufficient information, and much of what they gathered seemed uncertain. Statements from national or local authorities appeared abstract because they did not relate directly to what the firms observed in their physical environment. An industrial area containing many firms that were felt to be 'compatible' (that is, having similar characteristics to these small firms) gave out a message that these firms could survive in an out-of-centre area. The concentration of such firms, with common references and similar languages, reduced the cognitive uncertainty of the small firms.

Acceptance of a higher price is therefore linked to a cognitive characteristic of language. Firms pay for access to a system of tacit knowledge generated by repeated contact with others through apprenticeship and proximity. There is a real market in the cognitive, something that was not recognized by the public authorities in charge of these two areas (Hogarth *et al.*, 1980).

These two examples show that cognition is important for firms. More precisely, the key to running the hybrid and the complex lies in there being a shared cognitive system at the heart of the organization.

Shared cognition in fact liberates the organization from coordination managed from the top; more generally, it sets it free from coordination maintained in an exogenous fashion. It brings order and control, both collectively and individually. The units and people can coordinate their actions and choices without instructions from above. The language for action contains signals that record the activities of an organization in a single register, while at the same time allowing all individuals to carry out their own work autonomously.

Take two distinct operational units, one concerned with commercial matters, the other with R&D. If there is no cognitive communication path between them, if they do not share sectors of common language, they will remain disconnected owing to a lack of common knowledge. Instead of a direct horizontal relationship between them, there is a coordination mechanism provided by an exterior third party, which has only partial knowledge of the two domains and may often be a step behind regarding their problems (Figure 3.1).

If, on the other hand, there is just some partial overlap in the respective action languages between these two groups, if they share the same cognitions, the horizontal coordination of their acts and choices occurs with a minimum of third party control or external arbitration (Figure 3.2).

What is true for the horizontal plane is also true for hierarchical relationships. Any organization that does not possess an overlap of language will face issues dealing with blockages and recurrent political games at the top. Committees multiply, bringing the parties involved around a table. Top management finds itself forced to increase the number of discretionary, detailed intrusions into the operational units. Despite this, there is no guarantee that the choices made and the reaction speed will

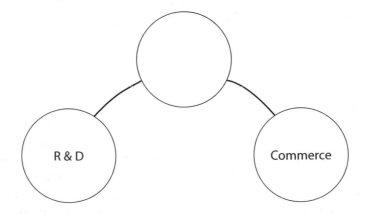

Figure 3.1 Exogenous coordination

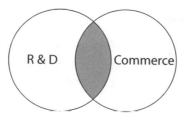

Figure 3.2 Endogenous coordination

be appropriate. Conditions such as these explain why those in middle management often become uncooperative, if not obstructive. This is particularly true when initiatives are proposed for ongoing training or consultancy techniques to assist in setting up internal networks and thereby establishing common references between the participants. Such substitutes take away power and control from these managers, who often see the control of information and language as an asset that they are able to use to their advantage.

When all is said and done, the lesson from this is self-evident. In order to manage the contradictions, top management or the centre must be able to reconcile in a single configuration of languages and destinies both the permanent review of the competitive advantages (regeneration) and the intelligent use of the currently available advantages (exploitation). There is little chance of winning the jackpot through some fundamental scientific discovery; a paradigm breakthrough is a rare event, even on the scale of a decade. Therefore it is only organizational continuity that makes possible the incremental experience and discontinuity that, while regenerating income, does not assume that the firm should adopt a policy of clean sweep and plundering third parties. What is perhaps less obvious is the lesson that the language of action is the key to this managerial imperative.

The nature, content and relevance of the cognitive cannot be understood as a phenomenon in itself: something to be interpreted by scorning or disregarding the specific situation with which a given firm is confronted at a given time. In our subsequent discussion we shall use two synthetic descriptors to qualify and simplify the huge range of concrete situations faced by the management of firms.

- The first (the strategic options) qualifies the external context in which a firm expresses its aims and policies.
- The second (organizational models) indicates the internal organizational model for the firm that is linked with this particular strategic context.

3.2 Strategic Options

The first descriptor is made up of the possible universes that confront the firm, the type of environment that it has chosen or aims to position itself in, now and in the future. For ease of examination this can be divided into two main parts: one is of cognitive essence and the other describes stated wishes that are at least fundamental for its strategic choices. These indicate and qualify:

- on the one hand, the perception that the firm is developing with regard to its context for action;
- on the other hand, the strategic positioning that it is adopting as regards success or effectiveness in time and in the long term.

The first deals with how the firm rates the level of pressure or threat in the environment that it is confronted with. This threat may be perceived as being strong or weak. If it is strong this means that, in reality, the competition will be seen and regarded as obliging the firm to surpass itself. If it is weak, there will be no incentive for such performance to be seen as strategic or as a priority; there is no appropriate shared requirement. This dimension is well known in the field of management and economic science research. Firms as so-called economic agents act according to the spheres, circumstances and rules that they consider themselves to be faced with.

A situation of hypercompetition therefore creates a significant and lasting threat. It quickly and permanently calls into question all competitive advantages, whatever their nature: symbolic, technical or advantages conferred by public regulations. There are no longer any superior weapons, such as inalienable and indestructible assets (D'Aveni, 1994). The threat leads to the need to change, and to the destruction of the firm's present advantages in the hope of creating others. Moreover, it ultimately affects every firm.

Similarly, the requirement for a firm in serious difficulty to recover, and the feeling that an essential task must be accomplished, produce pressures and incitement for individuals to look beyond their own interests, a collective desire that generates behaviour similar to that which follows from hypercompetitive situations. The effectiveness shown at certain times by public or semi-public services stems from the pressures, the sense of urgency, the perceived duties that mobilize behaviour of a similar nature even though they do not belong to the same sphere of competition as private companies.

Conversely, situations where competition is weak and tensions relaxed tend to reduce the pressure on everyone and loosen the ties of cooperation.

This state of affairs occurs because the dynamic of income X is available. An income X is an asset that provides protection against competition and is available at any given moment; it generates a monopoly and encourages the emergence of a feeling of security, timelessness and financial freedom. These circumstances stimulate individuals to behave in their own interests, leading to the appearance of internal pressure groups, the practice of systematic externalization of errors to third parties, and free-rider behaviour. They encourage bureaucracy, internal coalitions, cliques and internal struggles for a greater share of the added value.

The second dimension describes the policies or positions adopted by the firm in the face of its external context. At one extreme, the organization pursues exploitation of the current situation or short-term effectiveness. At the other, it pursues innovation and regeneration. In other words, it places its destiny in the hands of a policy of renewal generated from and within the firm.

Exploitation aims to extract the maximum from the business operations that make up the advantages and resources available at a given moment. Emphasis is put on the structures and procedures that produce short-term profitability. A product that no longer generates sufficient income is immediately dropped, a division that does not achieve the expected results is closed or sold off, a capacity or skill that is missing is bought in from outside. Competitors are copied by adopting their methods, even if that involves abandoning one's own roots.

In this context, the survival and development of the firm as a community, its identity and individuality as they really are, do not figure as priorities. In other words, everything is open to change or remodelling at will. In fact, it is the market that in this case determines the paths of action. As a social body the firm is to large extent exogenous in relation to the central player in the system (the general management) and, most often, in relation to the world of financial analysts whose expectations rigidly define the areas of decision making. The organization is like a kit whose components are interchangeable, particularly as they can be combined with third party elements (through acquisitions or mergers).

In contrast, the paradigms of regeneration and innovation are based on the idea that the firm must survive and develop through permanent renewal from within with a relatively stable configuration, especially in terms of staff. Regeneration is in fact a policy that comes from within the system, as it requires shared intuition and creativity. What is more, it assumes a minimum security threshold (Moss Kanter, 1997) in order to foster behaviour that will protect the environment while at the same time allowing for the risk of change. Here, the role of management is to construct an organization that permanently rebuilds itself and develops new assets while remaining largely endogenous.

It is for this reason that transformation systems operate in the long term and staff rotate positions internally. These systems accept fuzzy boundaries, and use apprenticeship and education to build a type of organization in which useful information can be captured and the strategic message can be decoded and interpreted. This type of organization can work with partly formulated objectives since the cognitive system allows them to be translated.

Its prime logic is not mimicry, cloning or 'me too'. On the contrary, it focuses on the pursuit and achievement of an imperative: the generation of innovation with value (Kim and Mauborgne, 1999). This route or ambition does not set out systematically to follow the path of competitors or build competitive advantage located in the same areas as others. Nor does it rely on segmentation. On the contrary, it tries constantly to devalue and marginalize the competition by offering new products and original solutions in the marketplace.

Such a policy thus assumes two capabilities at the heart of the firm: a capacity of intuition for needs still only vaguely identified, and attentive care for the subtleties of an area that are not easily submitted to the sectors of control and procedures of routine scrutiny. It is in this context that the endogenous and shared languages at the centre of the organization take on all their meaning. In fact, they encourage the slow structuring of intuition, for intuition is not simply an individual quality but indicates a collective capacity. It facilitates both the taking account of and the interpretation of weak information signals.

These shed special light on the problem of strategic formulation and implementation. If it is true that strategy begins with a detailed knowledge of a dynamic of the environment, continues with the definition of ambitions that are compatible with evolution in this situation, and ends with adapted resources, then the question of the level of compromise arises (Drucker, 1994). What happens if it turns out that the resources or the organizational system that were relevant at one time no longer correspond to the ambitions or do not deliver the results expected by the financial community? Posing such a question amounts to asking about optimization of the existing state of affairs and its capacity for survival. 'Every economic system that continually considers exploiting its possibilities to the maximum may ultimately in the long term be inferior to a system that never attains this end' (Schumpeter, 1942). Permanent transformation demands a long time horizon and fuzzy systems, requirements that do not correspond to those of short-term exploitation.

3.3 Organizational Models

The intersection of the perception of the environment by the positioning adopted by the firm allows four stylized situations to be established. For each there will be a descriptor of the organizational model that takes account of the internal method of operation of the firm. To be precise, it is here that a series of traits will be indicated and selected to characterize the collective behaviours and their deep-seated motives. They revolve around two key variables:

■ *The effective cooperation that is woven between the components of the organization.* That is, the way in which the individuals, functions and units manage their daily interfaces and interdependent relationships, the behaviour that they adopt, the content that they give preference to and the content that they are unaware of. This cooperation can be strong. All staff members integrate into their choices and actions the consequences that these may have for the objectives, stakes and situations that others confront. On the other hand, it will be seen to be weak if there is a culture of mutual avoidance, withdrawal and compartmentalization (see Figure 3.3).

■ *The level of common socialization that exists between these same components.* That is, the existence or lack of cognitive references and language in their choices and when testing the actions that they undertake.

3.3.1 The Type 1 or Organic Model

This model takes account of specific external contexts. On the one hand, the environment (the market, the competition, public regulations, technology, etc.) is experienced as unstable and threatening. The model generates a feeling of precariousness and weakness. On the other hand, faced with this environment, the firm may develop a policy that complies with two major characteristics. First, it focuses on the medium or the long term. Second, it is based on its own capacity for renewal and innovation through, for example, its range of products and skills.

In this so-called organic model, the socialization of people by the organization is intensive and of long duration. Their cooperation is close and is experienced as something obvious, even a moral duty. This model also encourages mutual loyalty among the operational units with regard to the firm. Its members reveal an enhanced ability to work together to resolve problems. Confidence in oneself and in others, when it is accompanied by an appraisal of the constituents that is broadly related to the community,

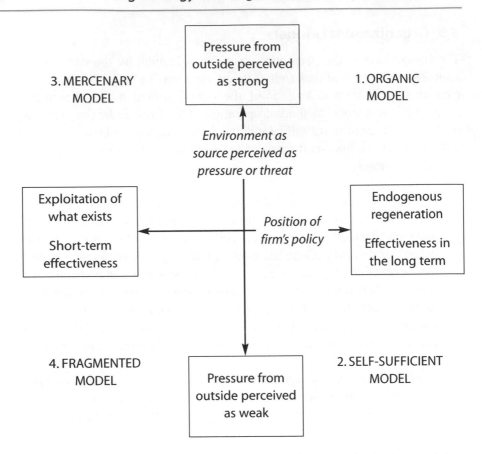

Figure 3.3 Contexts for action and types of organizational model

prevents the emergence of behaviour that is too individualistic and shows up the free-riders.

The Type 1 organization embarks on a shared adventure. The fact that there is loyalty and that a common destiny binds people together in their actions leads to a strong community pressure on the way individual behaviour develops. Cognitive channels spread and become established. This makes it possible for the whole social body, down to the units on the ground, to interpret and translate progressively the ambitions of top management. The improved structures also enable the senior managers to pick up embryonic ideas forming at the lower levels.

Type 1 is characteristic of those firms that anchor their policies on the establishment of internal networks and the building of communities of intuition and culture. Communities of languages and references are characterized by 'badgings': processes of recognition and marking similar to the way that animals identify and recognize each other and include or exclude accordingly. An organization that learns thus distinguishes itself by 'the nourishing soup of intuition, judgement, expertise and common sense rooted in the apparent chaos of day-to-day activity' (Vincent, 1996).

The organic model (Type 1)

- Strong internal socialization/mobility of staff.
- Active transverse networking.
- Diffuse and strong pressure to act collectively.
- Loyalty to the business.
- Common confidence.
- Shared criteria for choice and action.

3.3.2 The Type 2 or Self-sufficient Model

In contrast to Type 1, the Type 2 model refers to firms whose members experience a world free from any serious threat. They see their surrounding world as something calm and predictable, not uncertain or unknown. In comparison with what happens in firms that are controlled by an organic model, self-sufficient organizations suppose that they can find the means for innovation and renewal within themselves alone, and permanently.

The social and organizational configuration of Type 2 contains a high level of internal socialization. This is expressed through the sharing of emotional and interpersonal affinities, through references to common cultural traits, and so on. Innovation comes about through achievements or strengths developed informally or by dedicated departments, or it may be imposed through strong hierarchical pressure. There is little cooperation within the Type 2 firm in terms of the management of operational interdependencies, the collective resolution of problems requiring action, or the communication of everyday matters. Business dealings reflect to a greater or lesser extent the compartmentalization, the sequestered atmosphere and the maximization of everyone's autonomy. This model has two major characteristics of its operation that distinguish it from the other three types.

First, people get around segmentation and compartmentalization by ad hoc arrangements that are unshared and informal, or even secret. There are improvised solutions and special privileges whose peculiarity is to be invisible to the uninitiated. Second, and in particular, each unit tends to externalize to third parties the consequences of its own errors, both up and down the organization. Internal errors, failures in communication, delays or substandard quality carry no consequences for the units that cause them, they are passed up or down the line.

The self-sufficient model (Type 2)

- Strong emotional socialization and weak internal mobility.
- Restricted horizontal cooperation: each function or unit is an island in the organization.
- Extensive use of formal procedures.
- Ad hoc informal and improvised solutions to urgent problems.
- 'Someone else's problem' and what Goffman (1961) described as 'total community' syndromes.
- Externalization to third parties.

3.3.3 The Type 3 or Mercenary Model

This model applies to those firms whose external context is seen to be extremely threatening, but which, in contrast to Type 1, are positioned in the very short term and pursue a policy of exploiting the current situation. Instead of permanently recycling and developing innovation internally, the firm is continually compelled to import new skills and eliminate those that have become obsolete or are in decline. If need be, this practice extends to selling methods, and the acquisition or closure of entire sections. Such firms dispense with or take on staff where necessary, they abandon activities that are not immediately profitable; they buy in the market, especially through mergers, new solutions that can be immediately exploited. Attention is riveted on short-term quantifiable performance.

The organizational configuration therefore possesses a variable geometry. The spur to action is to be found in the engagement of professionals and the adoption of skills that come from outside, which are chosen because they are foreign to the social body of the firm and because they provide readymade new skills or methods. At the same time, it is understood and accepted that these people may leave at any time after the style of mercenary soldiers.

The Type 3 configuration possesses weak socialization and attracts limited loyalty. But there is strong cooperation, which depends on two mechanisms. The first arises from the insistent and sometimes obsessional pressure that justifies recourse to methods of domination and control based on immediate individual performance. The second flows from the existence of a common benchmark for management of standards of success and proficiency. These are exterior to the firm and can be dictated either by extremely structured professions (for example management controllers) or by external networks (former pupils of higher education or members of an elite group), or be supported by third parties (financial analysts, the media, etc.). At all events, for the staff involved there is no commitment to the firm or to the longer term.

The mercenary model (Type 3)

- No acculturation processes provided by the organization.
- Weak staff loyalty to the organization and its managers.
- Problem-solving management by designing new formal structures and procedures.
- Strong pressure for individual short-term performance.
- Compulsory or forced cooperation; coordination by the top and by command and control.
- Reference to exogenous benchmarks or action criteria.

3.3.4 The Type 4 or Fragmented Model

This model reflects calm exterior contexts, with no perceived turbulence or threat, together with a short-term positioning of policy for the firm. As a consequence, it neither embodies a vision of a collective adventure or a common destiny, nor does it give priority to a drive for renewal and innovation by the organization. It operates by being able to abstract itself from the demands of success in the marketplace.

Socialization and cooperation are very restricted. Avoidance and a mutual lack of loyalty develop, thus encouraging individualism and localized withdrawal. From the point of view of its internal method of operation, the firm also experiences a marked fragmentation of its identity and an extreme segmentation of its components. Such systems are often quite noticeably bureaucratic. Detailed procedures paradoxically encourage power struggles that remove any flexibility and prevent collective learning. In many respects, this model comes close to the bureaucratic type of operation that is so rigid that it is unable to adapt by itself in a spontaneous way to the changes occurring in its environment (Crozier, 1963).

The fragmented model (Type 4)

- Socialization by and loyalty mainly to the peer group.
- Individualism and mutual avoidance as normal ways of doing things; weak cooperation and high level of mistrust between units or functions.
- Strong segmentation and high level of specialization across the organization.
- High level of centralization and management through proceduralization.
- Importance of political games.
- No collective identity and vision regarding action.

3.4 The Dynamics of Renewal

The classification outlined above indicates a strong link between on the one hand the organizational model of the firm and, on the other hand, the nature of the dynamics and origins (endogenous or exogenous) of its renewal and regeneration. The models may be ranked on a kind of scale showing the relative degree of endogenous dynamic that belongs to each. They are radically distinguished from one another by their aptitudes for conveying the endogenous language.

The organic model (Type 1) is clearly the configuration where the endogenic is of prime importance. The mercenary model (Type 3) is at the other end of the scale. It reveals the primacy of the exogenic and, as a corollary, a rejection of the endogenic. As for the other two organizational models, they occupy intermediary positions between the first two. More precisely, Type 4 tends more towards the exogenic and Type 2 favours the endogenic.

In the sphere of the direction and economic survival of firms, Types 2 and 4 operate within and take account of contexts that show a relatively low level of competition. They are therefore not concerned with the world of hypercompetition. This is why they will receive less attention in what follows. The main focus will be on the organic organizational model (Type 1) and the mercenary model (Type 3), which relate to environments perceived and experienced as uncertain, unstable and strongly competitive.

Hypercompetition thus puts firms and their managements on the spot. In fact, the choice lies between two organizational models that are radically different: the organic and the mercenary. That is, a choice between two configurations that cross through renewal dynamics which are fundamentally incompatible and opposed to one another, namely the strongly exogenic and the purely endogenic.

Furthermore, if the classification suggests that there are choices or combinations of context, positioning and organization that are more sustainable or viable in terms of survival and effectiveness for the firm, this does not necessarily imply that there is by definition a causal relation between the various descriptors that is some kind of iron law of wages. For the time being it should be seen as statically indicating concomitances or covariations between the nature of the environment, the type of policy and the internal method of management of the organization. However, it seems useful to give some indication of the dynamic processes that encourage the appearance of languages for action, in particular the contributions offered by the economic sciences.

In the case of the organic model (Type 1), the firm is exposed indefinitely to a degree of instability. Success, particularly in the creation of income, tends to favour the emergence of a comfortable state of mind and a feeling of well-being. The competitive advantages, whatever their nature, drive the firm to exploit them, and therefore structure the organization and segment it in order to achieve the best results in the short term, or simply make the most of the positions acquired. All that remains of the endogenic are the formalities and the references, but not the principles of action. It becomes habitual to externalize to outside partners or to paid third parties. Ultimately, the culture of arrangements and cliques emerges.

This alteration, which is typical of many private companies, also occurs in the public sector. Sources of stress disappear, along with the sense of urgency and duty that vitalizes the energies and defines relatively clear objectives (objectives that are generally quantifiable and easy to understand and share). Pure innovation may continue to be valued and established as an imperative. However, it no longer takes its cue from the needs of the market or the community. Such needs cease to be endogenous to the market or to the community. They become exogenous. They express and carry the desires of specific groups that follow personal aims, technical challenges or scientific objectives: R and D labs which use the world as an opportunity to satisfy corporatist goals, marketers who want to keep their autonomy inside the firm, executives whose motivation is basically egocentric or status oriented. Along with the feeling of comfort comes the refusal to take risks. With the future apparently assured, people are happy with a management focused on the short term and on personal and particular objectives.

Apart from certain special circumstances, such a situation is not sustainable. It may turn out that the income from nature (for example, oil) or from the community (a public monopoly) proves lasting.

However, in the majority of cases, the breakdown occurs when new circumstances disrupt an organization with little capacity for renewal because of its too close adherence to a particular environment. This theory is strongly supported by the so-called population ecology school (Hannan and Freeman, 1989) which shows in a Darwinian perspective how an entire set of organizations acting in the same industry may die when some global economic or technical conditions change. The examples put forward suggest that the very survival of firms may be jeopardized rather by the strategic positioning and the vision that single firms, not cohorts of identical firms, carry and adopt in the name of effectiveness. Catastrophe theory provides a correct analysis of the rupture mechanism. It reveals the shape of a process by which a system slowly degrades while remaining apparently healthy up to the moment when a major shock occurs (Thom, 1991). This takes the form of the appearance of different competitors with new capacities. Alternatively, it may result from deregulation measures taken by state authorities that can no longer protect and guarantee the existence of organizations that are costly for the community. It may finally be due to a merger with or takeover by another firm.

In order to take advantage of the existing assets and respond to the expectations of demanding shareholders, the management of such a firm will divide up, restructure and above all dispose of assets and resources, whether they be business units, staff or goods. The short-term objective is to reduce costs. In the relationship between turnover and financial charges, in particular so far as staff is concerned, it is always easier to reduce financial expenditure quickly than to find new markets or offer new products. As a second phase, and in order to optimize the revenue from what is left, the firm then takes on external expertise. These experts, who have no knowledge of the firm and nothing in common with it, will use time-worn recipes, alleged good or best practice, all of which will be exogenous to the organization. Cooperation between professionals will ensure the necessary exceptional consistency. In these conditions, there is no need for the endogenic. Financial objectives and quantified criteria are all; any other objectives reach levels of generality that make them operationally difficult to translate into action, all the more because they are no longer subject to or relayed by shared cognitive links.

While the profitability extracted from such measures may well be high, the new group will however be faced with the progressive decline of the existing assets and the economic income that has been bought. Renewal can be carried out by the exogenic: the sale of failing units and the purchase of units created by others to bring in new income. 'It may well happen that classic beneficial competition gives way to a destructive competition, a battle at knife-point or simply struggles for control pursued in the financial markets' (Schumpeter, 1942).

Renewal can also be brought about in a quite different way, through the endogenous route. In contrast to a process dominated by cooperation between professional mercenaries (who are not united by the construction of types of long-term solidarity and who do not see a common future in the firm), this way lies in rediscovering the values of socialization. In other words, it concerns itself with reconstructing languages that, because they are specific, allow development from within.

The market model in the Walras or Pareto sense does not exist in this perspective. No economic market in fact operates without a certain number of organizational, institutional and cultural preconditions being present and satisfied. Competition does not mean perfect competition and a social optimum. The firms are faced with a game, a process that consists of establishing a permanent compromise that certainly bears on the market variables but also above all on their internal organizational configuration. Modern societies therefore do not boil down to market societies. They form organizational economies in which the firms can then develop and create value (Goshal *et al.*, 1999).

For those firms that position themselves on the paradigms of exploitation, the market must represent the reference for each part of the organization. Starting from what they perceive to be the behaviour of consumers, the competition and the expectations of shareholders, they simulate the market internally in some way, giving themselves a role comparable to Walras's auction bidder. Widespread decentralization is possible with little risk if such a framework is already in existence, for structures that are sufficiently divided up and small allow better control of autonomy by allocating resources according to a market model: that is, depending on financial performance. The decentralization is linked with a Taylorian universe, where the role of central management is to divide up and set the financial objectives, and allocate resources according to the results.

There are thus decentralized structures in the exogenic. The products, procedures and strategic market resources are largely external, their role being to obtain the best return by playing the role of production workshop or commercial department. In such a framework, decentralization in no way implies an increase in the specific power of the recipients. The autonomy of the periphery remains rather low. Production as well as sales units are still structured in a partitioned way and their respective roles are narrowly defined. Tasks keep being centred around carrying out orders, while decision making remains in the hands of the centre. In fact, throughout this process, it seems as though the centre externalizes to the periphery those decisions that were difficult to take, discuss and put into practice.

In such a system renewal is also experienced as something exogenic, the innovations being either bought in the market (mergers, acquisitions), or based on general scientific processes external to the firm. The latter thus simulates for itself the biological process of creative destruction (Schumpeter, 1942). The accent is placed on operational effectiveness, execution and procedural conformity. The combining and recombining of assets are generally experienced as exogenous to the whole and are consequently handled in centralized cells, often cognitively isolated from the rest of the organization.

There is in fact a contradiction between the anarchic development work of trial and error, even bankruptcy, and a so-called efficient organization according to the Taylorian rules (notably through the removal of overlapping functions and redundant staff). As the sociological theory of organizations shows, the chances of success in the case of an endogenous development increase when the areas of duplication and overlap are multiplied inside an organization (Landau, 1969). That said, duplication remains synonymous with redundancy and waste if it is judged solely from the point of view of short-term effectiveness and apparent cost (Jacobs, 1969).

Conversely, other firms deliberately withdraw parts of their activity from the market, at least for a certain period. This strategy allows them to play for the longer term without having to produce trading results in the very short term, to take risks and have fuzzier boundaries, that is, less clear-cut divisions and less bureaucracy. It allows partnerships to be set up with outside third parties using the model of a shared common language. It is also possible in this type of firm for research and development to establish roots in the scientific world while, at the same time, those who remain in contact with the consumers can capture and interpret the elusive signals of changing demand.

In order to connect the sections operating outside the market with those inside it, skills and practices need to be developed to produce or offer bridges, translations, negotiations, organizational compromises, all assuming the existence of endogenous languages, that is to say shared cognitive structures. These cognitive structures appear every day, through the problems encountered and through chance meetings. Knowledge, accumulated memory and intuition are very difficult to organize officially and keep on file. They are only expressed in particular circumstances and cannot become the object of archives decided upon outside the organizational system that controls them.

In this approach, decentralization appears as something significantly different from that associated with the standard market model that

Taylorism postulates. The centre still controls the periphery. Procedures and financial criteria are used to allocate resources. However the peripheral units are given greater degrees of autonomy and initiative. Experience is shared because overlaps and redundancies of roles are made possible. Such cognitive communication allows strong relationships of trust and cooperation to grow between the units that are exposed to trade criteria of performance and those that come under administrative rules of performance. It allows both the translation of strategic messages from central management and the codification and structuring of information from the grassroots. This way of working calls for consent, complicity and trust, all conditions for replacing a system of formal procedures with convergent behaviour that is based on shared knowledge, negotiation and compromise. It should be noted that the transaction costs are not necessarily greater than in the exogenous model. However, they are incurred elsewhere, and belong to a system in which everyone shares knowledge of the behaviour and expectations of others.

Common knowledge (that is, full knowledge shared by all the players) is defined by the understanding and confidence that others think in the same way and share the same references as oneself. It is one of the conditions for the operation of a competitive market system. Any failure to respect this criterion causes bubbles or deviations that, far from correcting themselves automatically, may cause ruptures and explosions. In the economic world as in the military world, shared knowledge 'defines the capacity to manage dynamic situations where rules are not enough in the face of ignorance or great uncertainty' (Raghavendra, 1995). The difficulty is that the establishment of a network based on shared knowledge takes a lot of time and a strong organic ability (that is, connection between its components).

This hypothesis on shared knowledge makes it easier to explain the flourishing of simplistic procedures and restricted corridors of freedom associated with situations where there is strong competition and a strategy of exploitation, with both under pressure. Insofar as the firm makes significant staffing cuts and disposes of operational units in order to reduce costs in the short term, the social network is torn and the latent memory amputated. Management carried out by people who have only a vague memory of the former networks is based on a simplification of the system in order to facilitate the application of largely standardized procedures and norms. But in reality activity in a dynamic universe is always complex, and complexity is hard to control with simple procedures.

This regression in the world of complexity explains why endogenous creation and leadership based on shared aims become problematical in this type of situation. The common knowledge necessary to the endogenous requires awareness of the organization's history, since it is only this that can connect people and ideas. But this requirement proves incompatible with the quest for maximization and optimization, to the extent that the latter almost always encourage the neglect of history (Nelson and Winter, 1982).

In brief, systems of exploitation and change differ profoundly in terms of the ultimate aims of the business policies that they embody. The ideal of exploitation is linked to theoretical demands of shareholders outside the firm who expect results – profits – without regard to the way that top management recombines and reconfigures the assets, or whether or not they ensure the survival and integrity of the group.

3.5 The Cognitive System Keeps Hybrid Models Together

Adopting a cognitive approach offers a promising way to connect the strategic aims and the organizational operation of the firm's management. It makes it possible to get round the obstacles and the dead ends that we have just described.

Pioneering work in the cognitive research of management has concentrated on the activities that managements engage in, particularly in situations of change (Daft and Weick, 1984; Thomas and McDaniel, 1990; Gioia and Thomas, 1996). Several studies therefore use concepts taken from attribution theories in order to profile leadership in the firm, in particular in the light of the arguments put forward by management concerning performance (Staw *et al.*, 1983; Salancik and Meindl, 1984). The arguments suggest that top management claims success is due to factors internal to the organization, while it attributes failure to external events. What is surprising is that such arguments find a receptive audience, to the point of influencing the perceptions of shareholders, persuading them to increase the value of their holdings and creating the feeling, especially in the case of difficulty, that management is in control of the situation.

Firms as organizations are also influenced by the way in which their headquarters take decisions and formulate policies. For instance research in management and in psychology shows quite consistently that process matters. Executives, whether they are aware of it or not, build and diffuse specific cognitive factors, in particular in face-to-face encounters or as members of work groups such as task forces (Schwenk, 1988). They manage reference frameworks (Mason and Mitroff, 1981), they model knowledge structures (Prahalad and Bettis, 1986), they act by using categorization activities (Dutton and Jackson, 1987); cognitive charts seem to guide their thoughts and to map their understanding of the environment or of the right way to proceed. Cognitive lapses do occur, which explains the irrational judgements made by top management in competitive contexts, and which lead to excess production capacity and even to bankruptcy (Zajac and Bazerman, 1991) or to takeover of other firms (Duhaime and Schwenk, 1985). The eyes become bigger than the stomach. For example, if leaders perceive actions or choices as potentially very threatening, it impoverishes the quality of their cognitive process, leads them to over-simplify problems to the point of caricature, to block out information and to proclaim reasons for their action that do not hold up in the face of events on the ground.

There is a risk in concentrating only on observing the top of the management hierarchy, as such approaches do. They perpetuate a kind of pious lie of management, namely the overestimation of general management's capacity, which is implicitly taken as the sole driving force of success or failure. This pious lie excludes all consideration of other levels of the firm. These are assumed to be passive players whose activities are marginal.

In reality this not the case. At Intel, for example, strategic decisions are the product of a more collective process that is not restricted to the beliefs and knowledge of general management alone (Burgelman, 1991). An empirical way of verifying the validity of this assumption is to regard the firm as a social and organizational phenomenon, whose interpretive and cognitive projects result from a more collective process that goes beyond the echelons of top management (Eden and Spender, 1998). The advantage of such an attitude is to give one a perspective on the literature devoted to the cognitive processes, which tends to concentrate on the powerful players – the directors – but is slower to comprehend the link between interpretive activities and concrete action.

The approach outlined here recommends that general management, and subsequently line management, make the proactive establishment of a link between knowledge and actions its prime responsibility. There are three dimensions to this:

■   Cognitions are not easy to detect, not facts that can be given as such. Nor are they pure and mechanical translations of discourses. How actors proceed, the references they use when acting, are not as such identical to what they say they do and to their arguments about how to proceed. Good reasons, presentations of self in everyday life, attitudes and values are not very reliable proxies of the content of actual behaviours. Cognitions are research problems, phenomena that need inquiry and analysis. They have to be inferred from observing what actors do, how they act, the tools and procedures they use, the specific organizational context in which their action takes place and is embedded.

- What might be called the cognitive domain of the firm goes far beyond the usual definition of the sole intellectual representations actors carry with them. Cognitive intelligence is not restricted to the sum of the IQs of the single persons or managers. Organizational models or structures as defined above are part of the cognitive assets of a firm. Procedures and routines themselves carry interpretative frameworks, induce specific ways of reasoning and acting. No managerial method such as an accounting system is a neutral tool. Any administrative technique can be linked to a specific theory of action: it postulates a certain representation or perception of actual phenomena and it implies causal linkages between particular causes and consequences.

- Thirdly, the approach regards firms as forming organizations that are relatively differentiated internally, being pluralist systems rather than integrated monoliths. They do not appear to be necessarily monolithic in action. They have to operate in complicated and unstable environments at great speed in a way that is appropriate to the current conditions driving the firm, competition and globalization. These environments cannot be ignored, because they have consequences for the firm. Finally, they are not controllable by procedural approaches imposed in a hierarchical fashion (the archetype of such approaches being detailed schedules based on medium-term strategies that set out plans of action for each component).

To bring together the firm's ambitions and the realities of action it is necessary to address two separate concerns. First, each component of the firm is expected to translate orientations or general instructions into actions and choices. Second, because the information on the environment and on action is known largely at the ground level, the operational units must be allowed a certain amount of autonomy in order to handle it.

The problem is in a way a classic one, both for scientific knowledge and for the practice of business management. It involves the management of sequential interfaces and, more generally, the ways in which the organization can ensure consistency in the actions it generates. The approach developed here has a much narrower focus. Action languages and policy references become the domain of inquiry as far as actors or decision makers adopt them in order to achieve some degree of compatibility between their behaviours, their acts and non-acts. This process could also be called a form of social integration. Common ways of doing things, which become implicit rules and taken-for-granted norms, spread inside the social and cognitive fabric of the firm. Their origins may be exogenous to the organization (by imitating or importing outside practices) or endogenous (constructed from the inside). In other words, firms as organizations appear at one and the same time as interpretation systems or cognitive systems (Pfeffer, 1981), and as action systems or relational systems (Crozier and Friedberg, 1977).

The endogenous language offers a firm and its management an unequalled advantage for building the link between the strategic ambition and the organizational operation, especially when there is a high level of decentralization: that is, where the operational units are granted much freedom of action in order to deal with a situation of high economic uncertainty. In fact, in contrast to exogenous languages or those imported from elsewhere, endogenous languages or those constructed within encourage two types of dynamic that are especially valuable and critical for success. The first is a cognitive and organizational recombination of the practices, choices and actions that appear permanent and shared and which integrate the collective aims of the firm. The second is an ability to recognize weak signals or unstructured data (qualitative, intuitive, uncodified in advance). These signals circulate throughout the organization; they are not blocked or removed en route. Moreover, they will interpreted in the same way by all those who receive them. Such properties are important. These signals in fact allow the firm to identify quickly (faster than its competitors) opportunities, threats or simply significant developments for its positioning.

Activating these two facets of the internal integration between the functions and the units of the firm is a challenge that is all the greater since it brings the firm face to face with numerous, dissimilar and dynamic external worlds: clients, suppliers, competitors, and so on. As a current view goes, even if everyone feels that he or she belongs to the same firm, not everyone necessarily speaks the same language, and everyone has his or her own picture of the world, which may not be the same as that of others. Shared cognitions create collective references, a virtue that cannot be taken for granted and does not emerge spontaneously in firms.

There are two difficulties at this stage. First, how is possible to translate general messages into concrete action? Second, how is the information sent from the periphery to top management to be structured?

In fact, each component of the firm needs concrete information in order to understand and be understood by others. It should be understood that a piece of information is here defined as concrete when it is compatible with the conceptual framework or schema of the person who receives it – or rather the person who is the addressee – and thus makes sense in the light of that person's existing knowledge. If the information received by the addressee makes sense it can be used as a basis for action. At the same time, the firm benefits from a process that protects it against being ignorant of a situation.

Another requirement that confronts the firm is to bring about a significant degree of compatibility between its methods of organizational division and its bounds of ambition, in the knowledge that this division cannot be avoided so far as action and the extraction of information are concerned. That said, if the division of tasks or segmentation of the human fabric is excessive, then the strategic objectives will be out of touch with the rationalities and with the reasoning that each component works by. There then emerges a method of organizational operation that is based on two complementary processes: differentiation and compartmentalization.

A challenge such as this, or its variants, boils down to fundamental choices with regard to plans of action. The firm may adopt either an exogenous or an endogenous way of thinking. The first, which often resorts to Taylorian models or to bureaucratic references, may sometimes appear effective, at least in the short term. The second, because it puts the accent on sharing and owning through joint construction that relates to the particular business context, offers an unequalled advantage for the medium and long term. In fact, it significantly reduces the firm's vulnerability in the face of fluctuations in the external world, because it lays stress on a broader margin of interpretation that allows more avenues for action. In other words, shared knowledge brings the firm stability, continuity, foresight and reliability in its action through time and space. It facilitates and accelerates the harmonization and coordination of multiple decisions made by multiple decision makers inside a single organization: a welcome function in contexts where the firm must mobilize thoughts that are sometimes contradictory and must integrate methods of organizational operation that are often complex.

CHAPTER 4

Cognition as a Major Asset for the Firm

The very word 'cognition' can appear to be an unnecessarily abstract neologism, difficult to fathom in practice and virtually impossible to manage on a daily basis. It tends to be reserved for use in scientific circles or by academics.

Yet any social organization that is goal oriented is structured around cognitive phenomena of some kind. Such is the case with the firm. It carries thought and knowledge at its core. It provides specific ways of thinking, perceiving and acting. It generates its own ways of interpreting events, situations, opportunities and problems. It gives sense and allocates reasons to act or not to act. These cognitive aspects are borne by the individuals and the groups that make up their members. Their content in time and space is relatively stable. They impose themselves on individuals without their necessarily being aware of the fact. They influence their behaviour in daily situations. If their effect is obvious and identifiable, their existence and their nature reveal themselves at the first encounter, arising from the order of the implicit and what happens naturally.

Cognitions are quite specific. Their content varies from one organization to another. In most cases they are the product of time; they do not change in a short period of time or because someone has decided to have them re-engineered. They are highly important, much more so than common sense would expect. They can hinder or facilitate the success of the firm; they can improve or destroy the capacity of headquarters to put strategic ambitions and organizational models into effect.

4.1 Shared References

The languages of action designate a particular category of cognitive phenomena. These are criteria of choice, theories in use and the ways of interpreting events and contexts which drive an organization through the actions and non-actions of its components: actions and non-actions that contribute to the realization of its economic objectives and strategic ambitions.

Do references exist that enable us clearly to detect and evaluate the range of choices present and the decisions taken when various functions and multiple services coexist in a firm?

This question refers back to an asymmetrical universe in which a centre responsible for managing the firm sets up mechanisms, and waits for the periphery to relay and translate the intentions, the sense, and the direction that these mechanisms convey. The strategy thus defined announces both a desirable or imposed development to be reached in the future – for example, to remain the leader for a particular activity or a particular market – and standard references, criteria of judgement and procedures to ensure its daily realization.

Furthermore, and this is often ignored despite the fact that it is crucial, the question also reveals how important it is that the centre – top management – demonstrates the capacity for listening to the peripheries and through them the environment, so far as the developments or discontinuities that may confront the business strategy are concerned. The reference to language for action therefore signifies that one cannot limit oneself to a perspective of disconnection between cognitive or cultural phenomena on the one hand, and organizational or structural logics on the other.

In order to appreciate the significance of such a remark, it is worth turning to the movement that is often called 'de-bureaucratization'. Rightly or wrongly, this is emphasized as being representative of business management, particularly when confronted with a set of demands flowing from the highly uncertain nature of economic environments and the pressure of profitability requirements such as 'shareholder value'. A process such as this becomes apparent through reforms or arrangements that are well known: decentralization of operational units, reduction of functional departments and levels of management, the adoption of individual performance criteria, and the like. It directly generates a series of challenges or demands that focus on information in particular.

Taylorism, combined with bureaucratization, feeds a self-sustaining cycle of reduction in the capacity of various levels of the firm to process information. This dynamic affects business units as well as headquarters. In fact knowledge about the causalities linking various parameters or linkages in terms of action deteriorates as it passes down the authority ladder. Causalities that were implicitly shared by the people at the top become fuzzy for the people at the bottom. Linkages between ends and means vanish. Orders are passed by the top emphasizing conformity to the means, while the understanding of the ends that they are supposed to achieve gets no attention. The cognitions about action lose their content. Those at the bottom of the organization, including the heads of business units, are aware of nothing more than the discretionary means defined by some top authority level, which they have to implement. In short, the cognitive capacity is restricted to the world of top management alone. What is more, because it is cut off from the organization, top management isolates itself in a universe of macro-information that is virtually abstract and that, in any case, does not make sense to those below (Crozier, 1963). The ideal of a seamless language for action integrating the whole social fabric of the firm remains quite absent.

Reliance only on business discipline and culture is not enough to mobilize and integrate the various segments and players confronted by the present and future context to which the firm is directing itself.

On the one hand, by making capacities for judgement disappear, the Taylorian and bureaucratic practices pass on two major handicaps. The first is demonstrated by a dramatic reduction in the capacity of managers to discuss matters with their staff. Top management may have done its best to talk, explain, communicate and try to convey what the rules are intended to achieve, but it will hardly be listened to, let alone understood. The second is revealed when the ability for collective action is held back by the suppression of intermediate hierarchical levels and by a high rate of executive rotation. The intermediate level fulfils a relay function, as an information channel between the bottom and the top, albeit of a sometimes debatable nature and at high cost. Even more significant is its dual role as a memory and means of socialization for new members, whether this be in terms of professional know-how, experience, intuition, or myths and rites that mould a collective solidarity.

On the other hand, by allocating the major responsibility for establishing tactical and economic autonomy to the operational units, firms gamble or postulate that they can generate and process sufficient information about the outside world and about action at their own level. Yet observation suggests that such a bet is far from being safe. Two prerequisites are needed for a capacity of this nature: an extensive focus on local experimentation, and a capacity for trust. However, Taylorian reasoning rejects or neglects the development of these two abilities. Its belief in the virtue of universal principles, which is claimed to be scientific, represses attempts to learn by trial and error made by firms at the start of an endeavour. It rejects the idea that a particular context or a contextual event could affect the developments that are set as targets at the strategic planning stage. Local initiative is forbidden, even if this incurs a risk of discontinuities between the centre and the periphery. The top levels may to some extent be willing to accept that the operational units are no longer transparent and in conformity with its policy, but only so long as they do not become autonomous actors. Its insistence on eliminating every element that allows for human choice drives it to confirm the supremacy of conformity to structures and formal procedures.

4.2 Interpretation for Action

Information constitutes a decisive factor for the firm. This does not relate merely to the dimensions of the transparency between participants, nor to the scientific reliability of data and their technical transmission. It is related to something else, which refers to the processing and the interpretation of the meaning of heterogeneous signals in many respects.

In order to give a meaning to the information and to link it to action, it is vital that chains of causality be developed and shared at the core of the firm. Such an aptitude requires learning processes, more precisely long periods of learning. This prerequisite may appear incompatible with pressure towards the short term (dictatorship by the financial markets, the poor loyalty of executives towards the firm).

The lack of such processes and of individuals who would convey this knowledge results in fragmentation, which is as much horizontal as vertical. This is why top management can transmit new messages, that is information, which remain inaudible and are treated as such by the operational units. In the other direction, the operational units on the ground become inaudible because their information does not make sense to top management: for example, it may be treated as anecdotal or considered as off-track or even unreliable.

The solution to the problem therefore refers back in a more general fashion to a perspective that views the firm as a universe subject to a basic and persistent demand that in theory is difficult to fulfil: the transformation of states of ignorance into schemes of uncertainty.

A state of ignorance is one that is difficult or even impossible to manage. On the one hand, ignorance generates cognitions of a secondary nature. Its management requires capacities of intuition. On the other hand, it is not based on what cognitive sciences would call a problem-framing activity. Problem-framing capacity is vital for success. It means that it is possible for someone, or an organization, to structure a problem so that recourse can readily be made to causality chains between information and action: in relation to events, territories or third parties, for example.

Management in a state of ignorance falls back on mythical or magical forms. One person or one small, directing group is invested with exceptional characteristics, such as prescience and intuition. Henceforth a privileged relation is maintained with the states of the world and their importance for the firm. Furthermore, the wizards or the fortune tellers attribute successes to their own projected status, insofar as they direct their firms. These characteristics are those of the genius warrior as described by Clausewitz or the entrepreneur as peddled by economic magazines. They refer back to the unique being or hero, who cannot easily be replaced.

In contrast to the state of ignorance, a scheme of uncertainty is compatible with the linking of a problem and an operational scheme of actions destined to generate effects that will contribute to its solution. In such a scheme, the situation can be recognized quite simply as one of unpredictability or low predictability. While an ignorance context is not manageable by shared reasoning, an uncertain state is manageable because it generates first-order cognitions.

Every kind of organization or profession assumes that there is a link between aims or problems on the one hand, and means or solutions generated by actions on the other. Sales forces for instance may play an important role in understanding the nature and the evolution of competition their firm is facing. Being in daily contact with buyers and customers, their representatives may notice almost imperceptible changes in the attitude of their partners, relating to how their company and its products are perceived and assessed by them. This may well be interpreted by the sales agents as problematic and raised to the status of an important signal. How successful will the commercial units be when transmitting such a qualitative or weak signal to the company's top management? Will the headquarters listen to them or does it only pay attention to the strong signals – statistics and the like – as a way of understanding the competition and following the market?

In a hierarchy, the time taken for the transformation from ignorance to uncertainty is generally quite long. The aim is to shorten this time. It is important to know how to classify the various signals and the numerous operating structures of potential problems in order to determine which of these are pertinent and which are not, especially if the firm is overwhelmed by data and if the world that surrounds it is changing quickly.

All processes of cognitive structuring of problems refer back to questions of an organizational nature. What are for instance the requirements that have to be satisfied to ensure that cognitive capacities for action are widely diffused and shared inside the firm and across functions? They have to be compatible with organizational differentiation factors such as a hierarchy of authority and a division of tasks. In other words, common sets of cognitions may develop, while at the same time those who share them belong to different hierarchical levels and fulfil different tasks. Such hierarchies and divisions of labour imply that their ways of allocating attention are not identical and that their interests are not the same. The difficulty lies in the fact that, in order to structure cognitions for action, problems have to be fragmented and referred to specific contexts. No cognition exists as such unless it is referred to time and space dimensions. Common cognitions mean that those who share them refer to identical time and space frameworks, a property that is not easy to achieve in organizations for obvious reasons. For instance supply managers tend to favour a rather mid-term horizon – their performance requiring stability and large volume – while manufacturing managers are more short-term oriented – their performance requiring low inventories and flexibility to meet short-term orders.

The firm can certainly put forward an outline of its strategic ambition. It then remains to translate this into operational activity. The difficulty lies in the fact that, in daily life, the participants do not detect the consequences of such an outline very well. Therefore the firm has to be divided into segments in order to take effective action. However, there is no guarantee that these segments will echo or become compatible with the goals that have been set, all the more because the segmentation may be long-established and even out of date. This amounts to a problem of an organizational nature.

Moreover, segmentation carries with it an inability to detect weaker signals, as in the case where territory, products and structures have been separated, for example. Intuitive capacities need to be generated to catch the weaker signals, yet the use of intuition tends not to be favoured by segmented firms, and is often seen as a last resort. One reason for this is that the people who use intuition are not party to the overriding analytical logic of the organization.

To sum up, the organizational and professional positions in the firm need to be modified to change the segmentation. Suppose that the firm's prime aim is to satisfy its clients, but at the same time that the clients' interest lies in having a product that works and causes no problems rather than having a product made in a particular way. Identifying and dealing with this requirement requires a sensitive ear that calls for a key role by those units that are in daily contact with customers, and that is generalized throughout the rest of the organization. It is therefore important that the various units at the heart of the firm do not operate in a way that is too segmented. But this causes problems when the firm itself is extremely segmented. What happens when it is not possible to manage from above without segmentation, when at the same time the customers' perception is of a company that is failing to coordinate its general activities at the bottom?

More generally, the firm is thus faced with two aspects or levels of action. The first deals with the tangible, though not always measurable, challenges of effective action. In this sense, effectiveness depends on identified processes. It is geared down from top management to the ground through segmentation of the problems. So, in this aspect the firm sets its norms by considering the customers' requirements. Their expectations are broadly anticipated in rational terms by the firm.

The second relates to what one might call intangible effectiveness, which is by nature less measurable, but is the process that builds experiments and future competitiveness. It deals with unsegmented problems and processes that are not clearly identified. For example, this aspect builds up the relationship in a more open manner than the first. The firm is able to interpret the many ways of satisfying a need of its clients.

This radical difference is illustrated by the case of the machine tool industry in France in the 1960s and 1970s. Most French firms in this sector consolidated every order to a combination of standard products. The client's requirement was thus treated in a reductionist manner, that is, a projection into a known world and therefore lacking a real understanding of specific needs. There was one firm that took the opposite approach and met the client's requirement in every respect by creating a specific machine. The reason for this different approach was that the firm had an experienced executive who was capable of translating clients' requirements into particular designs without needing these requirements to be segmented into preconceived elements. The difficulty was that this cognitive approach did not suit the short-term demands of the shareholders or the organizational set-up that required young executives who had not been immersed in this type of thinking.

The problems associated with languages for action are revealed by the differing abilities of the social body and the organizational system to pay lasting attention to these two facets of action.

4.3 A Definition of Language

A language for action appears as a collective construction internal to the firm, whose members weave relationships that are more or less asymmetrical and do not necessarily share the same objectives or the same interests. The language plays a part in integrating the components of the organization, for the same reason that the authority hierarchy and the instillation of moral values make their contribution. The language serves as a spur to action.

Thus defined, the language covers a class of phenomena that at first sight are the same as those referred to as "conventions" in the social and economic sciences. Recurrent patterns are observed in the conduct of human activity, which originate from collective norms and social rules. The latter are explained as stable forms or arrangements between the social players (Blumer, 1969). A convention is produced through an intersubjective agreement. It defines a world whose members share the same ideas, codes and experiences.

In many ways, our approach is in line with Becker's (1982): find out who interacts with whom to do what and on the basis of what conventions. But speaking in terms of the idea of language rather than convention implies more focused interests.

The word convention covers a great deal. It applies to facets as diverse as technical specifications, acquired skills, objects, codes for perception and judgement, styles of recognition, and so on. Our view is more restricted or less ambitious. It examines one particular factor: the aims, the policies of a firm, how these are constructed and how they are translated into action. It poses the precise question of how a firm – that is, a community that sets out to achieve an economic goal – adopts organizational models that enable it to tackle hypercompetition.

The approach through conventions, especially through economics, does not always avoid going down the wrong path when it works from empirical cases. It takes as proof of the existence of a specific social space signs and cognitions that it assumes to be rigorously identical and uniformly shared by all its components. But homogeneity is not a necessary condition for a cognitive community. The continuity of a social configuration, the fact that it appears as a whole or as a system, flows from other properties such as partial overlaps and successive links between two or more units that are juxtaposed in line. Moreover, the fact that the players share a language does not mean *ipso facto* that the boundaries between the firm and its environment are impermeable. If that were the case, it would affect the way it was controlled. General management would have to struggle vigorously against any appearance of shared language between its units, lest it should be cut off from the outside world.

There are but few studies and observations that deal rigorously and in depth with how average-sized and large multinational firms operate from the point of view of criteria of choice and codes of interpretation that are actually mobilized in their various components. The entry point is one question: how is continuity possible between the firm's innumerable parts when its environment is constantly changing? The standard theory developed by the sociology of organizations assumes that the authority hierarchy and the division of tasks explain how far the firm may make its environment secure and success predictable in order to achieve its strategic aims (Thoenig, 1998). An extended theory may explore another perspective. How are practices made compatible through the good offices of socialization and solidarity processes?

Our view is also distinguishable from a number of excellent studies made by conventional economists (Piore and Sabel, 1984; Salais and Storper, 1993), in that it does not take a given firm to be a representative sample in the statistical sense, nor as a place that is interchangeable with others and on which a conventional form produced by a more global society might come to be applied through some exogenous dynamic. It adopts a different attitude. Under certain precise conditions, a firm develops independently from the criteria for action that are specific to it. It constructs, assembles and mobilizes them in a broadly endogenous way.

A firm therefore takes on an appearance that is not like the market for creative works that Becker described in *Art Worlds* (1982). The art world comprises a group of players and organizations that are legally autonomous. Different functions, social spheres that are unaware of one another, intervening parties that obey the law of the market and others that do not, all somehow cooperate together to make a particular art form happen. For its part, the firm provides its components with a unique framework for control, a type of collective identity and allegiance to the central core and to a policy.

4.4 What Language is Not

A language for action is therefore defined as a set of references and positionings in situations of choice. It contributes to normalizing behaviours at the same time as it serves to create and share knowledge that is both substantial and procedural.

Understood in this way, this language has nothing to do with what is sometimes called a jargon belonging to a particular human group, a way of speaking in a particular firm, or a special vocabulary and collection of expressions that would only be understood by members of the same group. A language for action does not depend on linguistics. Nor does it blend with internal communications put out by management. It is false to assimilate cognition and speech and reduce the former merely to the explicit utterances of individuals or groups.

Oral and written output takes account of the rationalizations made by the players, the good reasons given by individuals and groups to explain and justify their actions. But the explicitly formulated rationalization of behaviour is an unreliable indicator of the challenges or objectives that lie beneath it. From the moment when individuals are linked through strong phenomena of interdependence, the attitudes that they express or adopt foretell little of, or take little account of, their effective behaviour. What players say about what they have done remains unconfirmed for an observer, at least if, on hearing what is said, this observer hopes to gain direct understanding of what the players are doing.

Similarly, knowledge – or the language for action – does not cover what is often described as the culture of a firm, or its folklore. A culture is revealed by a series of characteristics that evoke a feeling of belonging. It indicates a collective identity among individuals or among groups. It translates a representation of the self and others. It delineates a frontier between inside and out, and between insiders and outsiders too. It confirms an adherence to beliefs and myths. It allows the sharing of certain values and norms. It produces figures of chiefs or heroes. It expresses rites and customs. Defined in this way, however, culture does not mean much if it is not translated into principles for action and shared knowledge.

Knowledge refers to something else. It translates the relationships of instrumental causality that underlie methods of doing things. It is concerned with the methods of information that take account of facts that are significant for action. It carries the mental and technical constructions that are brought to bear in behaviour.

From a more academic standpoint, two avenues are opened up by the literature that associates organized collective action and reference to languages or to cognitive dimensions.

The first explores the nature, processes and functions of argumentation. The 'function of argumentation' covers a special class of phenomena. It deals with debatable situations, circumstances that give rise to controversies between positions or between people who are not *a priori* on the same wavelength. Argument and counter-argument are aimed, through a speaker interacting with an audience, at stimulating acts, whether cognitive or emotional, through a psychological or social effect. Their aim is the same: to secure the allegiance of the audience through persuasion or conviction (Paradeise, 1998).

The second view considers knowledge to be a set of models for perceiving and interpreting the world and for action that is borne by an individual or a specific group (Meindl *et al.*, 1996; Baumard, 1994). It is therefore possible to draw cognitive maps. This involves a method often used to produce a graphic or stylized representation of the models and variables that interviewed subjects are believed to carry in their heads. This approach supposes that this composition of models explains mental processes. How and why are problems formulated and choices considered? Experience shows that interpreting these maps is liable to be an extremely complicated task. Moreover, the reliability of this information depends on individual evidence that has not always been validated by observation of behaviour. Finally, there is the question – which is still far from being convincingly answered – that relates to several players operating in a context in which their choices are interdependent. At what level of similarity or congruence of their respective maps do two or more players share a common language? What happens when the time and space horizons in which each of them operates diverge?

4.5 The Role of Language in the Organization

The content and field of expansion of a language can be inferred from the behaviour and choices actually adopted by players who are linked by inter-dependent relationships, such as 'what A does has consequences for B'. The organizational language may be seen to have two main facets or dimensions.

First, it takes account of the way that an event or state of affairs is inter-preted. It contains a certain type of representation: parameters that are selected and others that are avoided, data that are retained as permanent and other data that are hidden. Representative activity proceeds through selective allocation of attention.

The ways of allocating attention are one of the surest means of analysing the type of objectives, reference systems and, beyond them, the cultural universe of an organization. An empirical research study carried out on four firms showed that firms with a strong internal growth and innovation had a distinctive capacity compared with others: acceptance that their staff members wished to pursue broad aims and objectives, thanks to greater attention being paid to them by the core of the firm (Hogarth *et al.*, 1980).

Second, the language takes account of methods of reasoning with regard to the factors that lie at the heart of this event or that state of affairs, and therefore with regard to ways of changing it in its natural or spontaneous flow. This second facet triggers causalities or explanatory links that join together factors or parameters that therefore allow an act, its content and even its development process to be qualified, through a relationship with consequences or effects that flow from it or might be associated with it. If you do L, M results. Or, in order to obtain M, L must be chosen.

The language is therefore identifiable and configurable through two main indicators: the parameters that an act chooses, and the causalities that link one parameter to another.

The language allocates meaning to behaviour, decisions and policies. Actions take on meaning through the work of representation of the world and of attribution of causality. They are directed to efficiency, they become intelligible and acceptable on the register of reasons. Mental grids that individuals or groups carry allow stability to be established. The latter arrange the criteria of choice and judgement. They also establish the possibility that actions will be seen as credible. In doing this, the erratic or random element in decision making is reduced, along with the impact that the decisions may have on the milieu that needs to be changed or on the environment that one wishes to control.

This is not to say that players necessarily reveal an explicit awareness of the cognitive models that guide them and that they adopt. The players internalize collective knowledge. Observation shows that, even at the highest management level in a firm, the language in its diverse facets arises rather from the order of tacit or implicit phenomena. Everything happens as though the players lived and interpreted their actions and the cognitive bases of their actions as self-evident. It is up to the observer to detect what the player takes for granted, and to make the player's cognitive universe explicit. Some managers show themselves capable of making such observations by paying close intuitive attention in their interactions. A more rigorous approach is to compare the data from an in-depth interview with data from observation of types of decision. This relates to the precise context in which the players make their choices, in which they bring their behaviour and policies into play.

Organizational language is therefore not just an entertaining artefact without any practical significance. On the contrary, knowledge as defined maps out the avenues for action for the person who bears and adopts it. It links principles to conjecture, and theory to context. It marks out the route. One of the major questions that is therefore posed for the management of firms is the nature of these markers. To be more precise, everything happens as though there were languages that closely and rigidly mark out the pathways for actions while others show a broader and less restrictive route.

A language is a phenomenon in action: that is, it is constructed socially and collectively. There is nothing else like it. It is the property of individuals who are active, who own it and who transform it. It is therefore not necessarily fixed once and for all, as if frozen by the past. This ownership is geometrically variable in time and space.

Of course, a procedure or a technique as such conveys promises, beliefs, or more exactly suppositions or theories as to the link between its content and its usage. This is the case for the choice of a criterion to establish a business strategy: for example, market share as a prime performance indicator. It is also the case for the measurement of the performance of operational units. A criterion such as the economic value added (EVA) conveys a purely financial and short-term idea of effectiveness, its yardstick being the profitability that the firm would achieve if it were to place its capital in the stock market.

While apparently technical and neutral, both tools are rather normative: they carry a theory or a vision of action and the world. A market-share-based prescription implies that the bigger the market share a firm controls, the more it controls the market and sets the competition standards. In other words, size is the cause of success. EVA likens the manager of an operational unit to a banker whose performance can be judged by the variation in the surplus profit that he or she achieves in comparison with the performance of the financial market. Adopting such a criterion leads the player to take into account instruments that mark out the action within quite specific representations and along more or less wide pathways.

At the same time, such devices provide scope for interpretation and even reformulation. For players reinvest the instruments with the help of their own cognitive schemas. More generally, languages do not exist outside a particular context. Their nature and existence are inferred from what a player does or does not do in a given context when faced with a precise situation. A particular cognitive method generates a particular consequence in such circumstances at such a time.

4.6 The Importance of Mutual Understanding

Sharing a common language does not imply that in an organization the language is uniform, the same for everyone. Common or shared does not mean undifferentiated, in the sense that a single reference number would be rigorously adhered to by all parties that make up the organization. No person, anywhere in the firm, possesses the same basic cognitive knowledge as those with whom he or she interacts. Describing a language as belonging to an organization is a shorthand device that needs to be handled with care.

A language can be defined as being common or shared from the moment when two players located in an interactive situation make use of identical cognitive references in the way that they carry out their respective actions.

When this occurs, the organization finds that it possesses a system of shared understanding. Step by step, more players, whose areas of overlap and cognitive content vary, are brought into the same cognitive configuration. Continuity is assured between functions and players whose dimensions in space and time are dissimilar. Bringing these together is assured by pathways of action that are, on the one hand, less narrow than those that

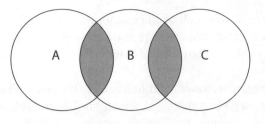

Figure 4.1 Linkage of shared language

would be imposed by too strict a codification system and, on the other hand, more clearly marked than they would be if total autonomy were granted to each player.

Partial overlaps of languages and cognitions allow two things to coexist. Strategies can be progressively translated into operational acts. Information that is generated by the units in contact with the ground can be interpreted more easily.

It is this that explains the confusion that often follows upheavals in which cognitive links have been dislocated or even broken. Persons, departments and functions whose language no longer overlaps with that of partners or internal contacts are thus deprived of access to concrete information that can be assimilated and makes sense to them. They are at risk of being incoherent. This often leads to the introduction of restrictive routines and procedures imposed by third parties, but this is an unsatisfactory solution; such an exogenous language leaves no room for intuition or adaptation on the part of those to whom it is applied.

4.7 Endogenous and Exogenous Languages

Here we postulate the existence of two different types of language for action, classified according to their original source in relation to the entity in question: exogenous language and endogenous language.

Exogenous language appears as a contribution coming from third party sources and impacting on the organization. Driven by their managements, and often in the authoritative style of command and control, firms resort to translation processes that are brought in from outside. These are, as it were, off-the-shelf knowledge that is roughly and insensitively applied to the internal social body.

Such exterior references have the advantage of being quite rapidly activated. Experience also shows that in the long run they are hardly satisfactory for a range of reasons. First, they only deal partially or from a restricted angle with situations of choice. This is the case with financial languages that only refer to visible shareholders (stock markets, financial analysts, boards of directors). They are concerned with the short term and work to very specific criteria.

Second, the external references that third parties establish in the social body of the firm (consultants, etc.) or that are borrowed from the supposed better practices of competitors or from third party firms in general (the phenomenon of institutional mimicry) sometimes hardly produce any competitive advantage and often remain cosmetic, or are even rejected like so many transplants. They do not relate to the peculiarities of the firm, the fact that it is already there and came before them.

This is the case with the management sciences that tend to provide systems that are more or less irrelevant from the operational point of view. The complete off-the-shelf package that the best-practice method brings with it arises from thinking that remains paradoxically Taylorian. Examples are marketing that does not integrate ethnological observation of different practices, and quality control measures that, instead of stimulating research into the improvement of contractual procedures, turn into a drive to conform to cosmopolitan standards (ISO or others). There is the risk of a vicious circle of confusion being set in motion in the organization because the exogenous constructs are not suited to the local requirements.

The endogenous language for its part is a code whose references and positionings are produced and constructed internally by a collective practice of the organization itself. It is a code that originates in and is legitimized by the core of the firm, not externally. It takes on the appearance of a locally mounted and contextually bordered project.

Six major characteristics distinguish it from an exogenous language:

- Endogenous language is accompanied by a process of activation, a task of collective appropriation and apprenticeship, that is diffused and long lasting and that is translated by shared cognitive capacities.
- It relies on the creation and/or existence of players and social processes that, at the heart of a firm, appear as carriers of knowledge and function like shock absorbers, particularly between top management and the operational units.
- It is made manifest through the existence of methods of regulation and adjustment that create competing logics for action at the heart of the firm.
- It extends explicit choice criteria through implicit norms.
- It becomes a collective asset that creates a shared identity, which is enriched through confidence and experimentation throughout the length of a relatively long time horizon.

■ The endogenous quality is thus translated by the development of a tissue of weak links that establish themselves in support of and in the interstices of the strong links in the organization.

4.8 Foresight

Under what conditions does a language become a collective property shared by the members of the firm? Also, under what conditions does it generate consequences that would not occur if all of the members brought their own cognitive schemas?

To reply to these questions we need to return for a moment to pragmatic evidence given on many occasions by theory of organizations. Firms are characterized by their continual facing up to a dilemma.

Internally, they are structured in two ways. The asymmetry of the relationships between their various levels represents the hierarchy of authority. Complementarity or interdependence between their various functions represents the specialization of tasks.

The challenge for them is simple to formulate in the abstract but difficult to deal with in practice. Organizations are error prone, they may be routine oriented or unable to learn. Their members generate risks to the common good of the firm, are over-sensitive to power and prestige considerations or avoid cooperation. How is it possible to ensure compatibility and continuity both vertically and horizontally when the future of the firm may be jeopardized by errors and risks whose source is endogenous? How are the units to be allowed a significant degree of autonomy in carrying out their respective day-to-day tasks?

In their business environment, firms are confronted with contexts of action that demand positionings and responses that are not only vital for survival or success but also decisive in relation to the firms' internal method of operation. The senior managers thus need the lower levels to integrate into their own choices and daily behaviour the visions and priorities that the management defines. In other words, two general questions arise.

First comes the question of foresight. In an organization that is often large, geographically dispersed, with numerous interdependences between the functions, units, hierarchical levels and trades, how is possible to ensure that what A does will be foreseen by B and what B does will be foreseen by A, and then even on to C and D?

Second is the question of coherence. How does one scale down vertically and horizontally the common pursuit of relatively broad or even different objectives by multiple decision makers who have significant scope for operational autonomy?

Quite obviously, the command-control binomial is not sufficient. It is even harmful when subordinates are expected to produce compromises between contradictory demands from top management on their own. There is at least one reason why relationships between head office and the operational units cannot be taken for granted. If the units are supposed to adopt the head office project and implement it in their actions, it is essential for more and more concrete and apportioned knowledge to be available descending through the hierarchy, and for the units or players to be brought into closer contact with the economic battlefield. In fact, however, there are considerable differences in space and time between the top and bottom. At the different levels people operate with different horizons and with different degrees of precision and abstraction.

Managing the interfaces between head office and the operational units both up and downstream constitutes a major concern for management from many viewpoints. Various functions are dedicated to holding together the choices and behaviours in such complicated and diverse worlds: for example, coordination, command, control, and integration.

Foresight is a quality. The firm sees the individual initiatives of its units fitting together in order to ensure continuity and complementarity, without any unit replicating the work of another.

An organization with a low degree of internal foresight is like a world where permanent uncertainty prevails with regard to behaviour and choice, and where choices are made randomly and arbitrarily. Reliability is never guaranteed.

A firm with a strong capacity for foresight is better at dealing with environments or economic battlefields, even ones that appear highly threatening for its performance and are very unstable. Internal transparency, which ensures foresight, allows the external opacity to be faced up to. On the other hand, the less this transparency is developed internally, the more the external opacity increases.

Foresight for actions and events is all the stronger when the languages for action employed by the members of an organization are connected through shared references. A common language is by definition a language constructed by the parts, individuals, groups and hierarchical levels or functions that share it. In other words, it is by nature endogenous, produced by the milieu itself.

4.9 Common Knowledge

Let us take two departments, A and B, located at the heart of the same firm. We assume that each of them sees its way of working, in particular handling the interface or interdependence between them, as being controlled by a precise codification, by rules and procedures that are dictated by a third party, C. In such a case, A and B are subject to an exogenous language. C imposes or introduces a device whose origin is foreign to A and to B. The codification or procedural rule prescribes extremely narrow avenues of action. By doing this, it reduces to a minimum, or totally eliminates, any flexibility of behaviour.

Taking the opposite case, suppose A and B have great latitude in their choice of action. In such a situation, it is probable that common areas of interpretation and meaning will develop through mutual and successive contact. This correlates to the often observed phenomenon that experts refer to as common knowledge, that is shared and implicit knowledge.

The existence of shared and implicit knowledge common to both A and B ensures flexibility and therefore creates broader avenues. There are common ideas about the ends that each department envisages in its actions and satisfies through the processes to attain these ends.

In other words, two ways of ensuring continuity and compatibility between A and B emerge. The first is the establishment of procedural codes that stipulate who does what, how and when. This is the work of a third party foreign to the two presumed partners. The second approach is based on the common knowledge that A and B share without any intervention by a third party being required. There are remarkable differences between these two approaches.

Codification through narrow avenues creates foresight through a grammar common to A and B. Prescribed processes, explicit ways of doing things are to be followed and are assumed, if correctly defined by their designers, to engender stability and certainty. In other words, formal and impersonal codes of action create a common framework between scattered contexts of action. It becomes more difficult to use rhetoric that underlines the uniqueness of each singular context, and that would therefore rationalize and legitimize the autonomy and discretionary authority needed to manage each of them. It follows a relatively strict pathway. It therefore allows little flexibility to whatever is subject to it, in particular in relation to the variability of the context to which it applies. Finally, it arises from exogenous language, because it is formulated by a third party. In this sense, it is much more liable to be fragile and unstable.

Intersecting common knowledge is made up of shared reasoning that bears on both the results to be produced and the means to be employed. It traces avenues for action that are more flexible and wider than average, as shown in the following example.

A is an executive of a commercial subsidiary. Suppose he decides in his sector to launch a campaign for a product, a campaign that will be launched at a specific time and in precisely defined conditions. He informs B, his line manager, but before launching his campaign he must be sure that B has received his message, that he has responded and that he will allocate the resources required, for example by supplying the appropriate products. An exchange of information is therefore necessary. On his side, the line manager is at head office. He needs to be certain that his subordinate, A, will have his response by the time that he launches his campaign. In other words it is important for the success of the campaign that both partners are in agreement, that this becomes endogenous to A and to B, and this in a context where they are not face to face in the same physical space and where they are not acting simultaneously.

The endogenous language created by A and by B has the advantage that the codification is minimal. It allows the actors who share it to react to surprises in contexts that they had not foreseen or anticipated. The subordinate has neither to wait for B to formulate a new norm nor to ask B for preliminary authorization to depart from the plan. The boss, for his part, takes a chance on A being capable of dealing with unexpected events, while bearing in mind the essentials or aims for which B is himself accountable to C, and that A will be able to find the most appropriate solution to the situation.

The existence of avenues for action is visible in an indirect but positive way. Everything happens as if all the individuals involved know more or less what they themselves need to do, and at the same time how the others will act, even if their actions are different. I understand and I know that they understand what I understand. In other words, there are no chance elements at play. No one is working in the dark. Everyone's competencies are measured by the same yardstick.

Under these conditions, the organization acquires a major advantage: an increased capacity for foresight.

In fact, organizations cannot create forecasts at their heart if their staff or those they work through cannot anticipate. This anticipation is made more difficult or even impossible to develop in two particular kinds of avenue for action: first, when the avenues are too narrow or rigid, and second when they are too broad and loose. If however the sector where the action takes place lacks stability and requires rapid reactions, then if codification is to be normal, the avenues for action must be enlarged.

To satisfy this need the endogenous language must be privileged in comparison with the exogenous language. In fact, between them they make compatible two avenues for action that are suitable for different players. The endogenous language is absorbed and internalized. The exogenous language becomes secondary and is not internalized.

There is another difference in the fact that, in contrast to the exogenous language, the endogenous language allows the players to interpret events for themselves, apply improvisatory skills, and explore alternatives around a common core: in other words all the necessary ingredients for launching a learning process.

4.10 Socialization and Trust

Adopting the same language for action, whereby the partners use the same words or even the same paradigms, is a useful and possibly necessary approach, but it is by no means all that is required. There has to be another element present for an interlocking common knowledge to become rooted. A must know that B knows that A knows.

Such a condition is not developed by techniques such as ongoing training at a management school or through experience gained outside the current workplace. It is obtained from other vectors: closeness to others, continuity of mutual experience. Personal proximity and professional continuity imply that the place of work and the process of resolving problems provide the matrix for learning and co-construction.

In other words, shared knowledge is not brought about through group therapy, nor does it develop merely from being together in a social context (eating together or sharing the same feelings). Common experience and problems managed together in a context outside work have little to do with the context of the workplace. Why? Because such contexts dissociate two facets that are in fact inseparable: socialization and solidarity. An illustration from team sports underlines theory.

American football tends to adopt an organizational model that makes little use of endogenous language. Many players who are specialists in positional play and at different stages of the game are linked throughout an impressive series of disconnected events, lasting only a few seconds. During countless breaks in the game, coaches spell out the details of the next play to be executed. There is little or no scope for improvisation.

Rugby, football and basketball are team games that flow with much greater continuity. They follow a quite different model. Here there is a somewhat intangible phenomenon, the aim of the game, with one or more players acting as trustees on the ground. This common aim of the group (which is something more than a collection of individuals who could be replaced at a stroke) is pursued ad hoc in an improvised manner that depends on the changing circumstances. This improvisation is not some random action; it is the art of collectively building variations suited to particular circumstances on a basis of common fundamentals. Finding oneself instinctively alongside a teammate in a phase of the game or antic-ipating the action or movement that a teammate will make are examples of the asset of common knowledge.

It is no accident that the best teams do not simply result from accumu-lating the best individuals in the market at a given moment (along the lines of the all-star games in professional basketball). They often emerge from a long history; they are relatively long established and they have experi-enced little turnover of their players before they come to fame. The phenomenon of the team emerges from work experience, including tempo-rary setbacks. Socialization is reinforced by solidarity. The coach keeps the same players as long as possible. He gives few detailed instructions. But he sees to it that confidence in what is being done is maintained and devel-oped by the group as it is and when replacements are taken on. The French football team that won the World Cup in 1998 and became champions of Europe in 2000 illustrates the performance that can be achieved through a process of common knowledge.

Knowledge that becomes common is knowledge relevant to content that is operationally relevant for the players. Turning cognitive content into a shared asset involves moving from abstract to concrete knowledge. This point is often misunderstood by managers whose good intentions result in bad disappointments.

Firms experience many situations of abstract or unshared knowledge. This is the case when the headquarters diffuses messages to the operational units that do not have real meaning for the latter. The top communicator acts in an egocentric way, sending content which make sense in terms of how the headquarters operates, but not for the units themselves. In such cases the latter perceive the message as information only, and as informa-tion related to the sender. To become shared and significant in terms of knowledge – that is, for the recipient to consider it as his or her problem too – messages have to be translated into contents and consequences that have a direct impact on what the targets do and how they should operate. Knowledge centred only on the role of head office does not activate the operational units for at least one reason: it remains in such general terms that it cannot be adopted by those that have to apply it. At best it seems an incantation. At worst it is seen as a whim of head office, to be listened to more or less respectfully but not of real consequence.

Moving to concrete knowledge assumes that cognitive overlaps can be established and are effectively favoured by head office, which dissemi-nates the paradigms in successive stages through the social fabric towards the periphery. For the values proclaimed by head office to be orchestrated, they need knowledge that is shared.

Furthermore, shared language is based on mutual trust that is apportioned *a priori*. From this point of view, trust does not flow from a kind of state of grace that might from time to time induce the alchemy of interpersonal affinity. A good deal of attention is often given to the selection and recruitment of individuals whose so-called deep personalities are compatible so that trust can more easily grow among them. While social psychology offers some serious approaches, too much reliance is often placed on factors such as charisma. Trust has to be de-psychologized to a large extent. Evidence from research strongly suggests that real trust arises when other conditions are present, such as common knowledge that is shared among the parties involved. Such cognitive aspects are causes of trust, which itself is a consequence of them. People recognize one another because they implicitly speak the same language when it comes to action. In other words, everyone's behaviour is predictable. Trust in fact prolongs and perpetuates cognitive styles. Above all, it allows them to be more quickly and more thoroughly learnt.

Knowledge becomes common to a set of individuals and groups from the moment that there is a state of reciprocal trust among them. In fact, trust creates room for the interplay and virtual negotiation of reciprocal commitments. Such spaces reveal an original property. They cause the relationship between A and B to stabilize.

This stabilization occurs even when A and B are not subjected to a group dynamic resulting from a face-to-face encounter or meeting between them and when they operate in a shifted time frame on different objects. The stabilization does not require any interpersonal interaction close at hand or the completion of a strictly identical task. Trust is not necessarily and uniquely associated with interpersonal or physical closeness. Nor is it associated only or mainly with common backgrounds.

Trust is not an absolute phenomenon. Only in an ideal world – which unfortunately ours is not – is it perfect and independent of any context. It is relative, it has limits. Trust relationships are not pure affective phenomena. They carry content. They apply in certain situations, not in others. They also carry obligations. The pressure to behave in a way that reinforces the trust of your partners does not apply everywhere and at any time. What is expected here, for instance in business matters, may not apply there, for instance in private life. To adopt behaviour that one's partners find reliable, and to make decisions that take into account their interests, becomes easier when both sides speak the same language and adopt similar grammars or cognitive codes of action.

CHAPTER 5

Agro: A Company in Transition

The cognitive firm is not an abstract topic of discussion, it is a working system whose real strategy is determined day by day. It is the result of operational unit activity, which does not necessarily coincide with the strategic rhetoric that is presented by top management and that the formal structures are supposed to put into effect.

How does a language present itself in everyday life? How can its content be gauged and its bearers identified? The following chapter gives an example taken from a real firm: Agro.

Methodological details on how to study cognitions empirically are provided in Appendix 1. It will easily be seen that there is no need to engage in long and extensive research in order to understand the languages in action. This can easily be done by managers who know how to listen to their organizations and to use a minimum of analytical intuition.

5.1 A Multinational Faced with Hypercompetition

A firm adopting extensive decentralization to the advantage of its operational units and applying virtual market principles internally between its various functions provides a good example of cognitive schemas at work. In fact, during this process, it is likely that the various participants, services and professions will benefit from a broad autonomy of choice, and that the way they behave in handling their mutual interdependencies will create positive-sum games. In other words, in contrast to a centralized and highly proceduralized organizational model, the decentralized firm made up of strategic business units relaxes the obligations passing through the hierarchical authority and codification. Coordination between the functions and services relies increasingly on horizontal interfaces, and therefore on the ability to adjust and make common decisions that the social body of the firm demonstrates.

The Agro company is a European multinational operating in the agrochemical sector. It employs more than 15,000 people based in 80 different countries. It manufactures and sells products developed from chemical and biological research on a worldwide market. It is composed of industrial sites, laboratories and commercial subsidiaries spread through the five continents. Its clients are specialized distributors who in turn serve farmers and the general public. It rates itself among the biggest in its sector, with a turnover of 3 billion, and is considered to be economically healthy and financially profitable. Agro is owned by a major and global pharmaceutical group, but enjoys a wide autonomy in the running of its operations. Its shareholder recognizes its specificity and respects its identity, behaving more like a financial investor than a hands-on operator.

The sector in which Agro has evolved is characterized by the high financial cost of newly discovered molecules and the clearly apparent risks to the environment and the population. This particular firm resembles many others in terms of the markets it tackles and the organizational model that governs it.

It operates in a market that is profoundly unstable, that stirs up waves of mergers and acquisitions, stimulates accelerated technological innovations, and experiences ferocious competition. In this context, as in many other economic activities, the ability that the firm displays on a daily basis to coordinate all the intervening functions upstream and downstream in its activities, together with innovation in after-sales technical service, become decisive factors for success. To prepare itself, Agro has adopted a formal three-point plan of action:

- Increasing the responsibility and autonomy of the operational units. The board of directors limits itself to designing of the plan of action and prescribing criteria for financial and economic performance, and keeps control of a small number of key skills (see Appendix 2). As a result, some of the commercial networks possess their own industrial capacity, enabling them to package the products that they sell on the external market.

- Resorting to virtual market mechanisms as references for unit decisions. Hence the commercial networks are free to establish their range of products and their retail prices, to buy products from the factories of the firm at their own discretion, and to negotiate upwards the price of new products. The units are linked themselves by interfaces resembling those between supplier and client. The functional departments bill their services to whoever can offer them a profit, and the executives are empowered to use third-party suppliers if these are less expensive. However, this principle does not apply in the case of two particular situations: research and development on the one hand, which does not form a business unit and whose budget is largely financed by head office, and on the other hand those molecules referred to as strategic or proprietary, the production of which cannot be subcontracted by the networks to factories outside the firm.

■ Regrouping into a single business unit called the AIG (active ingredients group) the strategic marketing functions, industrialization (the factories being autonomous economic centres also), and project management concerning basic innovations (new molecules) (see Appendix 2).

With the exception of R&D, each function is both autonomous and subject to the criteria of short-term financial profitability. It is therefore highly probable that a zero sum game will develop. Each department, each function, each executive will tend to give precedence to its own sector in the short term in its interfaces up- and downstream and with its colleagues. The result is little mutual understanding and few collective references to pave the way for choices for action. The formal design thus becomes based on a transactional scenario of generalized selfishness or even externalization to third parties.

Few staff leave the firm during their career. They are taken on very early and remain loyal. At the same time, few executives are recruited ad hoc from outside over the age of thirty. The Agro directors also pay great attention to social issues. Head office policy is full of references demonstrating a desire to avoid redundancies, to develop staff skills through internal training, to apply principles of respect towards people and a mutual willingness to listen. Finally, frequent opinion surveys carried out internally show an exceptional level of attachment on the part of the employees towards their company and their profession, as well as very high degrees of satisfaction about morale, interest in the work and working conditions. The generalized egoism of the formal design co-exists with a social body that is sensitive in itself and towards the logic of solidarity/loyalty and humanistic imperatives of which the firm aims to be the epicentre.

How comfortably do this second aspect, which evokes the existence of a strong, communal identity, and the first aspect, which maximizes the logic of opportunism, co-exist under the same roof? Which mechanism, albeit centrifugal or centripetal, has the greater, final influence on the daily choices of each function and the behaviour of the executives?

Close examination of the way Agro functions reveals remarkable contrasts, which can be summarized as follows:

■ Three main subsets emerge: one organized for research, one for which the epicentre is formed by those responsible for active ingredients, and one which groups together the commercial function.

■ Each of these three poles forms a world in itself, which distinguishes itself from the others by languages of its own.

■ The firm has a strong, limited degree of horizontal integration upstream and downstream, which corresponds to fundamental divergences between the criteria of economic and strategic decision making by its executives. It is as though an orchestra were to have its various instrumental sections play varying improvisations at different speeds from the one, shared musical score.

In other words, and here lies the interest of the Agro case study, a firm can favour cognitive networks and juxtapose heterogeneous languages at the same time.

5.2 Shared Cognition in Action: The AIG

An illustration of a shared language is given by the AIG (the part of the firm that supplies active ingredients). A kind of cognitive community links together individuals and departments that carry out different operations (strategic marketing, buying and selling of active ingredients and their approval, management of development projects for new, basic research of molecules up to their market launch and their purchase by commercial businesses) and that are controlled by quasi-market principles of transaction in their mutual relationships.

Two particular features emphasize the interest of this observation. The first is the relatively youthful nature of this function in the firm. The fact that the AIG is coordinated and communicates among its components by a common language is all the more striking because it is only four to five years old. While the other departments are more established and their age as specific organizations can be counted through decades, this operational unit is a recent creation by the current CEO. It brings together under one hierarchical banner services and functions that were previously separate and autonomous. Its employees, amounting to 60 or so, have experienced and carried out functions that are totally different from those that they have been carrying out since their arrival in the department.

The second interesting feature is the sharing perimeter of this common language. This not only includes the actual, named participants of the AIG, but also a certain number of staff and functions that are formally outside it, who are, for example, assigned to other departments. The boundaries of a cognitive community do not necessarily blend with the institutional status of members or the official sharing out of tasks. So far as the AIG is concerned, they overflow, and this creates, step by step, a network in which the different elements are linked together by partial overlaps and by common areas.

5.2.1 Criteria of Common Choice

Continuity is displayed in concrete situations that generate the choices and behaviour of individuals and services. To be more exact, the partners in an interdependent relationship adopt identical reference criteria in order to organize their respective decisions and transactions. A chaining of a cognitive nature links the interfaces step by step.

In Figure 5.1 the numbers show the content of partial overlap from the viewpoint of decision criteria that trigger the departments in their actions. In this way the six overlaps represent two functions that share one, two or three identical choice or action references on each occasion that they have to do business together:

1. The time for delivery, the cost price and the quality-reliability of a new molecule.
2. The capacity to produce products classed as strategic or proprietary; the delivery time and the cost of molecules; whether they are old or new.
3. The time taken for market launch and the commercial acceptability by the known key networks of new molecules.
4. The defence of all molecules classed as strategic.
5. The time to market and the commercial acceptability of new molecules by the networks.
6. The time to market and the commercial cost of new molecules.

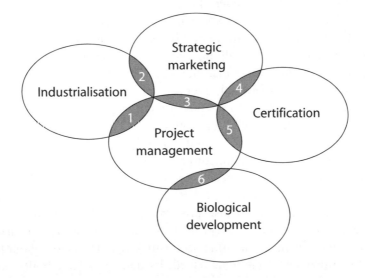

Figure 5.1 Linkages of language in and around the AIG

The interface between industrialization and strategic marketing at the core of the AIG is a good starting point.

Officially, the coordination between the two functions is established through the existence of a unique service, grouped in one place, subject to one budget and to the same evaluation indicator for the results. It extends itself by the fact that the industrial executives do not operate as factory commanders: the factories are separate and set up as autonomous centres of economic activity. The AIG is a buyer of their services.

This architecture in itself, however, does not appear to be a sufficient condition for crosschecking to be established between the manufacturers and sellers. The AIG is managed by two executives, each of whom heads up a specialized hierarchical line or a trade. The bonus on results offers relatively moderate financial rewards; annual remuneration per executive amounts to less than 3 per cent of the annual salary. More generally, when only the structural and procedural design is considered, there does not appear to be a firm basis for solidarity among the staff.

A more convincing indicator *a priori* is evident from the manner in which the manufacturers and sellers assess their mutual relationships, which are generally found to be pleasant. That said, the psycho-emotional affinities do not explain all the reasons for this understanding. Continuity is conveyed and extended in the content of the business choices and ways of cooperating.

Each person's priorities are internalized by his or her colleagues. 'I must bear in mind what my colleague in charge of industrial purchasing might do,' says the marketing manager. 'People understand my point of view, and don't ask the impossible or expect me to keep my mouth shut,' says a manufacturing executive. The annual financial performance of the department serves as the explicit rallying point that underlines the interdependence of the two functions. Once the specifications for launching a new product have been established, everyone trusts their colleagues and lets them get on with their job. 'It is up to my colleague to make the manufacturing decisions. All I want is for matters to be resolved as agreed and, if there are problems, I am sure he will have done all that he could,' says a marketing man. For the manufacturer: 'Marketing is not my business and I am not going to interfere, because the marketing department knows how to look after its own affairs.'

The active ingredients, whose procurement is a task entrusted to one group, are made available for project development, a task entrusted to another group. The manufacturing sector makes and tries to honour unilateral commitments without being asked. Its managers have built a kind of code of excellence which they implement in a recurrent way and whose latent function is to push its partners to offer reciprocity. In other words, a common threat unites the two parties: the reactions from downstream. The list of specifications attached to an active ingredient and in relation to which the AIG makes its promises to the rest of the firm is regarded as a priority challenge by its executives.

An example of this may be seen in the attitude to subcontracting. With new molecules, the way in which the pilot phase of their fabrication is set up reflects an approach shared by all AIG members. As one manufacturing executive puts it:

> There is a twofold risk: industrial and commercial. It may be that we have been too optimistic about development prospects . . . because at the beginning of a pilot project one cannot forecast the level of market acceptance at the end of two, three or four years. Then there is a technical risk: manufacturing a product, making this feasible, involves a type of chemistry that is still little understood. So, because of the uncertainty, my prime objective is to control the investment made by the AIG; I apply myself to this.

A decision is then taken to approach external suppliers 'as a reaction to bad experiences in the past when we wanted to do everything internally and when the factories did not know how or did not want to keep to the rules of technical innovation' says a marketing manager.

Common references are activated, these being significant resources or constraints for the challenge to be met by the respective parties. There may even be no need to discuss the matter. Manufacturers and marketing people are not keen on face-to-face meetings. Neither are they keen on writing memos filled with details about their mutual transactions. They are often away from their desks, abroad or visiting other units. So a project manager spends less than a quarter of the time at his or her office and only meets face to face the manufacturing staff concerned with the product five or six times a year. No contractual support is really needed. Written commitments and long conversations are not relevant in a world where people share the same action language. 'We understand each other *a priori*,' says a marketing manager.

5.2.2 Standards of Sociability

The common criteria of choice are mediated by behavioural rules. Tacit standards govern conduct and maintain good neighbourly relations.

For example, one rule concerns proper behaviour when there is a dispute or difference of opinion with a partner. It stipulates that the employee will not conduct the matter in public and will not appeal to any third party, whether hierarchical or up or downstream. It is therefore understood that problems must always be solved bilaterally, even if each person cannot win on every occasion.

It is remarkable that such ways of behaving develop, given the sometimes strong asymmetries in relationships of mutual dependence. If the marketing person relies on the industrial manager of AIG, the latter must manage an upstream for which he is the customer: the production plants that supply the active ingredients. Experience suggests that he basically manages the relationship with the plants as a buyer would do, which means according to a competitive and economic logic. He puts a lot of pressure upon the plant managers to deliver efficiently, on time and at low cost. While he is formally the supervisor of the plants, he nevertheless does not act as the representative of the cause or interests of the factory lobby. He makes use of comparisons of performance between Agro factories and outside suppliers. Only one restriction to his buyer rationale is imposed on him by head office: do not cause uproar in the factories (closures, lay-offs, social unrest) by resorting too hastily to subcontracting.

The rules of good neighbourliness between departments are supplemented by two powerful reinforcements: the high level of seniority of the firm's executives, and their experience of many operational functions. For example, the director of strategic marketing has twenty-five years' experience. He has held four positions in four different countries on the commercial side. His deputy has been with Agro for twenty years. The manufacturing manager who deals with subcontractors has been a senior executive in three factories, in addition to a period at head office.

In this context the managers are inclined to take calculated risks, such as making use of hybridization between the trades, even if this entails not conforming in an orthodox way to the original methods of the trade. As one executive put it:

> We have proved ourselves elsewhere. It is difficult to say to us: you don't know much about this or that's not the right way to do that. Because to innovate one has to have one's experience recognized and be freed from professional routine.

Moreover, they know personally many of their colleagues in the firm and the people their department deals with. They therefore benefit from an extensive virtual network whose members have shared active experience with them and are thus capable of anticipating the thought processes required for diverse functions. The employees are carriers of information that the relational interfaces do not transmit spontaneously. The first area of application for such resources is located within the department itself.

From many points of view, the strategic marketing sector constitutes the epicentre of the mechanism. Various occupations come under the heading of strategic marketing: biological development, market research, certification, and product protection. Cognitive schemes link them together. Biologists, certification experts, marketing staff and project heads share two common reference points.

The first is the delay in getting a product to market. For instance, everyone is supposed to act in a way that avoids any risk to the progress of a project up to its certification by a key country. Nobody is expected to redo downstream something that has already been done upstream (for example in terms of studies or tests) unless some vital question has been overlooked that could affect the viability of a project. Also, consideration must be given to the possible consequences that actions in one's own sector may have in other areas. For example, the toxicologist anticipates what effect the modification of a molecule may have on the environment.

The second register is concerned with the acceptability of a product by zones and by countries. This is achieved in three ways: percentage of market share obtained in a period, a retail price acceptable to the retailers, and securing a key region that acts as a yardstick for the other subsidiaries.

The existence of a common language becomes apparent from the strong urge to act collectively that people demonstrate.

Departments involved in marketing show versatility and overlap in their tasks. Thus, the person responsible for certification follows through the development of two new molecules in addition to his own duties. More generally, skills overlap. For example, the experts in developmental biology, soil science and certification are closely linked to common projects. Shared histories feed one another and information converges to consolidate individual contributions. It is difficult to personalize these contributions. An expert comments:

In my field, I can play solo. It is easy to want to become the king in a technical field, to rack up one's achievements. . . . But this would be suicidal. So, when I head up a toxicological study or when additional soil analyses are carried out, I subscribe strictly to two points of view: what is the global budget that the AIG can bear, and what are the business options available to the AIG as to the commercialization of the new active ingredient? I have obligations to the project head. . . . There is no room for personal technical gratification.

Another characteristic is the recruitment of employees. This receives priority attention. One director puts it this way:

> I personally choose the project heads. The key is to have credible people who can work with others without conflict while still conveying their point of view. This is because the timescale for the project is limited: two to three years. If the project head succeeds, he knows he will go on to something else, for example, to head up a region.

There is strong pressure for people to fit into an action community. The same goes for the experts who surround the project heads. The two partners are united through the common budget procedure. Studies that are contracted from other departments have to be paid for. They affect the common economic performance as well as the future of an individual project. On this point, experts occupy a position that makes them similar to their colleagues involved in manufacturing; they have to manage the compromise between the quality–cost–delay dimension of their purchases and the promise that the AIG makes to its internal customers.

However, there is no obsessive concern for profitability. This is seen as a safeguard, a marker in case something goes off course. The real error to be avoided, the challenge that unites everyone, lies elsewhere. 'We handle many uncertainties that are technical, legal or commercial. But this is not much of a problem when you compare it with other risks. The real catastrophe is the product with no market or the market with no product. . . . That is what has really to be avoided,' from a project head.

The pressure also shows in moral and behavioural requirements. 'The project head must be intellectually honest. . . . There is no point in exaggerating the potential of a market,' according to a biological developer. 'If we do not succeed in obtaining certification in the expected time period, we should be told quickly: there is no point in making me a promise that cannot be kept,' adds a project head.

The AIG is thus criss-crossed with elements of endogenous language, fashioned by the daily practice of its members. Reference to the product joins its functions together. Bridges made from partial overlaps link up chains of causality that in fitting together create sequences or bridges between functions. Thus, step by step, continuity is spread.

5.2.3 A Wider Network

The community of language is not restricted to the AIG alone. Interviews and observation show that it extends to people, functions and departments located elsewhere in the firm. The cognitive link indicated above in fact crosses the formal frontiers of work divisions and even ignores them.

Continuity is established between the AIG and various functions downstream, especially in the subsidiaries throughout the world. Apart from the 'strategic marketing' channels within the AIG, the network includes the executives of the areas that are concerned with certification and development studies and, in the different countries, the marketing managers as well as those responsible for technical matters and experimentation.

At first sight, such a network ought to be vulnerable to centrifugal forces. The financial interests of the supplier do not truly coincide with those of the client. Another obstacle arises from the technical studies (biological, toxicological, etc.) that are commissioned by one or other of the parties and are part and parcel of the development of a new molecule. These can be numerous, sometimes cost huge sums and are liable to cause delays. However, there is a community of references and criteria. This is made evident by the fact that the studies are generally well coordinated and are also kept within acceptable margins of cost and delay.

The first common denominator of this network concerns the priority allocated to the successful launch on the market of the innovations that the AIG manages within its portfolio. More precisely, the aim is to avoid delays and setbacks during the pilot phase. Everything works as though the new product under development was a major cause of the virtuous effect that would be the competitiveness of the national sales and marketing subsidiaries, and therefore of the firm. This causality operates in the medium term and assumes that the world is a kind of an outlet for innovations. As a corollary, the immediate innovation is relegated to second-level status so far as attention and the expectations of its strategic impact for Agro are concerned. The short term happens after the long term. A director of the AIG explains:

Every certification carries risk, for two reasons. There are the public authorities that grant permission to put on the market. It is not enough to have previous experience of them. For example, for one molecule in the USA we were confident of obtaining approval, but we were refused. Then there are technical surprises. For example, what works well for a particular soil or climate here is not suitable elsewhere. So, not only are the costs greater owing to additional tests, but because of the seasonal nature of use and sales, a year's trading is lost and one's reputation is affected.

An area manager for certification adds:

> We are all jointly responsible, because we are managing the key products
> for Agro. So everything must be done to ensure that things happen. No
> mess-ups or surprises. . . . That is a priority, and it is too bad if something
> else is delayed.

According to a marketing manager

> Commercial success is getting to market. I mean 'getting' to the market.
> There must be no hold-up with public certification for molecules and
> products. This requires complete transparency from us all: the AIG,
> certification, biological and soil testing. We put everything into it and
> give it our full attention – with good reason.

The second common denominator relates to the implicit concept of a
threat. If a major threat is identified, it is to be found first and foremost
in the outside world, in the environment in which the products are used,
with implications for the soil, vegetable and plant life, and human
beings. The policy adopted by the headquarters that Agro shall enter
biotechnologies on a massive scale has been widely and intensively
internalized and accepted by the managers and the staff. Such a
successful transition from a chemistry-dominated approach to a biol-
ogy-centred one was favoured by the fact that more and more people
were aware of two phenomena: most discoveries in the field of chemistry had already been made, and chemistry was becoming more and
more a source of danger and risk for mankind and nature. A marketing
man says:

> By getting ahead of the others, one can change everything. My job is
> to reach the point of persuading our distributors that with a new mole-
> cule they will have something unique. In their view that's a basic argu-
> ment. Competitors are then left with little to compete with us in the
> market.

In the words of a biological development specialist with the AIG:

> A well presented, honest case, having less product to spread and taking
> fewer risks with the environment – I think by controlling all of that we
> have done what is essential. It then remains to be seen what the market
> can absorb.

This cognitive schema appears as a particular view of the market and the competition. The ultimate customer, the farmer, is the structural reference. The service, which remains abstract, and the innovation, the work in progress at the AIG, serve as vectors for reaching the customer. This network leads back upstream from the ground to the development, to the definition of the customer. The customers themselves come to be seen as users who are first and foremost concerned with the non-economic qualities of a product, on condition that this product is seen as a true innovation.

In contrast, the dynamic of economic competition hardly ever leads upstream. Thus the strengths and weaknesses of Agro's competitors are ignored. There is scarcely a reference to them in interviews or the files examined. It can be said that the initiatives of other agrochemical companies are never mentioned by those engaged in the field inside Agro. If they are mentioned, say by the marketing staff and by the technical experts in the regions and countries, they are not linked to operational trends to be taken into account at their level and are not integrated with their day-to-day decision making; it seems just as though there was no risk.

Such cognitive schemas are taken as read; they are seen as truths and valid reasons that need not be questioned. If a third party were to question them, the person interrogated would justify them with arguments that shunned any alternative or refutation. This is the case regarding the status of innovation. For the members of the network, it goes without saying that a breakthrough is the one and only way for their firm to win the economic battle. The older active ingredients are not considered to be strategic vectors in the marketplace. 'Even if the agrochemists still earn their living with twenty-year-old products, our keystone is to build a better world with new things.'

The AIG possesses a lateral communication channel that links project heads in the regions and countries. This channel carries information about the medium-term total quantities of molecules under development, quantities that give an idea about the acceptability of internal transfer prices. This lateral continuity appears in many different guises.

For example, a certification expert attached to a country adopts the same criteria for action as his counterpart at the AIG and at the commercial subsidiary that he belongs to. As a regional toxicology expert explains:

> That test was fascinating, because it was a new toxicological problem. I would have liked to have had a complete and thorough study done on it; it would have been a first. I had the money for it. But I preferred to go for something less ambitious and less costly. . . . Too bad! I thought it

was not a good idea to add two months to the project, and it suited the
project head to have the results quickly.

In other words, the executive is prepared to compromise where necessary.

For his part, the marketing executive for a country anticipates the promises and constraints from the certification staff and the AIG product heads
when he prepares the launch, in his own unit, of a new product.

> At first glance I felt that this new molecule could be sold sooner that I
> expected in my country. I saw distributors who were ready to go straight
> away . . . but I let the project head at the AIG know before going ahead
> with the launch year.

The contacts are mutually supportive when surprises come up because
they recognize a threat common to all. For this reason technical delays and
economic setbacks (study cost overruns, etc.) do not cause recriminations
among the members of the network. Disputes are not publicized. On the
other hand, positive outcomes are made known.

The AIG is regarded by those concerned with certification and other
technical matters in the regions and countries as a unit that it is easy to
deal with, is competent and does its job well. Equally, the AIG finds that
it has good relations with the marketing staff in the countries. Their opinions are sought since they are the 'important element in the country,
without which all that we do would have no point', according to an AIG
executive.

Another aspect of the network is the exchange and sharing of resources.
There is a moral imperative to help one's colleagues to assert themselves
in their operational units, to help them persuade a reticent contact. A
certification specialist for one country says:

> From global studies I develop certification studies on finished prod-
> ucts as well as on conditions that are specific to the countries in my
> region. That's the theory. I pay all that is specific to my territory from
> my own budget . . . but it is the circumstances that dictate the funding
> for a particular certification. When the costs are very high, as is the
> case with active ingredients, I ask for financial help from the AIG, and
> I sometimes get it. That's the best solution. I could ask the [sales and
> marketing subsidiaries in the various] countries for help. But they are
> not usually keen. They are mean, or shall we say not very enthusiastic.
> On the other hand, when the studies only involve a formulation, the
> costs are lower. Often, the management of a country are more inter-

ested in a reformulation or a derivative. So I negotiate to establish who will pay in this case, and then the country agrees to pay.

Another says, 'I and the AIG manager work together each time we have to get a product certified by public authorities. We jointly approach the people, experts and politicians each of us knows and who might have a say or an influence during the process.'

Overlaps build up daily, with geometries that depend on circumstances. Even if everyone does not attend every meeting or is not invited, there remains the feeling that one is participating in a common task, which deserves one's trust. 'I do not attend all the AIG meetings . . . but that works well and I do not have to repeat anything,' says the marketing executive for a country.

The network enjoys the advantage of factors similar to those that facilitate the emergence of a common language within the AIG. There are people in the commercial subsidiaries who have a broad experience of the firm (through their seniority, their type of function and the number of positions that they have held previously). In addition, there are numerous task force groups that systematically bring together people from different units and function, experts, marketing personnel and others.

The collective scope within the network is expanded by the interest that all those concerned have in their own spheres of activity. For the AIG project heads, the advantage is clear. They have a lateral communication channel to the countries. The marketing departments located in the countries allocate services to the sales managements according to administrative criteria. Such is the case for free services provided by the AIG in the field of technical studies for certification. Commercial units assume ownership of breakthrough innovation in order to lend weight to the policy of the subsidiaries to which they belong.

5.2.4 A Marketing Theory in Use

Endogenous languages are theories of action in use. Once their content has been described, a further step is to determine how they are embedded inside the organization, to which activities they provide integration.

At Agro, the activity is clearly around and for the benefit of the development of new molecules. Old molecules hardly ever require people to come together; no endogenous language of any sort induces integrative effects. There is a reason for this; no common challenge causes them to join together. Each sales network states its requirements so far as they are concerned.

In the case of new molecules it is as though a very specific theory was constructed and applied, one which the executives thought quite normal and used to establish the transactions and define their sense.

The function of strategic marketing is in fact seen from a particular angle: managing projects around new molecules. The tasks are specialized and revolve around a particular new active ingredient. Furthermore, each new project has a dedicated timetable and a particular method of approach and handling. The project management appears to have skills across the board. A project focuses on a single task: this specific product. For every product a specific or specialized market is defined. The product is the solution; its market is the problem. But since the market is reduced to the exploitation of a portfolio of monopolistic rents, it hardly ever joins all its segments together.

The opposite approach, which would start with the markets as solutions and would try to determine the available opportunities – that is, find out the products that would suit it – is not the kind of thinking considered or taken for granted in the AIG. They scarcely ever go down the path of finding out, based on the Agro range of products, where the gaps are in the market, which are those that are significant and how they could be filled, either with new or adapted products.

In this sense, the strategic marketing theory in use at the AIG and its network only favours a single dimension type or addresses one question only. Will the market accept what the product offers in the way of advantages in performance and use? In this case, the pursuit of marketing becomes a gesture to accompany a process that consists of releasing what innovation is able to produce. Upstream checks the size and the relevance of its policy choices. The other side of the coin – identifying what markets may suggest – does not make any sense. Markets are not active but passive. The strategic dimension is blurred by the use of such implicit marketing theory.

According to another theory at Agro, only fundamental innovations are interpreted as valid, not local innovations. But there is nothing in the formal architecture of the AIG or in the directives given by top management that prevents or restricts attention to older products on the market. Reformulation and local innovation are neither penalized nor discouraged. It is as though the executives share a kind of common prestige hierarchy. The discovery of a new molecule relates to the noble rank of activities, a recombination of molecules belongs rather to the level of the common people. What really justifies the existence of the AIG and creates identity and legitimacy is the big fundamental discovery. Reformulation scarcely provides added value in symbolic terms and does not unite the social body. 'The challenges are what make us stick together. The real challenge is to find something new, a basic scientific discovery!' says an expert. According to one manufacturer, 'reformulation is just vulgar tinkering'.

The AIG's strategic marketing function, being positioned at the downstream outflow, gives priority to breakthrough innovation and provides services to an outside market set-up. It is in fact confronted with a dilemma:

■ It concentrates its activities on projects that are highly susceptible to breakdown, and is ready to take high risks (in terms of delays) in little-known, rather uncertain and poorly identified markets.
■ It is vulnerable in its decision making, especially when it is under heavy pressure, via head office, from an outside market allocation of financial resources. It then operates as a managed economy.

5.3 Cognitive Discontinuities at Work

If we now take a global view of the Agro firm, a quite different picture emerges, which is surprisingly full of marked cognitive and cooperative discontinuities.

5.3.1 A Set of Non-compatible Theories for Action

Three different logics or paradigms of action that may even be in opposition on certain points emerge in Agro at the interfaces between upstream and downstream units. These are summarized in Table 5.1.

These paradigms of economic management and action may be regarded as broadly implicit thinking whose complete linking up is rarely visible to the outside observer; they are considered by those involved to be self-evident. They filter the unfolding of events and their interpretation, simplify the complexity of possible alternatives, and translate taken-for-granted assumptions and implicit postulates about the world and about action taking. In other words, they are not sensitive to the test of empirical events for whoever carries them. Appearing as factual truths, resistant to a principle of reality, difficult to alter through experience, they spread through slow socialization inside specific micro-contexts. The problem is that they produce visible empirical consequences.

A firm such as Agro, like many others, is awash with theories that are applied in practice, at least as sophisticated and numerous as those found in management books, the difference being that they are unexplained and do not face up to the principle of reality. Table 5.1 contains a relatively

	AIG network	The sales units	The world of R&D
Theory for action	Functionalities of products under development ⇩ A market	A segment of clientele ⇩ A portfolio of existing products	A scientific discovery ⇩ An opportunity for use
The relevant indicators for choice	A potential global demand (volume)	A local opportunity	A gap in the range
	A reference region or country	A market segment established from experience	A functionality for use
	The medium term	The short term	An imprecise term
The strategic engine	Acceptability by the subsidiaries	Adequacy in relation to the distributors	A quantum leap or a breakthrough
The status of the innovation	A generator of monopolistic rents	A resource or a constraint	A federator for the firm

Table 5.1 Types of languages and action-related worlds inside Agro

detailed grid that shows four properties that they contain and which may be replicated as tools to study cognitive phenomena in other organizational settings and companies:

- the causal model on which they are based, that is the assumption that links a particular cause that acts as a lever to produce a specific consequence,
- the indicators and parameters considered to be keys or operating levers that are of importance,
- the strategic engine that moves through time and space,
- given its importance in the type of activity at Agro, the status that an innovation has in terms of management.

5.3.2 Isolation of the Bearers of New Projects

The cognitive community for which the AIG is the epicentre remains, so far as Agro as a whole is concerned, quite small and relatively isolated. In fact, downstream in relation to the commercial sector, and upstream in relation to R&D, there are sharp discontinuities.

For example, marketing is something of a function of its own, especially in commercial units in large countries. It is distinguished from other functions of the subsidiary by its assessment of the business opportunities. So, for a new molecule that it is expected to achieve 15 per cent of the market at the end of two years and increase turnover by about 10 per cent, there are two very different choices. The director of marketing believes that this is a remarkable lever, whereas his superior, the director of the commercial subsidiary, albeit reflecting the feeling of the sales networks, concludes that these criteria are insignificant so far as he is concerned. Does one only speak the same language depending on one's function?

Marketing is a relatively isolated occupation, especially for the sales representatives. Working together is not easy. Mutual comprehension cannot be taken as read. Face-to-face cooperation does not predominate.

Marketing in a country often fails to use the salespeople as a reliable source of information for its market research. It therefore deprives itself of the chance to receive any faint messages. At most it will get some feeling for the sales potential once the decision has been taken to include this new molecule in the catalogue. In contrast, the situation is quite different in the case of a recomposition, where there is a relatively minor modification to an existing product. The launch of a derivative is discussed at a biannual meeting during which the sales staff are invited to put forward their ideas.

There may, on the other hand, be occasions when the marketing department does not entrust the commercialization of a new product to the existing sales force, but creates a new network of salespeople from scratch to do the task. In other words, the old networks are short-circuited and the marketing people shoulder the operational tasks normally undertaken by the commercial management. Whatever the reasons given, such as image creation or quick access to a specific market, such an approach deviates from established practice.

By such action, the marketing departments of the commercial subsidiaries introduce an exogenous language into them: the language of the AIG. Through some institutional mimicry, they adopt an organizational model that is foreign to them, is based on teams with full control of marketing, certification, tests and experiments, each headed by a marketing manager responsible for either a product or a family of products. Its social and emotional isolation is cognitively strengthened in relation to the sales networks.

For it is a fact that the sales staff of national networks do not accept what is doubtful or, worse, unknown. The reason for this lies in their paradigms for action and the way that Agro evaluates their performance. The potential psychological regret that accompanies every change is a powerful constraint for the commercial staff. They deal with a peasant world, through the distributors (notably agricultural cooperatives), which, being rooted in the soil are suspicious of new things unless they are environmentally safe, among other considerations. There is considerable inertia in agriculture and a wariness about the costs of change, which are perceived to be high by those in the industry. The relationship between skills and products is strong. The end customers live in a very structured daily world of strong social and functional affiliations. The flap of a butterfly's wings here causes a hurricane there.

Particularly in the innovation phase, marketing is normally faced with ignorance and the unknown. In the cases already mentioned, it is isolated from the peasant world owing to the lack of links through the sales staff. What is more, it is disengaged from the constraints that bear on the sales staff such as performance evaluation. Finally, its skills are not linked to a particular product. Its challenge is to reduce organizational inertia and the costs associated with the adoption of new molecules through abandoning the old. It is therefore to transform ignorance into reasonable doubt and above all to show experience by being capable of making rapid adjustments in the launch phase.

In this context one can speak of a real tragedy for the AIG and its network. It is locked in a fundamental but uneasy role of transforming the unknown into the uncertain, while it is stuck between breakthrough research that is located outside the market on the one hand, and on the other a sales force that is rooted in the short term. The fact is that the AIG and its network do not understand, nor do they really like, the commercial set-up that they deal with downstream.

5.3.3 The Sales Force and the Primacy of Closeness

So far as local innovation is concerned, marketing in the countries is placed at the service and under the control of the sales force. The launch of a derivative, for example, is discussed at a bi-annual meeting during the course of which the sales force are invited to put forward their ideas. 'When the sales people have said what they are interested in, it is up to me to see to it that this product based on old molecules is supplied,' says the marketing director for a country.

Marketing finds itself relatively isolated at the heart of the subsidiary to which it is attached. This is because management and the sales network tend to form a block set apart from the other operational units of Agro. They are bound by common references such as volume, margin, yearly performance, and the priorities of established and niche outlets. Hence their attitude of rational prudence towards any initiative that might upset the channels of distribution. In their eyes, a good salesperson is one who sells volume, not customer service. The 'pull' approach that they adopt reflects their customers' rather conservative attitudes.

This isolation of marketing within its subsidiary also penalizes the AIG. It does not get on well with the management of the commercial subsidiaries. There are in fact two parallel circuits between the subsidiaries and the developers.

One of these connects the AIG product heads with the subsidiary market-ing managers. This circuit co-opts relatively isolated partners, is established on a narrow base (breakthrough innovation) and is deployed on the down-stream development phase (placing on the market). The other connects the AIG with the general management of the countries, mediated through head office. It is deployed on the upstream development phase, that is, the priority choices for new molecules. It is liable to serious breakdowns.

Whereas the first network functions well and with mutual trust, the second is beset with emotional tension and policies of avoidance. Quite evidently, the current does not flow. The directors of some countries communicate with the developers and strategic marketing staff through the general management. In other respects, they run them down professionally.

In fact, its formal design gives the AIG little scope to influence the commercial subsidiaries. It has no discretion in the fixing of market prices, in packaging, product formulation or the range of products offered to customers.

The way financial transfers are designed in the firm is peculiar. Their content is the outcome of a discretionary top-down approach. AIG's accounting starts from the assumption that the margin on an active ingre-dient, new or old, included in a formulation should go to the distributor, that is, the sales or marketing subsidiary in the country. By convention, this is fixed at an average of 35 per cent of an acceptable price. If one adds the fact that in practice acceptance, especially for new materials, is judged in terms of the subsidiaries where the retail prices are lowest, the rule when applied to other countries immediately creates a gross margin problem for the AIG. From that point, the AIG makes all or part of its margin by putting pressure, not downstream but upstream: on manufacturing, on its suppli-ers, whether Agro factories or independent companies. So, little by little, the countries, acting through the AIG, externalize the economic risk of product development.

Other minor decisions and procedures relativize the AIG's autonomy and strengthen the asymmetry of the dependencies to the advantage of the countries. An example may be seen in the purchasing function. All buyers will be located in the commercial subsidiaries. In other words, purchasing coupled with formulation further adds to the economic immunity enjoyed by the sales function.

5.3.4 The Fortress of Research

R&D operates in a segmented, internal and self-sufficient way in comparison with the other departments.

Internally, R&D is strongly partitioned. Sectors specialize in specific domains: herbicides, fungicides and so on. Functional hybridization comes up against teams grouped by scientific discipline: chemistry, biology and others. Sites are dispersed over several countries and continents. The summit of the hierarchy decides on the policies and orientations almost exclusively.

The director of R&D therefore spends more than 200 days a year away from his office on trips and visits to his units around the world. He describes his position thus:

> My role is to present my people with challenges. The researcher possesses only one thing: his methodology. Therefore he must be treated with respect. He must be helped. I am not the boss of science, I act as a mirror. So I ask my researchers to keep me informed and keep in contact.

This focus on one person, who has a discretionary allowance of financial resources for teams and projects, reveals the lack of transverse processes at the intermediary level and at the same time makes the problem worse. Centralization at the level of the director fuels a self-reinforcing process of marginalization of the researchers inside the labs.

Compared with the other functions and units of the firm, R&D appears like a fortress, a world apart, financially self-sufficient, impenetrable, hard to understand, not accountable in its choices and their consequences for the firm and not easily accessible to third parties. In fact, it is not organized as a business unit, is therefore not subject to the need to secure results from exploitation, and is financed only by a discretionary general budget from head office. In other respects, it keeps control of tasks and skills that are required downstream in basic research and that could come under the

control of operational units closer to the markets. This is true of the experimental farms when they take part in the development of a new active
ingredient for which the commercial subsidiary finances the test
programme. R&D hardly ever invoices its services downstream even
though it covers a broad range of functions for breakthrough innovation as
well as local innovation.

The AIG relies heavily on the services of R&D, depending on it as a
powerful player, as well as the outside market set-up. It is true that the
contributions from R&D come relatively cheaply, but the AIG remains
dependent on R&D's orientations and choices. R&D is associated directly
with the activities and choices made by marketing and the developers,
through services rendered once a project has entered the so-called application phase. It temporarily seconds experts and provides specialist services.
In a small number of cases, it even offers help with the budget, depending
on the appraisal of its management.

In contrast, the AIG has very little influence on R&D, at least so far as
the choices that the latter makes and that may concern it. The only contact
is at the top, between the chief executives at head office. The director of
the AIG is the only non-researcher on the board of the internal research
committee at R&D, which only meets twice a year. The subject matter is
relatively marginal. Important decisions are made on other occasions
between the head of R&D and the CEO of Agro.

When it comes to specification costs, such an interface is doubly restrictive. The co-opting of AIG partners by R&D is limited to one person and
only to the instrumental part of the service. In principle, the strategic
choices for R&D are discussed at other forums. On paper there is a so-
called Strategic Committee of Agro, which is supposed to meet at least
three times a year, and should discuss the research objectives with a view
to choosing new projects once a year. AIG is supposed to be involved, as
are the subsidiaries for regions and countries. In fact this committee does
not often meet; indeed in the last three years, it has only met twice. Moreover, it does not include the discoverers who are in charge of molecule
family projects. The only researchers who are co-opted are the heads of the
three research centres and the scientific managers responsible for application projects. In other words, knowledge or common language may be
created among participants, but to a large extent not at the right level in
terms of hierarchy of authority.

All of this reveals a way of interacting that is restricted in substance and
in intensity. While R&D may accept some compromise in the applications,
it operates autonomously in matters of finance and as an institution. It
rarely receives directions and not much information, except by way of

specification costs. Located outside the market, it concentrates exclusively on breakthrough innovation with discretionary attention to local innovation. It is thus able to contain downstream pressure. In the end, R&D reconfigures the firm, for example by devaluing the skills located in the downstream functions, without being made responsible in fact. The power that it wields in the firm confers permanent immunity.

5.3.5 Contradictory Paradigms of the Firm and the Market

The Agro firm sits on two stools, between two models of itself and the world. These models define the reasons for the choices made by the units and functions.

Downstream, the managements of the commercial subsidiaries established in the large countries vigorously relay back the sales forces' requests to provide products that suit the local circumstances at a low price and with relative continuity of supply. The thinking is that of salesmanship.

Upstream, the thinking is that of science. R&D drives for breakthrough innovation; more precisely (the nuance is important) the 'lucky find' that also happens to fill a gap in the range.

The AIG network is faced with dilemmas in its actions. If it tries to get closer to customers, it cuts itself off from R&D since this is not intended to be part of the latter's brief. Moreover, it does not become a relay for the countries, because its contacts in the network, the marketing staff, are not pushing in this direction either, and the managements of the countries go for autonomy. If it aims to fill gaps in the product range, it falls more in tune with the set-up at R&D, and may even be dominated by it. The AIG also follows the direction of its network. On the other hand, this takes it away from the countries, which is not planned to happen, and away from the markets. A director of the AIG described the problem as follows:

> For example, people say that we need a maize herbicide that is flexible to use, can be applied frequently, is selective to suit the methods of growing in such and such a country, with this toxicological profile or that environmental profile, in this dosage and selling at not more than that price per kilo. Now all that is easy enough in those areas that Agro knows well: vine fungicides and cereal herbicides. We already sell in those areas so we can segment the market. But we know nothing about the gaps: soya bean herbicides, etc., because Agro has never been commercially powerful. We live on clichés. Neither the countries nor the AIG know the market. So we amass a list of dreams: the lowest price in the market for the best poison at the lowest level!

The solution that is preferred by the AIG, with the tacit support of general management, is to go for the gap in the range of products. The outside market and the unknown attract it, albeit reluctantly. It has two weak resources to help keep it on track. It can relax the internal virtual market by subsidizing the transfer prices. It is able to take advantage of occasional exceptional circumstances: where, for example, a commercial subsidiary, for its own strategic reasons, wishes to make use of a breakthrough innovation that has been produced ad hoc by an intersecting network rooted in the country and that allows market approaches and scientific thinking to be combined. An AIG director explains:

> When I arrived at the AIG I found a gap-filling project that was the stuff of dreams. No one knew the market. But I knew that, in Thailand, Agro had an executive who came from a competitor and who knew this market. I decided to introduce him to the people in France and Germany who looked after areas that come into contact with this product. I brought them together for a day, there were also people from other countries. There were exchanges between marketing and technical experts, myself and the head of products at the AIG. The researcher said: here are the families of molecules that I have studied and the characteristics that one can expect them to have. The sales people said: this is what the market expects from us. The result was a recommendation very different from the initial proposal.

The radical discontinuity that is typical of the relations between departments in the firm thus has a direct and lasting affect on Agro.

There are two ways of representing and interpreting success. One is downstream – that is, local innovation – and is based on certainties. The other is upstream, that is breakthrough innovation, which tolerates uncertainty. For the Agro executives, they are perceived as necessarily opposed. One must hold sway over the other. The firm cannot support both at the same time as priority axes of its strategy, even though both are legitimate and necessary in day-to-day business.

Furthermore, it seems as though the price of active ingredients sold by the AIG, both old and new, formally established by the AIG, was in fact fixed downstream, largely by the sales networks working in the most important countries in terms of their sales volumes and turnovers. The virtual market set-up, albeit adapted and modified, benefits the buyer, with the seller making use of hybrid and opaque arrangements to ensure a profitable deal.

In short, at the end of the day the responsibility for strategic marketing is assumed upstream, that is, by the management of R&D. The nobility upstream knows what is good for the common people downstream. It is the trustee of the global compared with the local. The Director of R&D discussed his objectives in the following way:

> What are the objectives of R&D? One must start with one fact: marketing wants tomorrow what was discovered yesterday. My role is to make marketing's dreams come true. You would like a herbicide for the American Midwest? Here it is. That would be the jackpot. When the marketing managers come to see me, they want to see how the knowledge is progressing. I initiate them with new products.

R&D, perched on its mound, and guided by an extra-market logic, chooses the solutions that the marketing people properly speaking will then have to carry out. And it instructs the latter to take account of a factor that R&D is happy to leave to them, namely the competition. The sales and trade personnel are not relevant in this context; they are relegated to the secular arm of the chain that ensures the outflow of products. At most they have to sort out with the help of local innovations the economic and tactical fluctuations that the firm encounters locally. Breakthrough innovation originates in the essence of the strategy. It marks out the future that is important, it writes the history and the essence of Agro as a firm. Innovation in derivatives patches things up when there is a system breakdown.

In such a representation of the world and of the firm, the market looks more like a mythical construction. R&D, enjoying the trust of head office, is assumed to know how to decode the market's evolution and to meet its demands through its sense of intuition. So the ultimate performance reference flows from R&D. The customers themselves do not represent a major criterion. They have the status of second rank dependants and passive players, whose well-being is looked after by the researchers, and whose care is devolved to the sales force. Their demands and characteristics have scarcely any impact on the decisions considered to be fundamental by Agro as a whole.

CHAPTER 6

Managerial Fine-tuning

How does general management operate when facing choice situations that require heterogeneous solutions, or when implementing action plans that may be contradictory? Integrating heterogeneity when not managing contradictions is quite a common fact of life. It is not always comfortable for managers, whose ability to sustain dialectical approaches may be low. Others may not understand why they do what they do: decentralizing at the same time that they control more, cutting the R&D costs while asking the researchers to focus more on breakthrough innovation. The present chapter deals with one major skill: building complexity as a solution to the problems of heterogeneity.

Management sciences pay little attention to methods of building and using complexity. It is regarded as some kind of resourcefulness, something magical or anecdotal, a craft that is acquired by birth or embedded in the deep personality once and for all, a set of gestures that is hardly worth studying. This seems amazing when one knows the extent to which the success of any action is played out in the chinks that appear daily under the pressure of circumstances between the orthodoxy of the models and the reality of the situations.

In their actual work managers reconcile two cognitive abilities that are often used in a disjointed way. One is of a theoretical nature or causal, in the sense that a policy or an organizational model implies *a priori* a vision of causalities, ways and means for the future success of the firm. Causalities are implicit theories in action. If A is done, then B follows as a consequence. The second ability is pragmatic or opportunistic, in the sense that success is measured *a posteriori*; it depends on the capacity that the manager shows for tackling the events and contexts whose content and appearance cannot be fully understood, that cannot always be bent and moulded as one would wish, and that therefore represent constraints on the manager and flaws in his or her theory. Pragmatic cognitive abilities allow the use of unexpected effects as resources for successful or purposeful driving of action.

Blending the two registers may be defined as fine-tuning. Opportunism is not erratic, while planning is open to flexibility. Fine-tuning becomes crucial in a context of hypercompetition. For general management it means that three registers receive attention at the same time:

- *Ensure that a strategic aim is shared through internal renewal*; therefore adopt a Type 1 or organic model as discussed in Chapter 3.
- *Guarantee the short term through the aim to exploit what has been acquired*; therefore adopt measurements and organizational skills that arise more from Type 3 or the mercenary.
- *Find day-to-day solutions or compromises that establish a minimum of compatibility between the two positions*, but which at the organizational level do not irreparably obliterate the endogenous capacities of the firm to be competitive in exploitation while performing excellently in innovation.

The purpose of this chapter is to analyse more precisely how general managers operate when fine-tuning. How are compromises elaborated? How are they made compatible with strategic and lasting success requirements? More precisely, starting with a Type 1 or organic model – that is, a configuration that is suited to the development of endogenous capacities, especially those that are cognitive – how does one identify the margins of flexibility that at the same time allow one to do what the strategies and conduct associated with Type 3 require?

General management is often unprepared and ill-equipped for fine-tuning, improvisation, hybrid solutions and trial and error as ways of learning. It is not a question of doing something, somehow and whenever. Any old solution is not good enough. Ad hoc solutions must be formulated and validated by simultaneous reference to two imperatives. First, they must strengthen the competitive capacity of the firm. Second, they must be sustainable by the internal social body of the firm. Sustainable is taken in the broad sense, namely that they have a good chance of being accepted while also being intelligible to the staff of the firm that they relate to. It also means that they are performed empirically, becoming manifest through behaviour and decision-making.

6.1 Dealing with Contradictions

Combining an ambition to exploit with an endogenous type of regeneration policy demands considerable savoir-faire, tact and attention. This approach is certainly the least easy for general management. At the same time, the endogenous process is the most effective for firms in intermediate positions, neither the smallest nor the leaders in their market, especially in a hyper-competitive context.

The task for top management is to ensure compatibility, day after day, between three types of contradiction: setting up exploitation and regeneration-oriented organizational models, using trade and non-trade (administrative) references for the allocation of resources and for inner transactions, and relying upon endogenous and exogenous change processes.

6.1.1 Exploitation and Regeneration

The first contradiction concerns exploitation coupled with regeneration. Intensive exploitation clearly provides the financial resources for regenerating the firm. That said, such surplus or profit, if a necessary condition, is not enough by itself. Here regeneration is taken to mean that the firm ensures that the income exploited is regenerated from within, not abandoned as soon as the surplus has been creamed off (witness the example of the practice of burning off agricultural land in Africa). Nor is it dissolved away in a process of takeovers and mergers of third party firms, avowedly innovating but less rich, like the pillage of one tribe by another.

Exploiting what one has in an intensive way is a policy that finds favour when the centre or head office adopts a specific organizational model for the firm:

- extreme simplification of structures (few hierarchical levels, etc.),
- a high level of staff interchangeability, thanks to the use of standard procedures and routines,
- highly specialized functions, clearly marked boundaries between the internal sectors, precise and compartmentalized responsibilities, detailed procedures for financial control and reporting,
- limited knowledge-based systems and restricted intuitive sharing,
- little attention given to a spirit of solidarity, cooperation or horizontal support.

Regenerating, on the other hand, means recreating, or transforming what already exists into something else. Such an approach requires the centre to subscribe to a movement for involvement, co-construction and sharing:

- Adding complexity to structures that through trial and error allow processes and opportunities for discoveries to emerge.
- A low level of staff interchangeability, to the extent that regeneration is based on processes of intuition, of interpretation of weak signals,

and therefore of complicity between individuals and groups sharing a common cognitive asset.

- A search for versatility in experience and tasks. This is achievable mainly by two processes: through a high level of internal rotation for executives, and through the declaration of fuzzy or even porous boundaries between responsibilities and functions. In both cases the idea is to allow as much intense and rapid cross-fertilization as possible to develop.
- Strong cognitive systems, to make it possible to deal with phenomena such as the intangible, the unexpected, the weak signal, and the tacit.
- A high priority given to the collective, to socialization and to solidarity in action.

6.1.2 Traded and Non-traded Goods and Services

A second source of contradictions whose operational resolution is the responsibility of top management is represented by the content, treatment and priority accorded at the heart of the organization to market and non-market spheres.

The non-market sphere relates to those activities, functions or transactions internalized by the firm within its own organizational structure that are not treated according to the same criteria of immediate profitability as others. In their case, general management accepts a more distant, more diffuse and more uncertain profitability. They more or less reflect or conform to some discretionary or administrative reference. On the other hand, the non-traded sphere or logics understood in this does not mean that these activities or these functions are not deployed on the market. In contemporary economies, with a few exceptions, practically all products and all services are placed on the market in the sense that they can be challenged and replaced by other projects and services or rejected by the consumer. From this point, to speak of income does not mean that such and such a product or service is outside the market, in the radical sense of the word. The facts indicate something else: assured protection from competition for a relatively long period.

A market activity therefore entails two concrete and distinct properties. It has an obligation to be profitable, and it is accountable in the short term. Market activity is generally found in situations that arise from paradigms of exploitation. It is what generates the profit and surplus of the firm.

In contrast, an activity that is of a non-traded nature is an activity from which the centre expects a return in the future, in the medium term at best, or from which it hopes to gain some indirect benefit, surpluses generated in an indirect way, not predicted in advance or not necessarily of an immediately economic nature. Regeneration is typical of this type of activity. It includes a not insignificant amount of risk. As a consequence, it is incubated for a relatively long period, which corresponds to the duration of a project, and allows it to escape the measurement criteria normally applied to performance.

Moreover, the organizational system that is associated with an extra-market activity includes and describes boundaries that are less precise and more fuzzy than the boundaries of a market activity (the latter being shaped by a tighter fragmentation and by more formalized controls). The aspect that comes under the heading of the tacit, arising from the nature of the intangible, is also much stronger. What is non-traded is accompanied by and structured around communities of language for action that are much denser and stronger. Working together is less subject to the procedures of the centre and less focused on a narrow range of skills and preoccupations. It relies largely on the exchange of shared intuition. More than any traded activity, an activity arising from non-traded mechanisms appeals to the collective memory and activates the internal and external networks of the organization.

6.1.3 Endogenous and Exogenous

Management faces a third and final source of contradictions in the endogenous and the exogenous.

Exploitation and the non-traded rationale occupy a common position in this respect: how they are treated arises largely through an exogenous process. This is brought into effect first by the fact that performance is measurable and is assessed by reference to criteria that are simple, take account of the short term or even the immediate in a very direct way, and by explicit indicators. Established procedures and clear operational standards allow organizational life to be clarified and simplified. In addition, people can to some extent be substituted one for another. Finally, identification is quite unequivocal with regard to the products, markets and areas for which the organization is responsible.

Such a world opens the way to the best practice approach, an approach that entails the introduction and adoption of methods of interpretation and behaviour brought in from outside the organization. In short, complexity can be and is reduced. More precisely, devolution allows the organization to be simplified since, for a unit, a department or even a given manager, the products and the procedures are exogenous. That is to say, they are not the fruit of the regeneration efforts that this manager, this department or this unit would have taken account of and undertaken at its own level. A best practice approach makes sense when sales networks do not master either the technical definition of the product that they are selling or the marketing function that ensures segmentation of the market and positioning of the product on offer.

In contrast, what arises from the endogenous reacts much worse to this type of treatment. The internal generation of knowledge, its diffusion and the sharing of experience (not the duplication of third party practices) is transmitted poorly in an organizational mould that is made up of well-defined boundaries and narrowly targeted individual responsibilities. The world of the endogenous needs to be deployed in a spatial and temporal continuum. Such a requirement may appear paradoxical to the extent that the endogenous is charged with producing discontinuities and breaks.

In fact, the discontinuity has two sources or causes. It is generated either in a brutal and exogenous way, or in an endogenous and sometimes incremental way. In the first case, the market world of exploitation may be discontinuous to the extent that it is scarcely linked to the history, and not at all the outcome, of a kind of quasi-biological impregnation process of the organizational cognitions by factors such as the product or the clientele. Products that are relatively continuous, quite stable over time, and exogenous may be linked to discontinuous teams, such as a rapid succession of mercenaries employed by the firm. In the second case, products that are continuously being transformed and subject to perpetual adjustment for their part require a situation of organizational and interpretive continuity.

When it comes to the function of research in the firm, the endogenous presents a real problem: in what type of paradigm is it located? Frequently, R&D is perceived to be and is positioned in an extra-market set-up. The bearer of innovation, it finds itself entrusted with the key to the regeneration of the firm in an almost monopolistic way. But how endogenous it is and its real method of operation depend to a large extent on the mission the centre entrusts it with. Is it to invent or to innovate? Depending on the axis chosen, the implications for action and vigilance from the centre are not at all the same.

Research that is concerned with innovating – that is, recombining and improving what already exists by applying known scientific or technological principles – often arises from small-scale adjustments by individuals, from tinkering. It is characterized by the fact that the absence of the unknown makes dialogue between different parts of the firm easier, including those parts that do not strictly speaking belong to the world of R&D. This has consequences.

To a fairly significant extent, innovation understood thus fits perfectly in a non-traded status and in an area of continuity. In fact, it produces a limited discontinuity since, in essence, it is incremental by nature. It is this work on detail and its corollary, an orientation towards the incremental, that give it an intangible aspect. For innovation to be deployed, there must be continuity. The key lies in the fact that innovation through endogenous tinkering gives the firm an advantage of an exceptional nature. Its largely intangible quality in practice turns out to be difficult to reproduce by third parties and therefore cannot be copied by competitors. It is because it is linked to the whole of the firm, to a shared knowledge and to tacit collective experience that it offers appreciable income, income that does not have to be defended through legal or other means. This type of research is to a large extent endogenous in the sense that the tinkering (the 'me too') connects it with the firm's strategy, and therefore with the market.

For its part, scientific research that is focused on invention and has little or nothing to do with what already exists is managed in a non-traded way. It is thus largely exogenous. History, contingencies and even in certain cases the markets on which the firm is located are largely foreign to it. It is detached from what makes the specific quality of the organization that shelters it and feeds it financially. The inventors and researchers belong to human networks and professional communities that extend well beyond the firm and whose epicentres are foreign to it, such as academic associations. The activity of invention is ultimately relatively difficult to protect from the covetousness of third-party plunderers and imitation by the competition. The results – scientific products and paradigms – are tangible as soon as they are published and therefore less easily defensible. Being exogenous, invention also runs the risk that the firm that has financed it hardly really owns it, if at all, as it paradoxically remains the concern only of the researchers and laboratories that produced it.

General management is expected to be able to reconcile these deep divisions. More precisely, the challenge for the centre is to make two inseparable gestures. It must at the same time generate non-traded and traded spheres, exogenous and endogenous processes, innovation and invention activities, all in proportions that vary according to the circumstances. Equally, it must also manage them: that is, find ever-changing compromises in order to avoid being made a prisoner of contradictions that are too fundamental. The firm must be capable of exploiting its income and assets in order to produce surpluses. It must also assume battle order so that it may ensure regeneration.

Of course, this regeneration can be ensured externally, rather than within the firm. This is what would happen if it sold what became commonplace and bought its new assets and new products from outside. In such a case, general management resembles the management of a financial portfolio. It fulfils a strictly limited range of functions. It acts like a merchant banker or a shareholder who is quite independent of the products that are manufactured by the firm he or she owns, as well as the people who compose it and the organization that structures its actions and knowledge. General management does not regenerate itself; it will work on something else if it can get hold of it.

The firm must put into the market set-up everything it controls for the purpose of exploitation. It must also, however, preserve some non-traded activities, either because this element provides a positive external source, or because the non-traded brings regeneration (in the second case, there is also an externality). The art and skill of top management has something of the know-how of a chemist. It lies in its ability to ration and combine, in an evolutionary way and according to the needs of the firm's strategy, the ingredients of the exogenous and the endogenous, the relative elements of continuity and discontinuity. This subtle chemistry also takes into account the fact that the formulations adopted can be borne by the people involved and by the finances at the heart of the firm.

There is therefore a challenge of complexity and hybridization for the internal organization of the firm. If the firm wishes to avoid profound and lasting trauma by ensuring its own development and its own long-term survival, the task is neither clear to conceive nor easy to guarantee. The different management paradigms that must be brought into play involve references, principles and cultures that, even when they are compatible, are not identical. This implies that the core function of a general management goes far beyond the usual stereotypes such as command and control. For the centre the type of mid-term horizon that it adopts, its ability to manage hybrid systems, the networking of people and products that it helps to bring forward in the firm, all become parameters that represent all the stakeholders' rights.

6.2 Setting Out Principles for Action

The hierarchy of authority rests on an asymmetry of the positions of the various grades, such that those at the lower level are dependent on the higher grade for what they must do. In order to determine the actions of the lower grades, the higher grade has two chief means of intervention.

First, it sets out principles. These can take various forms, from setting rules through formal structures and operational procedures, to the dissemination of beliefs backed up by visions of the shared future and the objectives to be achieved. These decree cognitive and behavioural conduct. The centre, explicitly or not, consciously or not, defines ways to perceive, think, and act: when, what, how, for which purpose.

Second, the higher-grade managers use their discretion. They intervene whenever they wish and with every right, even to the point of deviating from pre-existing principles that they themselves may well have set out. In the eyes of the lower grades, the management is then doing the opposite to what was originally laid down. This sense of arbitrariness felt by the lower grade, the non-foreseeable acts from above, results entirely or partly from an act or a decision that management explains as an exception made in a context or circumstances that did not match with what the higher grade understands as being the normal conditions to which their principles apply. The legitimate source of authority violates its own principles.

Observation confirms that general management's recourse to the binomial of principles–discretion is in everyday use. American, Asian or European firms all behave in a similar way. Value-oriented CEOs behave like the more cynical of their colleagues. Deviations if not violations are committed by the legitimate authorities in relation to the principles that they themselves impose. Observation shows one major factor of their occurrence. Such practices are the daily fate of those firms in particular whose managements position their aims in terms of endogenous innovation strategies, but that are not controlled by a Type 1 or organic organizational model.

Does tinkering reflect some kind of disease? It is tempting to come up with explanations that would explain it by the attributes of the people in authority: erratic behaviour, a disturbed personality or an ignorance of good management theory. But irrationality among the players is not a satisfying answer. The actions and non-actions of head office make sense if they are referred to a series of contextual constraints.

A good example is provided by the Agro company examined in the previous chapter. The story of its CEO, Albert, is certainly quite specific to the company, but the facets of his activity are similar to those found in many head offices. In this sense it provides a useful illustration.

The organization chart and the handbook of principles set out, in more than 50 pages, the duties and responsibilities of the operational units (see Appendix 2). In theory, according to these documents, general management devotes itself exclusively to exercising a short list of supreme functions: formulating the strategic goals, developing the systems of control and audit, choosing performance indicators, selecting and nominating the heads of the operational units. Exclusive responsibility for a domain falls to head office from the moment that domain is classified as a firm priority. The CEO does not have to delegate in the matter (which does not mean that he does not consult or involve the operational units under his direction). By establishing a drastic division of the spheres of competence and by assuming a virtual monopoly over some of them, Albert hopes to give some substance to decentralization, as though decentralization occurred through the fixing of clear boundaries between respective jurisdictions of head office and the operational units.

Agro illustrates a much more general case. Top management underlines its uniqueness compared with the remainder of the firm, reserving a triple role for itself:

- It shows the route to the future that the community will follow. It sets the strategy; more precisely it formulates and propagates visions of the future, whether they be vague or detailed, reasoned or emotive.
- It sets out the values that the community must respect. It develops codes of conduct in order to improve civility among staff. Hence Albert's insistence on such topics as the drive for security or management's respect for the individual. 'I believe in humane management. One cannot guide others unless one also fulfils the criteria than one sets for others. That is my condition for action.'
- Finally, it writes the constitution for the community. It formulates the rules and procedures that serve to coordinate the various parts and to determine the references of the individual choices. As a result, head office, or even the CEO alone, regularly monitors and updates the organization chart, job descriptions covering the two senior management ranks and approved methods of performance measurement.

Managers are somewhat reticent and moderate when it comes to subscribing to the virtues of tension and fuzzy divisions between the different spheres of action. While they may often go along with this, it is quite another matter to portray it as a legitimate practice.

For example, Albert does not believe in the virtues of the fuzzy or the advantages of overlap. 'In my firm badly drawn boundaries make us lose sight of long-term concerns. We therefore need good rules that are clear and accepted; those are two essential conditions.' As a result, top management is totally unequivocal in its marking out and defining of boundaries. It separates the traded functions from the non-traded ones, the long term from the short term, the continuous from the discontinuous, the centralized sphere from the decentralized sphere. It makes this task almost exclusively its own, on the pretext that the units must not be taught to do 'whatever they like' at their level and so free themselves from the principles that head office asks them to respect.

6.3 Principles Are Not Enough

Head office writes the constitution for the organization. At the same time, it must ensure a means to reconcile the world of principles and the handling of problems, between the control of conformity and the efficiency of the real choices made by the units, between egoism and altruism, between the local and the global.

The outside observer is surprised by the emphasis that Albert places on hammering home slogans and moral codes of conduct in the management of his executives. 'Decentralization without the counterweight of values such as security or the respect for other human beings cannot succeed. Otherwise, I would only have managers who only believed in figures, in quantitative performance that was individually identifiable. Would it get results? Yes, but I would not want them at any price. Take those people who produce high performance at their level but who mock our values in their behaviour and in their style of decision making; they must not stay with us.' The values are therefore partly conceived of as a means of facilitating integration between, on the one hand, the operational choices made by each decentralized unit and, on the other, the strategic aims of the firm as expressed by top management.

Another lever chosen by Albert lies in the policy of leaving directors of operational units at least five years in their posts, especially those in the eighty commercial subsidiaries around the world that are profit centres. He hopes that these directors will not just concentrate on realizing their economic objectives (measured in terms of economic value added [EVA]), nor base their decisions on what will be profitable within a year, but will also see themselves as trustees for success in the medium term. This being the case, they will agree to launch initiatives and be responsible for the costs of development, formulation and certification, such commitments and costs having a time horizon of three or four years to appearance on the market and profitability. At the heart of general management is the capacity to manage the two worlds of action through recourse to a system of force and counter-force and maintaining equilibrium between different types of demand.

Head office at Agro is very compact, with fewer than a hundred staff on the payroll. Albert has very few departments and staff that are directly and exclusively attached at his level. He relies on an inner group of advisers and intermediaries. This consists of three executive directors, who also manage operational units and are long serving members of the organization. He confides in them and involves them closely in his style of management of the firm. They include the director of R&D and the director of manufacturing. There is also a 'centre', consisting of the CEO and his personal network, which appears to have remained relatively stable over the years.

An example illustrates the strength of this type of management. After he had spent a little more than four years as CEO of Agro, Albert was promoted to an additional post within the framework of the pharmaceutical and chemical multinational company that owns the firm. While remaining *de facto* the boss of Agro, he was made director of the animal and vegetable health sector of this company. This newly created position is responsible for the strategic supervision of three subsidiaries in the group, including Agro, that are otherwise separate entities. The chairman of the group at the head of Agro has named a replacement for Albert.

Albert now has two offices, one in Agro where he spent two to three days a week, the other in the headquarters of the company that owned Agro. In addition, he took on oversight of the investments and disinvestments made by his commercial and manufacturing units, with his successor having the freedom to control a budget of 15 million. Finally, Albert has taken his inner group with him, while they still retain their activities within Agro. So the director of R&D, like Albert, has a dual role. He is responsible for managing Agro in his field of expertise, and he supervises part of the R&D policies in the controlling company. Agro pays part of his remuneration, including his profit sharing from the results. The other executive who joins the sector has for four years been the director of manufacturing for Agro. From now on he will supervise the manufacturing of the three subsidiaries in the sector.

These dual affiliations certainly contribute towards restricting the autonomy of Albert's successor at the head of Agro. Similarly, the director of R&D in the sector controls its departments in the subsidiary, since he has been the undisputed head of science in Agro for more than fifteen years. These double hats to some extent act as a contradiction to the decentralization that Albert otherwise advocates. However, he hopes this arrangement will help develop a more collectively shared vision of the strategy and choices, and a more rapid dissemination of firm's aims to its lower levels.

He wants head office to be in touch with the operational units and the subsidiaries. 'My new sector will not just be a holding company. If it supervises and the subsidiaries manage, that is if the domains are structurally distinct, one needs paradoxically to create links between the people. So, my sector pays the whole of the salaries of the heads of the three subsidiaries because that makes them feel that they belong to the sector. I want to make the executives exogenous in relation to the unit that they manage and endogenous in relation to the sector or the wider community to which they belong.'

He also wants to facilitate closer coordination and more apparent compatibility of choice between the downstream and upstream functions at the heart of Agro, which is the most important of the three subsidiaries that he is responsible for. In fact, R&D and marketing pursue a policy of mutual avoidance. Their respective top and middle managements generally refuse to accommodate the requirements and systems of their partners on a day-to-day basis. Owing to this lack of a satisfactory cross-departmental relationship, the CEO ensures direct access to the two internal instruments of his strategy by co-opting two of their operational managers. Thus top management creates organizational complexity in the hope of obtaining a substitute for the deficiencies in horizontal cooperation at the base.

Here we can see a quite typical example of how top management secures for itself the formal and informal means of more closely monitoring the affairs of such and such a subsidiary or unit, either because it is perceived by the head office as a problem, or because it is defined as a highly strategic unit. At Agro, the mechanism is sophisticated. In other firms, it is often run in a simpler manner, not made explicit and not displayed. In its crudest form, it is ensured by the fact that the person who is put in charge is personally chosen by the CEO, has the CEO's ear, and will be more protected or on the contrary more closely monitored than his colleagues. In this sense, the resulting discrimination between hierarchical peers reveals, even though moderately, a style of management that operates by amending the principles of decentralization and internal virtual markets.

6.4 Transgression or Compromise?

Head office indeed implements the dynamics of exchange and quasi-negotiation, leading to compromises with regard to the official division of responsibilities between general management and those assigned to the operational units. Head office may override its own operating principles and legitimize ad hoc arrangements.

Albert, a man thoroughly aware of the moral requirements of a position at the top, does not hesitate, at times, to deviate from or even go against the principles that he advocates. What is important is that these deviations or adjustments should be accepted as legitimate actions without the operational units losing confidence and themselves departing from the principles too much and too frequently.

This can be exemplified by the case of the purchasing function at Agro. Whereas Albert more generally advocates a high level of decentralization, he has been led to consider personally coordinating the purchases of raw materials at his level. His reasons certainly include the lower costs incurred in higher volume purchasing. But above all Albert wants to control the process and prevent the emergence of instances where subsidiaries fail to take account in their choices of criteria for strategic objectives propounded by head office (non-closure of Agro factories through social plans, purchases from suppliers that may even be competitors, etc.). That said, Albert in the end abandoned his aims of centralization in the matter and has broadly delegated the purchasing function to the commercial subsidiaries. However, as a counterbalance to this autonomy, he requires the heads of these operational units, hitherto reticent, to give tangible and lasting support to the endogenous strategy of innovation and renewal that he wants. The CEO uses a combination of persuasion, coercion and quasi-negotiation.

The management of human resources is another domain where head office is confronted with the task of making principles and reality compatible.

At Agro, human resources are managed according to a centrifugal system. Of course, there is a central office that exercises the formal responsibility of setting out the frameworks and objectives to the subsidiaries. But it struggles to provide a full service, even though it is supposed to provide its services to the operational units on a supplier–customer basis. The units in fact baulk at accepting coordination, or even simple technical assistance, through the head office department or through any other unit. In practice, they rely on informal resources such as personal networks to identify and shortlist candidates from other units of the firm. There is certainly an internal labour market that ensures a minimum of horizontal movement. But this market is not formalized or transparent, and does not share the same criteria as those laid down by the head office.

In short, individual transactions are the fruit of local circumstances. So this contradicts one of the CEO's principles: that of maximum autonomy in the framework of shared explicit criteria (transparency and coherence of executives' careers, etc.). What counts is the weight of the power factors and the 'political' positioning of the centre's areas of intervention. In part this makes more fragile the embeddedness and the influence of the centre. It narrows the autonomy of the CEO whenever he makes single decisions that relate to his formally supreme spheres of action. Principles are not enough in the face of an organization that remains centrifugal, struggles to become civilized along the lines of a Type 1 organizational model, and takes a long time to get resolutely involved in a renewal strategy focused on the medium term. At the same time, the short term applies pressure.

Where human relations are concerned, in the end head office adopts a practice that is similar to that followed by the directors of the operational units and is at variance with the principles. The CEO keeps a domain to himself that he controls without help or interference from anyone. He takes it upon himself to select his immediate colleagues ($n - 1$) and even his second level colleagues ($n - 2$). He chooses them using his own discretionary criteria, some of which are intangible and call for trust and loyalty, while others focus on previous interpersonal relationships. In effect, using the principles of filiation, he creates a core of links based on common knowledge.

The position adopted by head office with regard to the operational units can be partly understood by referring to the type of shareholder base that controls the firm. In the case of a subsidiary controlled by a group, the relationship of subordination that its general management maintains with its controlling partner affects greatly the relationship of control that this same management employs with regard to its own subordinates. When it comes to the way that adjustment is made between the principles and the realities one fact is obvious. The margin of discretion is enormously in favour of head office.

So Albert benefits from direct access to the CEO of the pharmaceutical and chemical group and from his personal trust. Moreover, he was the person who named him successively as director general of Agro and head of the sector. Albert therefore believes that he has some freedom in comparison with the rest of the general staff in the group. 'It's a joke, but only just. My president has only one right over me; that is to fire me.'

In addition, the fact that he assumes control of the departments and conduct of policy at R&D as a reserved domain is not a neutral act. Through this exclusive and direct ownership, requiring daily a strong dose of discretion in the allocation of resources and little transparency in scientific and technical matters, head office is able to be simultaneously autonomous when dealing with the group and with the operational units.

It is a fact that R&D provides opportunities for trying to counterbalance the consequences of any short-sightedness shown by the commercial subsidiaries. The latter are spontaneously oriented towards the single aim of exploitation in the short term. Head office relies on R&D in the hope of injecting the cultural elements and the concrete instruments – new molecules – of a dynamic for the long term and for innovation.

By protecting R&D in this way, Albert creates in addition a source of legitimacy for himself in a domain where *a priori* he is perceived to be inexpert. By training he is an agrochemist, whereas the researchers are chemists and biologists. Finally, he can hope to distinguish himself from his predecessor at the head of Agro. The latter is now a personal assistant of the CEO of the group and looks after long-term technical and scientific policy. By having his own doctrine, Albert can hope to establish his own legitimacy. For example, is it necessary for Agro to maintain a strong presence in chemistry? Should priority be given to the biotechnologies? What needs to be done in plant protection by 2010? The fact that the director of R&D at Agro ('someone who has power and who is listened to in the group') has been co-opted by the CEO into his own inner group becomes a significant advantage.

One of the interesting aspects of exercising the function of general management is to be found in the way that its staff organize their daily dealings with the operational units. This approach also has consequences for arbitration and the application of principles.

Albert prefers direct contact. In management jargon, he uses the technique of wandering around. He devotes a significant amount of his time to visiting numerous sites, units and senior executives of his firm spread around the world. More than half of his time is allocated to such activities. He expects his colleagues to do the same.

The centre is therefore often away from the office on trips. By contrast, formal meetings, bringing together in one place and at the same time around Albert the whole of his first level of subordinates, seem much less important, rich and integrating. Apart from his R&D director and the director of the American subsidiary, Albert does not regard his first line of subordinates as his favoured spokespersons inside Agro, or use them as trusted relays between the centre and business units. He operates through various intermediaries, via devices of variable size: occasional large meetings with the executives, face-to-face meetings with middle management, and similar events. Top management, led by its head, is positioned at one and the same time as being detached from its first and second level executives, but easily accessible.

This pattern of operation induces particular perceptions and attitudes in the relationship of operational managers with head office. Two characteristics emerge. First, the centre invests the person who represents it with charismatic legitimacy; second, the centre becomes the resort for the solution of unusual operational problems.

Almost no one challenges Albert. He evokes striking emotional support from the service units and the operational units. He is said to possess exceptional qualities of attention, common sense, vision and influence on the course of events and, above all, of inspiring people. 'He is my personal friend. . . . I give all I can for him, not for Agro,' admits a director of a country. He is made a hero in the face of adverse events. He operates as a facilitator; he provides a counterpoint to the administrative complexities.

For an outside observer, such loyalties however cannot be taken for granted.

A contrast is established between the personage that is Albert and the system that he has put in place. The 'barons' who run the large commercial subsidiaries openly criticize the strategic and organizational principles Albert promotes, while they also claim to be won over by his personal skills and charisma. They expect from their chief first and foremost one role, but nothing more; they want him to behave as an arbiter, as a last resort, not as a master of foxhounds or as an interventionist proprietor.

That is how it is with the climate of strong hostility that the R&D department arouses. While R&D is supposed to subscribe to the breakthrough strategy wanted by general management, and its director enjoys the personal and overt trust of Albert, it suffers from persistent rejection and denigration so far as its effectiveness and privileges are concerned (financial resources, exemption from EVA criteria, etc.). One director of a large country does not hesitate to produce polemical memoranda against R&D, expressing the clear hope that the 'top boss' will know how to settle the question.

Head office appears as a level that is attentive and easy to reach when a manager has a problem that he or she considers insoluble at his/her level, or attributes the cause to another unit, or wishes to pursue a cause of his/her own that his/her immediate superior will not consider. Albert is positioned as a last resort for when partners cannot reach acceptable compromises. The magistracy of general management induces a strong level of community feeling, provides collective meaning to scattered events, and acts as the major integrator between selfish units. For, in the eyes of the thousands of employees of Agro, it can be taken as read that the unique and legitimate role of the centre is, at the end of the day, properly played out in the arena of the unusual, the abnormal and the case-by-case, not as controller of the strategic constitution, or architect of the economic and organizational models of the firm.

6.5 Behaviours Inducing Paradoxical Effects

The CEO bases his legitimacy on a paradox. He wants to make the firm evolve fundamentally by pushing it to abandon a Type 2 or self-sufficient model and by transforming it into a Type 1 or organic organization. But his legitimacy in the eyes of the departments arises from the fact that he shares common characteristics with the rest of the firm, which has a Type 2 organization and strategic positioning. When top management deviates from the principles and embraces the cultural sensitivity and methods of operating that develop at the middle rank and below, it sets a paradoxical phenomenon in motion. The more discretionary it becomes, the more the subordinate ranks gain an impression of familiarity, and the more easily they are able to decode the contents. In other words, the discretion shown exceptionally by head office in order to accommodate a temporary problem becomes the yardstick of what is normal for the departments, especially for the most powerful, which are R&D and the commercial subsidiaries.

The absence of shared languages between the top and the bottom is the major reason for this phenomenon. Such is the case at Agro, whose general management finally has to adopt a command structure that comes close to the vertical management used by the operational departments.

An enquiry carried out with a representative sample of sixty executives belonging to hierarchical levels $n - 3$ to $n - 5$ shows that the support of the head is on principle taken as read (Burt *et al.*, 2000). In contrast, the support that the individual receives from others located in other departments and hierarchical lines cannot be taken for granted. It must be negotiated on each occasion. It is therefore a permanent source of uncertainty.

In comparison with horizontal relationships, the vertical hierarchy therefore appears more reliable and much less fragile. Lateral interaction and interdependence is approached in a restrained, selective and temporary way. It is very difficult to develop horizontal coordination. As for clubs or networks created around technical, administrative or commercial subjects, which according to head office principles are defined as common to various departments and involve representatives from a variety of units, their impact, though not insignificant, is subdued. It is undeniably true that verticality remains the main anchor for day-to-day affairs.

In fact, the immediately superior manager is the person who counts most for an executive. But at the same time this applies within narrowly defined boundaries. The relationship is a personal one between two individuals, not between two positions or two roles. In contrast, peer groups or the nature of work problems are second order references. In addition, interactions are not necessarily frequent. There is no need to meet often to be sure of relying on the other. Verticality signifies first a contract of mutual trust between the head and the subordinate within which each manages independently so far as possible. What would be unacceptable would be to place a colleague's job at risk as a result of actions that one has taken oneself. Communicating information, developing a team spirit and sharing ideas in themselves contribute little to verticality. However, the duty of mutual support in times of difficulty is important.

The social networks made up by the executives at Agro have the peculiarity of being rooted in relationships of affinity based on mutual understanding between individuals. In comparison, work situations do not provide a lever for building an ad hoc but specific network. The social asset is thus the property of the individual; it is not linked as such to the task, the unit of attachment or the position held. When an executive changes his or her job, unit or hierarchical position, he/she takes his/her network with him or her. On the other hand, he or she cannot expect to add significantly to it or change it in future. The constraints and resources that prevail at a given time are managed through the major resource of experience gained in the past.

These observations explain the benefits provided by seniority. At Agro executives have an average of more than 20 years' service. Individual performance plays a small part. Three-quarters of the variations in salary are predicted by the combination of rank and age of the person, which correlate with the speed of promotion.

Now on the one hand, Albert does not call into question these characteristics by his choices so far as policy for executives is concerned. He does shake up the salary structure a little by adopting the EVA and reintroducing differentiation through performance, but in amounts that he considers reasonable. He appears reluctant to recruit massive numbers of experienced managers from other companies. Albert has a dream of transforming Agro in an endogenous way, through its current staff and from within. On the other hand, general management is obliged to get involved in the daily round and the operational. The point to note here is the fact that general management takes initiatives that are disconnected from the principles that it otherwise proclaims and institutes.

6.6 The Dilemmas of Complexity

Two lessons may be drawn about the management of a transition towards the organic model.

The first relates to the division of skills between the supreme domain of head office and the supreme domain of the operational units. The decentralization operated in Agro gives the units significant areas of autonomy that top management respects as far as possible in practice. For example, the centre does not control the choices so far as distribution is concerned. Country A divides its sales networks into two autonomous units that deal with the sale of 'commodities' and the sale of house 'specials'. Country B adopts another way of handling its sales force. It separates it into managing the big accounts and dealing with local retailers. In country C, the sales function remains based on geographical territories, with each salesperson being responsible for all the buyers in his or her area.

The diversity of the operational units in increased by the use made by top management of general principles to write the constitution of a firm that is established internationally. Agro therefore has more than eighty subsidiaries that differ in their size (from tens to thousands of employees), their portfolio of products (climates and agricultural crops that make it difficult to provide identical or universal products), their local markets, their activities (some for example in addition to selling also formulate products, their factories then being suppliers to other subsidiaries, or they provide trialling services) and in their turnovers (France, the large historical market, represents more than 40 per cent of Agro's turnover in Europe and enjoys a 25 per cent market share). By definition, the EVA technique makes more sense for huge units like the United States or France than for the smallest commercial subsidiaries in the poorest countries. On the other hand, some subsidiaries attract more attention from head office than others. Either they are an economic burden in the short term, or they appear as small markets with strong development potential.

A second lesson concerns the way that head office carries out its role as organizer of principles and architect of procedures.

In Agro, the boundaries of jurisdiction or competence set out by general management cause it to balance from day to day the formal rigour of the proclaimed principles, bypassing if necessary the single first rank authority (or area) present at the executive committee and dealing directly with matters specific to a given country under pressure of time, challenges or local specificities. In other respects, the interventions of head office reflect selective concerns that are peculiar to it. For example, Albert asks the US subsidiary, despite its own wishes, to entrust the certification of its products to a single person, not to each brand in its range. Another example is the location of a future factory to produce a new active ingredient discovered by R&D. Albert's colleagues propose to locate it in country A, strictly in accordance with the reasoning of the EVA, namely that production costs will be lower there. Albert imposes another solution that entrusts it to country B, a less economically attractive proposition but one that he judges more socially prudent. Top management remains in control of the criteria, becomes opaque and rules with discretion.

At another level, it can be seen that the content and degree of decentralization are managed in a flexible way by head office itself in the hope of accelerating the launch of new products and renewing the range. In tune with its endogenous renewal strategy, head office agrees to allocate discretionary financial support to help the efforts of the weakest. Such is the case with departments entrusted with developing products using new molecules. The rationale displayed by Albert is to give a financial incentive to the weakest in order to counteract the inertia of the strongest units, that is, the sales networks, which are accustomed to give priority to subsidizing through their own budgets products that use old molecules. The strategy–organization dilemma for head office is thus resolved through respect for the principles of positioning the firm in its market and by a violation of the principles that control its internal functioning (the development upstream is financed by the commercial subsidiaries downstream).

Any organizational model of inner management that relies upon quasi-marketing principles looks like an economic market. There is a limit to free competition, and the need for some form of regulation, in order to maintain collective cohesion and effectiveness. Every head office therefore finds itself exposed to setting in motion a process that, unexpectedly, creates a dual, if not schizophrenic, type of management and relationship with the operational units. The top lays down the rules while at the same time it exercises discretionary power on a day-to-day basis. Principles and exceptions to the principles cohabit in its range of action.

The important point at this stage is that, starting from a certain threshold and if there is no shared language, a general misunderstanding may be set in motion, which may emerge as a wave of cynicism. At the point where top management invokes the need for pragmatic flexibility, which in its eyes in no way detracts from the rules and principles that it promotes, the operational units develop a quite different interpretation that proclaims that the legitimacy of a principle is highly relative and in fact top management itself does not believe in it. The principle then becomes a promise that only binds those operational units that want to believe in it. Experience shows that they are few in number.

Without the existence of any prior condition, such as interpersonal networks sharing similar action cognitions or languages, head office can only fall back on rather poor weapons such as authoritarian pressure, centralization and the threat of personal sanction (sacking or pensioning off) to convince those who misinterpret or are recalcitrant.

6.7 When Cognitions Become Confused

The fact that top management becomes involved in the daily business strengthens a specific phenomenon. The interfaces between it and its first levels of command are loosened. A self-sustaining dynamic begins. General management comes up against a verticality that we have referred to as restrictive and against a truncated transversality. To remedy this deficiency in shared knowledge and to contain the centrifugal effects of the high degree of autonomy allocated to each unit or department, the management is driven by urgency and by the units to intervene case by case in an authoritarian and discretionary way.

This requirement has two effects: first, it provides a strong incentive to the units to have direct recourse to head office, and second, it weakens the credibility of direct mutual adjustments between the units as a process able to find agreements and to set up decisions. In other words, in such a case, nothing promotes and accelerates the spread of a common language, either between general management and the units or among the units themselves.

Integration therefore rests on the shoulders of top management alone, either the CEO or the director general when it comes to individuals. The main board close to the chief tends to be oriented towards a prudent and individualistic approach. It gathers together single individuals or stakeholders more than it unites a cohesive group. The collective references remain largely a priority task for the director general alone, while the subordinates pay selective attention mainly to the local implications of these references.

The firm's project is not shared much at this level. The problem is less one of a relaxed discipline, of a laissez-faire style of leadership unable to induce conformity, or a problem of ethics or morality, than one of an individualistic and fragmented positioning of knowledge. The discretionary exception tends to be regarded as a godsend that one hopes to see generalized.

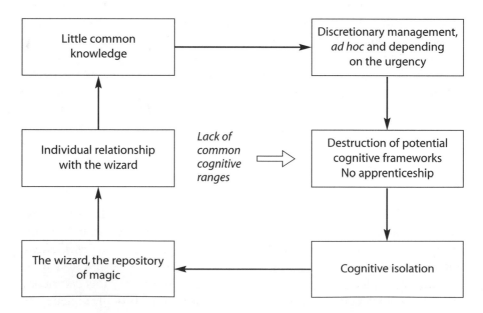

Figure 6.1 The vicious circle of the lack of common cognitive ranges

To return to the example of Agro, if A receives an urgent allocation of funds from Albert, why shouldn't B benefit from the same treatment? Moreover, as the horizontal networks are weak, as regards creating solidarity in action, top management feels obliged to intervene, which only strengthens struggles for autonomy and crystallizes the discontinuities, both cognitive and behavioural.

Such a dynamic is punctuated with relatively numerous paradoxes. The financial subventions granted to make things easier for departments developing and putting innovations on the market destabilize their relationships with the units upstream and downstream. Partners become jealous or suspicious. The parallel and informal circuits of contact that open up between head office and the units take away the relevance of the authorities, committees and units that could otherwise help and accelerate the diffusion of the strategic projects and management principles that Albert would like its organization to adopt. Bypassing them destroys their credibility.

The process is not however out of control. Top management possesses many resources for preventing things from going off course. Hence the unusually high levels of legitimacy and loyalty that the charisma of the director general arouses in his troops. However, these are poor substitutes. By nature they promote a content confined only to emotional control or to psychological dependence. They also do not disseminate references or contents for action taking. The director of Department A does this or that not because he necessarily shares and interprets at his level the strategy from the centre, but because he feels admiration and trust for the personality of the chief executive. Emotions, not cognitions, drive the managers.

This style of management clearly induces a generalization of ad hoc arrangements and encourages single deal making.

Faced with a top management that finds itself to be virtually the only promoter of a collective perspective – that is, isolated when worrying about the medium term and continuity – the operational units develop cognitions that favour a specific rationality horizon: the taking of relevant action is approached as basically referring to the short term and taking disjointed spot decisions. Continuity and linearity are not pragmatic virtues. In the minds of the managers, what counts is what brings immediate and local tangible results for everyone in their departments. Hence the selective nature of the information sent by the operational units to head office. For example, the director of an Agro subsidiary notes that 'the centre does not at all like negative information, difficulties, setbacks or problems. It is only receptive to good news. . . . At my level one soon understands this and takes it into account.'

Mapping and interpreting business as a sequence of disjointed deals also leads the managers to believe that success or failure is to a large extent the outcome of luck, personal gift or non-repetitive ways of behaving. At Agro this is the case with some R&D managers and quite a number of sales executives. They are proud of some technical *tour de force* or some spectacular commercial achievement they were able to perform, but without referring it to the strategy of the unit or the firm they belong to. Therefore they hardly ever explain to themselves or, more importantly, to third parties such as subordinates or colleagues, how and why a deal was successful or failed. They explain even less how the deal fits into a whole framework, or is relevant to more global or strategic objectives they are supposed to serve, or how it justifies the resources consumed. While this may encourage passive and superficial imitation, it does not at all encourage learning processes and attitudes. Learning means that linkages or causalities are made explicit between what is done individually and how it contributes to collective aims or goals. Without such a learning process, no progressive construction of common benchmarks is possible. Making deals prevents the accumulation of shared experiences because it turns its back on one essential aspect: the public explicitation of what the individual does, the ability to argue and therefore to translate experience as a source of knowledge shared with others.

Agro, for example, operates a commando tactic. Headquarters often acts operationally when situations are defined as urgent, while at the same time there are no contacts between R&D and the commercial units. In this culture of the ad hoc, the empirical criterion of success that a manager considers lies in satisfying his or her immediate superior's opinion or assessment. On the latter falls the task of finding solutions to the subordinates' problems, but without necessarily having to establish and explain to them what the link may be between the superior's own solution and the more collective principles that they should satisfy. The higher ranks may free themselves from principles that they are otherwise likely to promote and prescribe to their staff.

Decentralization expands and autonomy proceeds on a day-to-day basis throughout the organization without being based on strong and stable principles, which are simply reduced to rules and procedures, to a set of tools or means where the ends are no longer considered. Discretion provides the margin of flexibility that allows these rules and procedures to remain acceptable and realistic in the context. All the same, the reasons for this go largely unexplained and are non-understandable, so little is learnt. Because of this, the firm remains in the world of the magic.

As a result, the boundaries between the short term and the long term, between the continuous and the discontinuous, between the traded and the non-traded, become fuzzy because they fluctuate according to circumstances. Although the principles proclaimed by top management promote a cognitive function, it is very difficult for this to contain the behaviours and choices of the operational units. Values are reduced to slogans or petitions of principle. They fulfil a cultural function, but not a knowledge function. They establish an identity and mark the membership of the same firm at same time that the firm creates a barrier to learning and shows preference for the 'someone else's problem' syndrome. On the other hand, no link is established between the image of the community and the practice of the firm. The members of Agro feel that they are a culturally homogenous community while observation suggests that they are a rather heterogenous organization at a cognitive level.

In such a context, information assembled for choices and decision making enjoys a revealing position. Theoretically speaking, the prior availability of relevant information on prices, costs and details of products should allow the manager to derive a range of possibilities numbered as to the alternatives to be considered and favoured in order to launch a new active ingredient. In such a case, the arbitrary and discretionary aspect is restricted, and this allows the use of planning procedures in order to decentralize head office's strategy for the operational units.

However, this approach is not in fact adhered to. Head office puts forward ideas, designs routes and suggest visions. To a large extent these are transparent. But the business units have insufficient operational information to interpret them. They know what Albert thinks and wants in his role for Agro, but do not understand what implications his ideas, routes and visions may have for each of them. Thus head office acts in quite a solitary fashion, if only because the relevant information does not get through properly from the units and because their horizontal fragmentation is not compensated for by an intermediary level, for example the executive committee, that would ensure a minimum of integration. Therefore its discretion is strong. It operates by decentralizing not the group strategy, which is a cognitive system focused on a coupling of ends and means, but only the execution of its ideas, which is a system of conformity and discipline focused only on the means. This helps explain why a strong rhetoric arises and is legitimized and strengthened as to the uniqueness and specificity of each operational unit. Sales forces are supposed not to be like marketing people. Herbicides have nothing in common with pesticides. French people are by definition different from North Americans.

This phenomenon has two consequences. It increases the centrifugal tendencies inside the organizational fabric. Owing to the lack of learning and the deficit of collective debate, Albert has difficulties sharing with others the burden of the collective rationale of the firm. He is to a large extent the sole and lonely level that takes account of synergies and cohesion, and this is the reverse of what he would like to achieve.

The interplay of recourse and arbitration builds externalization behaviours by the operational units towards head office. Since referrals of this type are not forbidden, the obligation for each operational unit to internalize falls away. In a way, this accounts for the common view held by the commercial subsidiaries in Agro that it is impossible to discuss anything with R&D. In fact, the behaviour and reasoning of others become difficult to interpret and appear random, because they cannot be decoded owing to the lack of common areas of knowledge. In addition, mutual exclusion and sectoral fragmentation between units discourage the repetition of interplay and choice, even though this is a prime condition for a dynamic of common learning and therefore of becoming endogenous. It is significant that the authorities at general management level (executive committee, etc.) have difficulty in collectively generating a legal framework so far as criteria of choice are concerned. The principles remain relatively procedural; they do not refer to any meaning or content.

In order for the principles to convey content, they need to be institutionalized. More exactly, a principle that conveys content and meaning fulfils seven criteria at the same time:

- it is shared by head office and by the operational units,
- it is credible,
- it is experienced as legitimate and has value in itself,
- it is perceived as self-evident,
- it results in sanctions in the event of deviation, these sanctions being bearable,
- it can be communicated to third parties through discussion,
- it is acquired through a process of debate and learning.

6.8 Implementing Two or Three Organizational Models at the Same Time

Headquarters deliberately refuse to adopt a mercenary type of organizational model for the firm. That choice has major daily consequences for the business units.

At the same time, its CEO is faced with a heritage that he is not responsible for. His firm operates in way that derives from the self-sufficient model, but he wants to introduce a third organizational model arising from the organic type.

This stance brings top management up against the problem of management in situations of different time frames. In order to bring about such a reconfiguration, quite a long time horizon, three to five years, is necessary to set a learning process in motion. However, so far as the conduct of business for the operational units is concerned, the time horizon is much shorter: one to two years.

As an organizational configuration, Agro operates with a range of characteristics that refer rather to the Type 2 or self-sufficient model:

■ *A remarkable stability among the executives.* There is a policy of taking on young people in search of their first job, annual staff turnover is less than 1.5 per cent, and the staff stay with the firm for more than 20 years' service on average. Despite the extremely wide dispersion of units around the world, executives rarely leave the firm, which lets very few people go in the course of their career and is very reluctant to take on outside people in mid-career.

■ *A feeling of belonging and of distinction* that correlates with a stress placed on self-reliance. Agro is spoken of as a family, in comparison with other competitors that are not. 'Here it is not like other places,' says a senior executive. 'One must first be loyal to one's firm,' from a manager. On another subject, executives shrug off consideration of competitors in the marketplace. Quite literally, it is as though they scarcely exist, or not at all.

■ *A strong asset of shared knowledge among staff* that senior staff in the firm enjoy from the developed relational networks. But this asset increases and changes very little as the jobs of individuals evolve. This characteristic is perpetuated by the fact that trust is delegated *a priori*, preferably to the individual that one knows personally, and, in contrast, by the fact that explicit arguments based on the content of issues and tasks are not brought to bear as a decisive step for making decisions and concluding consensual arrangements between the parties involved.

As inherited by Albert, Agro in many respects resembles the so-called 'organized anarchy' model (Cohen *et al.*, 1972). New orientations that the top wants to inject into the company are diluted by complexity and become lost in the hazards of everyday life. At the same time however, not everything is erratic or unpredictable. If the firm that the CEO takes over seems to be quite anarchic or complicated to understand when seen from the outside, it possesses stable structural characteristics. The lower grades have relatively a good deal of power. The sales networks, for instance, autonomously control direct access to distributors; each salesperson covers his or her territory as a virtual monopoly.

This autonomy at the bottom has consequences for the circulation of information and sharing of knowledge. The weak signals about the market hardly ever get through. If the lower levels try to open a channel, the hierarchy is not listening or does not decode the signals. The latter are not very audible and often become badly interpreted because the voice of the sales staff on the ground is disregarded by the hierarchy, the marketing staff or the department of R&D, who see the reports as mere anecdotal evidence with no wider relevance. This voice is labelled as suspect for its supposed lack of detachment; it is denigrated as being both incomplete and biased. The situation is even more deadlocked because the sales staff is assessed according to the volume of their sales. The old and established products that form the basis of the tonnage are both the resource of their autonomy in the face of the hierarchy and the preferred commodity in the sales transaction. Therefore the staff have many good reasons to play down prospects and new business opportunities.

The relationship that is played out between the salespeople and the hierarchy illustrates a more general property of the Type 2 or self-sufficient organizational configuration. A loose cognitive collective goes with a weak relational collective. The salesperson thinks in terms of individual customers, local distribution, volume and, above all, priority conservation of existing products and brands. The marketing team think of global markets, alternative end consumers and distribution channels, prospects for renewal of the ranges. They do not perceive the same world and they do not speak the same action language.

The CEO is not blind nor a fool. He takes into account that, before his arrival, his firm, as an organizational configuration, had neither a history nor experience of substantial transversality on which to rely. In other words, the absence of a sufficient minimum level of common knowledge between the units and between the departments – R&D, commerce, etc. – makes it difficult for any spontaneous engagement in a virtuous circle of cooperative transversality to occur in a now decentralized framework. The new CEO must bear in mind that too long a period of lethargy and disorder would be risky, on account of the effects it might have on economic performance. Thus the introduction of a new configuration that generates more integration will be made from the centre, after first carrying out a phase of designing the new principles that the CEO wants to be very participative. More generally, he remains vigilant. A measure of ambiguity still seems to him to hover over the firm. Nothing guarantees that the game is won.

It is true that the executives and leaders of business units appear to have accepted a new organizational configuration, at least so far as the principles are concerned. The same goes for middle management. For their part, decentralization, new rules for the conduct of affairs and the adoption of EVA have won the day. That said, two intuitions temper general management's assurance and relativize its confidence in government by polls.

The first concerns the very status of a favourable attitude. Verbal support is an insufficiently sound indicator in terms of predicting behaviour. This is confirmed by a closer analysis of the remarks of middle management. EVA is expected above all to have technical effects: a simplification of costs monitoring through the adoption of a single criterion for all departments, and a reduction in their work since less time need be devoted to reporting. As for decentralization, the architecture goes in the right direction because it is perceived by the managers as strengthening their autonomy in relation to their hierarchy. On the other hand, these same people believe that their firm is already notable for the quality of its transversality and its horizontality, through its lively lateral communication and noticeable cross-fertilization of references and jobs. In other words, the new principles proclaimed by the CEO are not related to something that is an objective weakness in the existing organizational configuration, namely centrifugal autonomy coupled with references for action that remain narrow and localized.

The second intuition held by head office concerns the senior directors who are the heads of the large commercial units. Their attitudes are certainly more favourable. But they trade their support for something equivalent, such as more autonomy in purchasing. Alternatively, they limit themselves to the role of charismatic dependence: 'If the chief executive has pronounced it, I accept that he is right.' All of this gives head office the feeling that their behavioural support remains fuzzy, and there is uncertainty about their translation of the principles and visions into cognitive rationality, as used for action mapping.

Albert interprets the signals that reach him wisely. The question of decentralization remains open. He does not want to strengthen local micro-identities. He aims for an organizational fabric that is more transversal and better integrated. Therefore, managing the fundamental misunderstanding that surrounds decentralization becomes his major challenge. The question is whether the CEO can carry through alone, or almost alone, the dynamic of such a reversal; it being assumed that, in the units and through decentralization, suitable characteristics for a Type 1 configuration or organic are put in place: that is, a configuration that puts more pressure upon single managers and local units to play a much more collective game.

Two factors come together to complicate control of the course taken by the CEO.

In the firm the starting point for sharing cognitive references is very low; this makes it difficult and slow to establish a virtuous circle of transversality in a decentralized framework. Not to be under a time constraint is a major resource for Albert to ensure that an organizational apprenticeship gets under way.

On the other hand, the strategic restructuring of the firm fits into a horizon that can only be reached in the medium term. Sooner rather than later, general management will have to watch very carefully and ensure its financial performance. Albert is aware that he will not be able to keep on using year after year the excuse that modest economic results are due to the firm and the strategy he took over.

6.9 The Usual Nightmare at the Top

Albert interprets the keys to strategic success by considering two alternatives for the renewal of the product range: 'me too' based policies and breakthrough-driven routes. In doing this, he assumes the two strategic positions that are current in his industry, agrochemistry, and that are also adopted by the pharmaceutical sector where he gained his experience.

The 'me too' policy starts with products that are not unique, that are generics or derivatives. It is based on rapid and flexible adaptation according to market needs. A 'me too' product tends to have a short life span. Such an alternative requires a lot of flexibility. A breakthrough policy is very different. The firm's R&D has consistently to generate fundamental innovations that provide a longer-term rent because they are exclusively owned by the company.

Derivatives and the recombination of existing molecules for which new applications are sought are the routes chosen by the leading firms in agrochemistry. Their advantage is that their starting point is the market, and therefore the uncertainty if not the unknown is reduced. They rely heavily on marketing support to guide the process of R&D. In other words, R&D is integrated into the firm in an endogenous way. On the other hand, this approach has two disadvantages. It appears as an incremental process that emphasizes routine. In addition, it demands many resources, and so is restricted to the very largest firms; the number one firm in the agrochemical world employs more than 400 chemists working on local innovations and derivatives and controls a budget that is of the order of five times the amount that Agro allocates. For example, about twenty-five people are employed simply to analyse the products of competitors.

The example of the world leader leads Albert to conclude that the necessary capability correlates with the size of the firm. The fact is that Agro is much smaller than the leader. In addition, beyond a certain threshold technical experience shows that derivatives become more and more complex and uncertain, with the modification of a term in the chemical formula running the risk of unpredictable consequences. In short, any position based almost exclusively on derivatives seems unachievable. Albert gives all kinds of good reasons for not adopting it: 'Agro has not been able to do it in the past and will not be able to do it on the same scale and in the same style.' To this must be added the fact that Agro is witnessing the erosion of its market protection. The virtual cartel agreements between competitors are falling apart. The certification processes are becoming internationalized. Movement towards genetically modified organisms (GMO) threatens to reduce the consumption of pesticides and fungicides to a large extent. The old products are considered too harsh for nature and for humanity.

These considerations lead to adoption of a breakthrough strategy. It seems less expensive in human and financial terms. It is also more uncertain. Since it is of a non-traded nature, there is no guarantee that what is discovered will be acceptable on the market and commercially viable, despite all the indications that might be gathered together downstream. The breakthrough advocated by head office will rely on a certain number of technical resources. These include the expected advances in biotechnologies. Better understanding of the internal processes in plants leads to better control of the 'black box' that contains the links of causality between the various elements that go to make them. By this means the high degree of uncertainty that appears as a 'lottery' of effects produced on nature through molecules discovered in the laboratory is reduced. The other resource relates to new methods of screening molecules, borrowed from pharmaceutical R&D. The target is to be able to move from 15,000 to 200,000 molecules per year.

In fact, until now Agro has not truly been positioned on either of these alternatives. The portfolio whose supply the country commercial units ensure is essentially made up of two categories: common products that are made out of molecules or active ingredients that Agro owns but that are close to falling into the public domain, generic products, imitations and 'me too' products. In the latter case the firm produces some derivatives, but only to a moderate degree and not systematically. As for bringing new molecules to the market, this is very limited. Agro is emerging from a long period during which there has been only a single fundamental and significant breakthrough.

The CEO chooses breakthrough as a long-term strategic route, but without abandoning derivatives suddenly and in the short term. So far as the latter are concerned, he recommends and implements the subcontracting of skills and activities, in particular towards third-party suppliers located in Asia whose costs are lower. All that remains is to introduce the break-through choice operationally at the heart of the firm. This poses the question of the compatibility between the strategic principles proclaimed by the CEO and organizational configuration formed by the firm.

In theory, the answer is clear. The coupling between the two excludes certain combinations. A breakthrough strategy requires an organizational configuration either of Type 1 (organic model), or of Type 2 (self-sufficient model). In fact it brings two main resources into play: solidarity and socialization. So far as Agro is specifically concerned, this implies the following:

■ R&D becomes the strategic heart of its organization, confronting a market dominated by technology.

■ Marketing does not play a major strategic role, since the product is supposed to make its own presence felt.

■ The commercial side retains some importance on two main counts: selling and informing customers. In a general sense, the operational units have no independence of strategic choice.

■ Cash is generated by the nature, speed and reliability of monopolistic income derived from technological and scientific breakthroughs.

■ The key instruments for strategic choice arise from two domains: finance and R&D. Either the firm puts its own discoveries on the market, or it buys other companies that have breakthrough products in the pipeline.

A policy of derivatives relates rather to the organizational configurations of Type 3 (mercenary model) or Type 4 (fragmented model). It adapts perfectly to internal methods of operation that are fragmented or bureau-cratic. In such a case, there are two essentials for success: the accumulation and handling of information, and the fact that everyone is replaceable and is judged on short-term results. When applied to Agro, the implications of this requirement are:

■ Marketing predominates in a context where product domination is achieved through market share and cost rather than through scientific advancement or technological breakthrough.

■ The commercial side becomes a fundamental function. It is in direct contact with the environments; it has grassroots information; it sees the weaknesses and gaps, but also the opportunities.

- R&D is guided by the information from downstream, from the commercial units.
- The commercial subsidiaries established in geographical areas are really autonomous and independent.

Before Albert's arrival at general management, Agro was focused on a strategy broadly similar to exploitation of the existing portfolio of products, relying on an organizational configuration of Type 2, or self-sufficient, rather than a configuration of Types 3 or 4. After his arrival, the firm does not truly come within the scope of either schema. Everything appears as though the reorganization announced and put in place under his charge has produced a hybrid model:

- R&D is kept in a Type 2 system.
- A sector controlled by Type 3, namely the commercial subsidiaries, is created.
- Mediation between R&D and the commercial sector is confined to a Type 1 sector, the AIG.

R&D continues not to produce much, either from breakthrough or from derivatives. In addition, it remains internal, subjected to a self-sufficient organizational system or Type 2. Head office leaves R&D out of the internal reorganization through decentralization and the introduction of EVA and does not immediately call into question its internal organization system.

On the other hand, the new principles give strong autonomy to the commercial subsidiaries. There is also implicit recognition of a strategy of derivatives for the most important countries. This is in contradiction with the fact that R&D retains broad independence and is clinging to a policy of breakthrough.

Finally, the AIG is not proving the catalyst for initiating a process of transversality between units. Hope for an immediate, short-term dynamic of increasing learning has been eroded, for the AIG itself embodies the contradictory injunctions addressed to the units. It cannot by itself solve the dilemma of building bridges between a strategy of exploitation and one of innovation, between derivatives/cloning and breakthrough, between the short term and the long term.

Of course, on paper at least, it has a card to play. This relates to the price of active ingredients that go to make the final products, which head office decrees can be neither bought nor subcontracted freely by the operational units to outside suppliers for reasons of strategic control. In fact, the countries control the situation by imposing their language and their local interests. They have market information that relates to derivatives. All they have to do is to wait for the fatal weapon of the breakthrough without having to pay for it in terms of engagement. The country remains a free-rider. It is not able to reconcile upstream and downstream forces, owing to its lack of authority or, at least, of full and complete ability to arbitrate, something that head office should have granted but in reality takes away through its discretionary interventions.

Head office holds on to the resources necessary for the solution of the dilemma. Although it is certainly against the principles of the internal market, head office helps to lower prices to the commercial subsidiaries by providing discretionary subsidies to R&D and to the AIG for the development of new molecules. The subsidiaries, with the help of EVA, are encouraged to offer these new molecules to their external customers. The new range of products appears to be successful because its strategic adoption by the commercial subsidiaries entails no share of financial risk, the risk being largely borne by head office.

The confusion managed by head office may be analysed in another way, by examining how the interaction and exchanges that are traded and those that are non-traded connect with the heart of the firm. Two types of situation are visible.

A breakthrough schema (Figure 6.2) implies a 'push' type strategy. In other words, everything is externalized by the firm onto the consumer. Such a schema is viable so long as the monopoly enjoyed by the whole protects each of the units that go to make it up, including head office. In such a case, the non-traded sphere dominates the traded one through a centralized organization model. R&D controls uncertainty; it is the repository of the essence of the game, which is the non-traded approach, and it dictates the game through the supply of innovations and breakthroughs that restructure the policies taken care of by the collective. Located at the very end of the chain of dependencies, the commercial units are restrained by the magic product that is supposed to be developed upstream. This implies that they have no autonomy. It is down to them to generate and

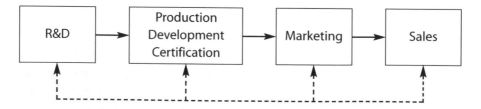

Figure 6.2 Non-traded approach and breakthrough policy

provide the financial returns on the products that the firm controls in a monopolistic way on the market, products whose price is high and cost is incidental. The financial returns are put at the disposal of R&D on receipt through an automatic feedback effect. However, there is a problem with this schema, namely repeatability. Breakthrough innovation is not at all easy to repeat and to programme.

A derivatives schema (Figure 6.3) is distinguished by a 'pull' type of strategy. Here the customer is the uncertainty and the traded approach dominates. It is the so-called downstream functions that interpret the opportunities and dictate the game to everyone upstream. Three dimensions are involved which serve as reference frameworks to be shared by the units of the firm. Costs have to be reduced at all levels over and again, if possible below those of the competitors. Products have to be renewed often and quickly through the recombination of the materials and their functions. The third major dimension is organizational: much autonomy of choice is granted to the operational units on the ground. This implies that at their level there is a broad understanding of events and alternatives through face-to-face cooperation between marketing and sales. In addition, the upstream of the firm is subject to strong discretionary dependence with regard to the financial flows generated on the ground. To these are added information flows that the operational units collect and to which upstream must submit itself in order to make its own choices.

The solution adopted by Agro's general management aims to reconcile the two systems of downstream traded and upstream non-traded logics of action, with the AIG acting as the mediator between them. The way this is implemented may be characterized as follows:

■ The AIG is cut off both from the non-traded sphere (breakthrough oriented) and from the traded sphere (sensitive to local markets).
■ The specific perspective of marketing as a way of reasoning is diluted because it is appropriated by each of the three poles (the AIG, R&D and commercial subsidiaries).

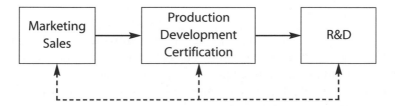

Figure 6.3 Trade based approaches and sensitivity to local markets

- Each pole seeks a third party on which it can externalize. The result is a vicious circle of subsidization.
- The flows of information are weak between departments and the financial flows between them become intermittent.

Now the rift between the traded and the non-traded poses an enormous problem of how to maintain global coherence. This provokes a movement of recentralization for the benefit of general management, even though this contradicts its own principles of decentralization and economic empowerment for the operational units. Vertical lines become the answer to weak transverse lines. The challenge that creates the centre's nightmare is to be found at this level. Lacking coherence through transversality, head office and the operational units resort to management of coherence through a restrictive verticality, namely action solely through general management.

Centralization of the decentralized dynamic is also caused by the fact that the AIG is not by itself in a position to achieve sufficient integration capacity between R&D and the commercial units, between the push and the pull, or between breakthrough and local incremental adjustments. In reality, general management ensures a large part of this integration, by giving a boost where necessary and offering to arbitrate.

Such intervention is effective in the short term, because in the case of new molecules it enables them to be transformed from breakthroughs into products that fit local market and customer needs. However, in the medium term it strengthens the power of those who argue for localist incrementalism and further marginalizes those pursuing the breakthrough route. As a reaction to this, we have seen the role and attention given by head office to ensuring room and funds for R&D, in line with its proclaimed breakthrough policy. The paradox is that the more support is given upstream, the more the salespeople are driven to focus exclusively on short-term incremental and local adjustments to products and market needs, and the stronger their incentive is to care about their own firm and only their own firm (Beuzit, 1999).

6.10 Trusting to Luck

For the management of a company, resolving contradictions takes place in a setting open to unexpected circumstances, surprises or deviations from theories behind the proclaimed principles, and is affected by factors linked to a particular context at a given moment. In this sense it is an art rather than a science, a significant element being down to chance, on the one hand, and to pragmatic opportunism, on the other.

For example, Agro functions like a firm focused on reactive local and incremental opportunities (what might also be called a proximity positioning: business strategies resulting from the fact of being very close to short-term market events and explicit customer needs), but one that at the same time allows a breakthrough system to operate. Head office plays on the two themes because it wishes to reconcile two requirements with different time horizons. The locally induced policy allows short-term goals to be met. The breakthrough policy serves to satisfy the medium-term pressures. They relate to different areas. The first responds to the requirements of the owners; the second arises from the firm's size and therefore from its position in relation to its competitors in the marketplace.

The proximity-based policy is consolidated by the method of performance evaluation of the operational units (in this instance through the EVA criterion) and through decentralization. In reality, the countries externalize on the AIG. The latter in turn externalizes on to manufacturing. This has a major consequence. A lot of pressure emerges through costs, quality and delays, whose epicentre is manufacturing. The AIG from now on appears like a lever whose function, at the heart of the value chain process, is to bring considerable pressure on production, in particular through massive subcontracting. Plants and workers bear a major part of the economic uncertainty. With this amount of pressure externalized, head office is quickly able to satisfy the financial requirements of Agro's owning group. The creation of value, and therefore immediate economic rent, provides the CEO with relative autonomy. He is significantly successful in improving profitability and creating value for his proprietors. At the same time he can finance his breakthrough policy.

For its part, the breakthrough system represents another type of pressure. Agro is a firm that, within its sector of activity, does not rank among the two or three largest in terms of size, global market share or self-financing capacity. The strategies of derivative innovation and being close to local opportunities cover a large range of products and require substantial sums in relation to its budget and thus in relation to its size. To this must be added the fact that it is affiliated to a large group whose core business lies in other areas: agrochemistry carries much less weight that pharmacy or chemistry. It therefore does not rank high in the priorities of its proprietor.

Breakthrough is the weapon of a small player among the big players. The creation of economic rents through technological innovation offers the hope of reconciling (but only in the long run) strong competition in the marketplace with relative marginalization within the group headed by its proprietor. The wager is difficult to win given that breakthrough is itself by nature unpredictable.

Agro's general management works as strategic architect and organizational guide that attempts to hold together two separate systems: a decentralized model of the downstream market type, and a centralized model of the upstream extra-market type. If Albert does not rush his decisions, but relies and gambles on a progressive dynamic, it is because he is confronted by at least two other major pressures, a situation that many other firms and sectors are familiar with.

It is a fact that his firm is emerging progressively from a protected market, especially in the major countries of Europe that would ensure the major share of his economic performance.

In the first place, the detailed regulations of the public authorities were quite favourable for agrochemists. The fact that each country had its own specific procedures and criteria in terms of safety or tests made bringing new products onto the market slow and costly. But it also allowed the firms that were good at handling such a complicated and disparate regulatory scene to benefit in a spectacular way from capture relationships with the regulators themselves. Public authorities were often more confident of firms that they knew well, and whose technical know-how they may have used as a reference for their own expertise and decision criteria. In its own country, the firm was regarded as a national champion that would receive the most benevolent attention from the public authority responsible for the approval and certification of products.

In the second place, Agro benefited from a historically consolidated proximity to the end users of its products, especially the distributors at the heart of its large historical markets. In addition, mutual feelings of non-aggression among the agrochemical firms in their respective base markets encouraged a calmness in the markets and allowed affairs to be managed with a quite strong degree of secure predictability. In the view of general management:

> All of our competitors shared with us the tools of common knowledge of the markets; this created shared references. . . . There were also codes of good conduct between competitors; I do not touch my colleagues' products, we do not attack each other on matters of toxicology and the environment, we avoid publicly taking sides with third party groups (environmental groups, etc.).

The end of the twentieth century has seen growing uncertainty and increasing unrest, including the Europeanization of approval procedures, the intrusion of new constraints (on pollution of soil, air and water), the emergence of public debate (the media and genetically modified crops, the mobilization of ecologically sensitive people) and the accelerated globalization of competitors.

Such a transformation helps one to understand an apparent paradox. By proclaiming a breakthrough strategy for the future, the CEO returns to a theme endorsed by his predecessors, even though, during their period of office, the breakthrough strategy was really no more than a fiction or, more precisely, the product of rhetoric. The breakthrough strategy served as a shield for the general management of Agro when making promises that kept the owners at bay. In reality, things were different. In its actions Agro revealed a strategy and configuration mode organized around proximity, derivatives, imitation and cloning. The largely autonomous commercial subsidiaries drew the rest of the firm behind them, with the exception of R&D. The only difference between the past and the present is the matter of size. It lies in the fact that before Albert's arrival as head of Agro autonomy was vague and concealed, and went on behind a façade of a centralized and procedural style of management. After his arrival, this autonomy became established as a principle that is explicit and delegated to the countries.

One can then better appreciate the question of R&D. In the recent past, it has not produced much. The rhetoric of breakthrough still allows it today to rationalize its autarchy, if not its immunity, at the heart of the firm and to protect the budgetary resources that the centre at its discretion allocates to it. However, it is now increasingly confronted by its lack of success and by open criticism from the country sales units. While the pressure is mounting, R&D cannot respond to it in the short term. It is the CEO who takes it in hand. But he does not treat the issue in an irreversible way. He buys some time and wants to keep some options open. Therefore, he works out compromises that he perceives as acceptable. While he promotes breakthrough and obtains the benefits of credibility or protection of that in the face of the board and the owners, he at the same time struggles with internal bureaucracy.

In theory at least, there are two ways of sweeping away bureaucracy. The first is to make a total break. For example, company A takes advantage of an acquisition in order to fulfil another goal, which is to reform itself. An exogenous dynamic is established either in A or in A and B. The acquired company B, though it is now under the control of A, becomes a benchmark for the latter. Its language for action is introduced and imposed even inside A. Another form of total break involves a global reform of A and B, by calling in consulting firms. Head office reviews everything from scratch through a global and immediate reform, redesigning structures, procedures and the tools of management, even redistributing staff and positions. The fact is that Albert deliberately avoids this approach. On the one hand, he does not want to make an acquisition of importance. On the other hand, he stimulates the change in an endogenous way, by closely involving his executives, by increasing project groups and giving them full scope to get the general principles translated into procedures and structures.

The second approach, which is the one that Albert adopts, is a process of progressive or incremental reform. Head office progressively abandons a certain number of prerogatives to the advantage of the operational units. In a case such as this, decentralization is not experienced as the death of the old organization, but as a transformation generated by the dynamic of the social body itself. It is constructed in an endogenous way. The condition for its success is that it requires two factors that must be confronted: time (a horizon of three to five years at least) and surplus resources (spare human and economic capacity). If these are not available, the removal of bureaucracy can only be achieved by the total break or exogenous approach.

The problem of the dilemma between a pull and a push perspective arises often from the size of the firm. But size must be interpreted from the perspective of a lever that it gives or does not allow to be given to action by general management. In the context of Agro, a comparatively small size clearly becomes a strong constraint, as the case of the R&D department shows.

Suppose the CEO were to choose the market strategy. In this case, R&D focuses attention on development: that is, derivatives and cloning. But Albert does not have the resources for this. Agro is not large or rich enough to be able to afford quickly a critical mass for local development apart from in its already established research centres, which also have a tendency towards academic and fundamental research. Furthermore, he does not go for a merger or acquisition that would allow him (once again quickly and significantly) to integrate firms that have products already well advanced in development, so that through an exogenous process he could reduce the level of uncertainty about its strategy and lower the risks. To a large extent CEOs act like gamblers who take decisions now so as to enable the firm to face a future that remains, if not unknown, at least uncertain. They also try to reduce the risks of their bets.

The CEO's action is the result of a compromise: a breakthrough strategy coupled with a recombination tactic. The recombination requires much cash to be available, while the breakthrough requires the firm to have a relatively large number of new products to introduce at brief intervals onto the market.

The dilemma for its CEO is that, in comparison with its competitors, a firm like Agro does not have enough money or enough products to take either route. It cannot simultaneously summon the resources for its tactic and its strategy. What is more, its proprietor allocates financial priority not to agrochemicals but to the development of its pharmaceutical activities, which prevents an increase in the range of products through the purchase of third-party firms that might have them. From now on Albert's strategic position remains doubly fragile. The adopted strategy, breakthrough, is more or less irreversible, while at the same time the number of proprietary products at an advanced stage of development remains small in the medium-term horizon.

There is a lesson to be drawn by top managers from uncertainty and unpredictability. The chance factor and the lottery effect play their part in the strategic nightmare. They are even a condition for resolution or a way out. The art of management at the top is based on the seizing of opportunities as elements for integrating contradictions. It depends partly on at least three factors: flair, intuition, and being in the right place at the right time.

The nightmare for top management, however, hardly ever reflects the skills of the CEO alone (his 'nose') nor the sole effect of the lottery of events (his 'luck'). One thing is certain. The loneliness of top management will be all the greater and the burden of fine-tuning will be all the more overwhelming if the operational units do not share the same language as the top. Sensitivity to organizational cognitions, which means the ability to understand the real situation inside the organizational fabric of the firm and the skill to set up change processes, is a decisive facet.

CHAPTER 7

The Role of General Management

Every general management plays the role of cognitive architect of the company for which it is responsible. Cognitions, knowledge, languages of action are factors that are as key for economic success as technologies, brand or cash. Observation suggests that not many CEOs or head offices are aware of their importance, and that even fewer are good at managing them. How the architect proceeds depends on the cognitive references that are diffused through the core of the company, whether they are shared or not, and whether or not they are common to the operational units and to the company itself.

This situation becomes a sensitive factor when a strategic ambition is pursued through an endogenous renewal process while at the same time it encourages a dynamic of organizational decentralization. For if knowledge is not shared, it is very probable that a partial, informal and paradoxical recentralization process will replace the initial decentralization in quite a short time.

7.1 The Cognitive Architect of the Business

What happens when strategic opportunities emerge or new visions are elaborated that are not compatible with the organizational model dominant in the firm? The answers are not easy, as many executives know. Quite often head offices try to address the issue by adopting new business policies while not changing anything inside the organization fabric and its cognitive frameworks. Or they have the illusion that issuing decrees is enough to change these dimensions successfully and swiftly. What happens when surprises occur, for example when routine activities cease to generate successful outcomes? Do firms and their head offices accept that solutions may be used that are not in line with the repertoire of action they are accustomed to, or that even violate the principles they consider constitutive for the whole organization? The way in which such events or surprises are resolved is often decisive, especially with regard to how head office acts at its own level, how it approaches ad hoc or improvised schemes, and helps or hinders common language sharing. For ease of argument we will examine two situations where decentralization principles are displayed.

In the first case, the organization supervises and guides the behaviour of the units by combining two main approaches. It designs quite narrow corridors of action. It also defines highly specialized action jurisdictions that apportion partitioned action territories among different business units. Decentralization as managed by head office is nothing more than the devolution of extremely simplified implementation schemes. Major difficulties arise when action contexts or contents emerge which do not come within the corridors of action for which the players in the company are prepared. The organization experiences what is unexpected or new, what is non-anticipated or non-planned, as a constraint, not as an opportunity. No attention is paid to anything that cannot be handled by the cognitive structure. In such a circumstance, head office will feel obliged to intervene. It will recentralize, that is, by applying a system of handling exceptional circumstances and by legitimizing this. It will be all the more ready to violate the decentralization principles it displays if it has already used codification widely in order to manage the business units.

In the second case, the less codification has been developed, the greater the likelihood that a difficulty will be handled and resolved in some other way by head office. The latter does not behave like a decision maker intervening in a prompt, discretionary and distant way, but like a teacher, a facilitator in the process of learning, allowing knowledge to be shared with the directors of operational units. It works for the emergence and diffusion of an implicit and non-proceduralized precedent in an open if not interactive way. Each problem treated thus contributes to the establishment of a process of accumulating cognitive frames of reference. The adjustment therefore goes well beyond the definition of an immediate solution adopted at a particular moment. It allows the world of principles, both objective and constraining, to be activated, to guide and indicate the behaviour of the centre, such as its vision of the long-term strategy for the firm. It makes it possible for the operational units to understand the strategy's contents while at the same time they are led to commit themselves to them, each in its own local context. In such a case, top management works to ensure that a cognitive apprenticeship operates through confronting the realities of action.

Top management therefore plays a dual role as a cognitive architect of the human organization it heads. On the one hand, it defines the general long-term interest of the firm. Such a definition is exogenous with regard to the units and to their staff; it does not arise from a mutual internal apprenticeship. On the other hand, it acts as the integrator of the multiple units and functions inside firms. In order to achieve some acceptable level of cooperation between them, it has to make their behaviours predictable. Observation suggests that top management has two alternatives. It can help construct common languages or it can prescribe narrow corridors of action.

What makes life at the top difficult is the fact that these two alternatives are mutually incompatible from the point of view of the strategic positioning envisaged by the firm, as already underlined above. They also call for types of intervention from the centre that induce contradictory effects on the units.

In contrast to management through codification, management through shared knowledge is not decreed by a speech or by an order. Three aspects have to be considered. Shared knowledge construction emerges through time, in a mid-term perspective. It also implies another skill from the CEO and the general managers: allocation of attention. It requires a continuous and sustained series of explanations that make explicit what managers usually keep tacit in decision making or when making transactions. The third aspect refers to autonomy. It has to be understood emotionally as well as behaviourally as a general and specific principle. Autonomous business units and staff are *a priori* by definition supposed to have the right to make decisions and act according to criteria they define, provided that they are accountable for achieving goals assigned to them by their hierarchical superiors. Such a principle is radically opposed to the principle of planning that lies behind codification.

While quite easy to define intellectually, autonomy is much more difficult to enact behaviourally. For instance, a thorough decentralized organizational style of management, occurring moreover in a dynamic environment, assumes that the firm delegates a high degree of autonomy to its operational units. The corollary is that the situation becomes fuzzy. The issue for head office becomes how to avoid disintegration when facing a fuzzy action structure. By far the best solution is provided by knowledge that is clearly shared between head office and the operational units and among the units themselves.

On the one hand, innovation or adjustment is usually generated in the peripherals of the firm. It is not head office, at all events not it alone and permanently, that is in direct contact with the realities on the ground, visiting customers, detecting faint signals, and anticipating opportunities and incompatibilities. On the other hand, endogenous language cannot develop unless the boundaries between internal players are fuzzy and there are partial overlaps inside the organizational fabric. It would be a major mistake for a firm and its head office to declare war on such phenomena, for instance by considering tension as such to be a disease, by narrowing the corridors of action, or by defining over-precise boundaries among the units and between the units and head office. The consequences would be dramatic. The business units and the staff would not think and act as if they had a stake in or were responsible for success requirements, such as permanent adjustment to the market and competition, long-term survival by renewal or the role of the non-traded sphere. On the contrary these factors would become exogenous to them.

Moreover, without shared knowledge, what is measured quantitatively by the management systems becomes the ultimate norm in relation to which the players make their choice and from which they will only deviate on direct orders from their hierarchy. The hard, that is, the routinized element or any other technical convention, drives out the soft, or intuition and information about surprises and news. A short-sighted firm is an organization that does not look at anything except what it has learned to look at once and for all. Short-sightedness is a feature of bureaucracies; they encourage the alignment of their internal conduct with the principle of conformity, to the point of not allowing anyone the practical challenge of anticipating and interpreting the world.

7.2 The Tools of Cognitive Management

Cognitive architects have four main tools at their disposal through which to act and enhance the level of shared cognitions for action internally: empowerment, the diffusion of threats, control of relevant uncertainties, and the activation of networks.

7.2.1 Empowering the Operational Units

Empowering the operational units means that handling transversality and defining ways to achieve collective goals are taken in hand by the subordinate levels.

To a large extent empowerment is not a gift, but a constraint. The main reason is not so much the related accountability but the fact that subordinates have to cooperate in taking action. For the units located on the ground, managing transversality at their level can appear as a risk of losing their own autonomy or having to accept the challenges of partners more powerful than them. 'Why take it on myself when no one above me is interested and no one supports me, except general management, which by the way is not very accessible?'

Basically empowerment means that units and staff have to find solutions for coordination at their own level and to make trade-offs for action. It is a process that implies learning and appropriation by those who are empowered. The more head office decentralizes these activities and leaves them to the units without interfering even as a court of appeal, the more the units are empowered. In contrast, the more top management intervenes or takes the burden of horizontality on itself, the less the units assume empowerment.

Empowering for the sake of building some common language means something very specific. The superior level has to empower the immediate subordinate level. This implies that the latter no longer acts as a simple relay between the top and the bottom, basically carrying back and forth information, and in worst cases acting as an information filter. The reason why head office needs an empowered $n - 1$ hierarchical level is that, just like any superior, the CEO needs immediate collaborators who gear down the principles and get them translated into more operational terms. Intermediate hierarchical levels that are empowered allow the centre of a company to counter one dramatic problem: front-line units and staff who may be tempted to care only about their own business. Withdrawal and egocentricity are deadly behaviours for firms in hypercompetitive contexts.

A head office may suffer from inadequate channels of information and may be led to respond with crisis and commando thinking, in a reactive and immediate way, when faced with any lack of transversal coordination between the business units. A centre that cannot follow the action on the ground from day to day appears sensitive only to those actions that are immediately intelligible and visible. Its own interventions appear as exogenous to the units. The discretionary behaviour of the CEO thus comes into conflict with his or her own pronouncements on values such as respect for people or economic empowerment. For, through their intangibility, they assume on the contrary that an endogenous system is established.

Disempowerment is exacerbated by discretionary alterations made by head office, to the performance evaluation procedures of the units or to the allocation criteria for investment funds for example. Such interventions are experienced by the units as ad hoc fiddling, as sudden and unexpected apparitions. If the endogenous entails foresight, such practices, whatever the good reasons behind them, are characteristic of an exogenous approach and interpreted as a flurry of blows with no coherence about them.

7.2.2 Using Urgency as a Threat for the Firm

A second instrument stimulates internal mobilization. Head office puts the organization and its staff under pressure by spreading the idea that the firm has to meet threats and by diffusing a climate of permanent urgency.

Collective challenges are often perceived as efficient stimuli. Strong emotions and some dramaturgy are ingredients that induce unusual consensus and mobilization. They designate the periods when the collective future of an organization is on the line, either on a defensive front ('the exterior is a grave danger for our integrity and our survival') or on an offensive front ('we are going to beat the competition, to become the leader or the reference for the market'). The positioning of a firm in the organic mode requires that a threat can be used by head office and that it is perceived as exogenous.

To be efficient the threat must be exogenous by nature at the same time as it must generate endogenous mechanisms. In the case of Agro, the lack of such a threat seriously inhibits head office's capacity to mobilize the units and causes a new organizational configuration to emerge through practice. Even if the prospect of internationalization of the firm presented a threat, but head office only used it in moderation, the same weakness of capacity would ensue. Thus the CEO must have recourse to his personal charisma and charm if he is to win over the executives of the business units. His first lines of command perform not so much because they are driven by a common challenge as because they are seduced by a leader they admire as a person. They fight not because they share a common outside enemy but because they individually are willing to follow their leader.

Charisma does not in any way replace the use of the threat that allows the organization to internalize and appropriate the challenges. For charm carries with it the seed of a threat that is by nature endogenous. It contains the potential for conflict or emotionalism that is often counter-intuitive. Head office wishes to make itself wanted by the staff. Unfortunately, this does not work out as expected. The managers are disappointed by their CEO. They like and admire him but they feel frustrated by the fact that they do not get what they would like him to deliver.

7.2.3 Controlling Major Uncertainties

Being at the top of the hierarchical pyramid does not suffice. In order to be a strong player in the organization, the centre needs actual power to back up formal authority. A third lever of cognitive management concerns the sources and amount of power that head office can deploy.

As is clearly shown by practice as well as by the sociology of organizations, authority without power is an empty shell; it has little capacity to influence the behaviours of the other players in a social system like a company. The amount of power particular actors have is linked to the fact that their own behaviour becomes a source of uncertainty for their relational partners. The latter are dependent on the way the former handle their tasks, the alternatives they choose, the impact their own acts and non-acts have on their partner's stakes or goals. Powerful head offices are actors whose behaviours have major consequences for their business units. The content of their decisions is to a large extent unpredictable by the latter, which means that the decisions and behaviours of the centre matter for their subordinates.

Controlling tasks, functions or issues whose content matters is a major precondition for the centre if it is to influence third parties inside the organization it heads. CEOs who are not powerful, whose behaviours and roles are not uncertainties for their subordinates, will face difficulties in influencing their cognitions. Therefore, cognitive architects must also be actors who control relevant sources of power. The more top management controls by itself and at its level the issues or tasks that are relevant uncertainties for the units and for the company, the better it mobilizes the units. The less relevant they are, the greater the risk that a system of organized anarchy will become established. Such is the case when head office has become almost totally transparent, in other words when it does not any longer control any uncertainty. The CEO at Agro has granted formal autonomy and has defined rules that make the role and the decisions of head office, including his own, transparent and predictable. On paper the centre may have lost most of its former power, except what it allows itself to handle in a discretionary way, for example, through the allocation of subsidies to the business units in specific situations (giving incentives for new molecules, etc).

This discretionary behaviour that infringes the principles does not rank as a real added value on the part of head office. It is perceived by the operational units as a sign that head office behaves as a free-rider in its relations with the collective set-up. Arguments that may be rational for the top become destructive for common cognitions inside the organization. The operational units have a biased view of how transversal coordination and interfaces should operate between the domain of the traded and the domain of the non-traded functions. The link between upstream and downstream appears to them to be monopolized and controlled by a centre that has become even more exogenous. Consequently, managing the conflicts in a horizontal mode by seeking a solution between the units involved becomes pointless and impossible to achieve directly. Decentralization of the transverse coordination and cooperation does not occur. Because they are stripped of the responsibility for coming to an arrangement between themselves without the mediation of head office, the various departments lose many opportunities of sharing knowledge.

In the case of Agro, the CEO simultaneously adopts a breakthrough strategy and a tactic of derivatives by managing improvisations or arrangements that in principle ought to emerge from the base units and that Albert handles without knowledge of conditions on the ground. His acts therefore appear fuzzy. Contradictions seem to be a usual practice in his decision making. His unpredictability means that people inside Agro, while admiring him, remain rather cautious or even passive. At the same time he does not have full power, given the fact that he does not control in a monopolistic way major factors that may matter for building success of the firm, whether short-term (the sales forces are in control) or medium-term (R&D has the upper hand). Improvization means that he may well have a vision but not a strong power base of his own to make things happen just by his own will. In other words, people obey because they admire the person rather than because he controls a major uncertainty. Besides the CEO, many other players inside Agro are key players for success.

In contrast to Agro, the head offices of other firms base their way of working on an uncertainty whose origin is specific. If the decisive factor of the strategy is the brand, the image or the reputation, it is handled by marketing. In this case, head office directly controls this department. If the key uncertainty for success or survival is linked to good knowledge of the clients, to the fact that close contacts with distributors matter for the strategy of the company, if the markets are local, then the sales forces have power. How they act induces major consequences for most functions of the firm. In such a case power is in the hands of the front line and uncertainty lies at the periphery much more than at the level of head office.

7.2.4 Activating Networks

A fourth tool is provided by the constitution of specific network configurations across the firm. Is head office able to rely on the interpersonal networks that exist between the managers, so that it can through them mobilize this social asset to develop and consolidate shared cognitive learning? A network can effectively function as a vector for knowledge if, and only if, three very precise conditions are satisfied.

First, networks shorten social and functional distance. They have to be considered by cognitive architects as opportunities insofar as they provide non-redundant connections between people, units and functions that are also non-redundant. In other words, 'structural gaps' are bridged (Burt, 1992). If the contacts between units or departments are redundant, and if the interpersonal network only reproduces the normal transversality of the units, the information exchanged by the network is the same as that exchanged in the usual dialogue between units. Redundancy of contacts does not produce added value in terms of 'advanced' perceptions (weak signals) and does not initiate cognitive apprenticeship.

Second, networks based around structural gaps develop if at the same time there are fuzzy boundaries, duplications and overlaps in the organization, as well as broad corridors of action that guide or contain the behaviour of the players. When it comes to carrying out their task and managing departmental interfaces, managers only invest in interpersonal relationships if these already exist. The drama of bureaucratic organizations lies precisely in the paradoxical fact that they give top priority to isolation and 'everyone for himself', thereby discouraging networks linked to the job.

Third, a network must be endogenous to the organization. It must not become the exclusive property of a single person or the business of a clique, apart from a group of connections around a single centre such as the people close to the CEO. Life without contact with the outside world and networking with sealed boundaries do not generate significant cognitive consequences. Information generated and conveyed within a self-sufficient relational space does not produce much originality, chiefly because there is no hybridization or cross-fertilization.

The nature of the asset that social networks bring with them allows one to complete the classification of organizational configurations. This can be shown by highlighting their cognitive differences.

The organic or Type 1 model is characterized by a specific combination of properties. The attention span is wide. Networks are diversified. Cognitive systems are interactive. Their boundaries are fuzzy. The corridors of action are wide. Varied origins and experience are welcomed and treated on an equal footing. Mutual trust is highly developed. The organization is very market oriented. Primary references are the consumer, the company and society.

The self-sufficient or Type 2 model carries cognitions that are not very market oriented. The main references for action are the members of the organization. Corridors of action are narrower. Boundaries inside the organization are tight, but still allow some exchange flows to occur. Cognitive learning is not easy. Some apparent common language exists but on the surface only.

The Type 3 or mercenary model favours the shareholder and the customer as the main cognitive references. The span of attention is rather short. Corridors of action are quite narrow. Internal cognitive systems are many, specialized and highly partitioned. Networks are poorly diversified. Learning capacity is very weak.

The Type 4 or fragmented model derives from the purely bureaucratic model. Market orientation is absent. The span of attention is extremely narrow. Corridors are rigid and poor. Networks remain underdeveloped. Mutual trust in action is lacking. Knowledge is neither useful not shared. Cognitive systems remain extremely scattered and static.

7.3 The Quest for Foresight

How is foresight produced in an organization? By what processes of mutual and intersecting knowledge is it disseminated? Do voluntarist steps initiated by top management exist, and do they facilitate the creation and development of shared cognitive schemes?

The academic literature pays relatively little attention to the spreading of languages for action. Organizations theory distinguishes three main types of approach: discipline and conformity, the instillation of values and the handling of the preferences or duties of the players.

The classic theory of organizations assigns a task to the hierarchy, in particular to the managerial staff located on the front line: ensure that staff carry out and respect the procedures that govern their work. Conformity is supposed to ensure that actions are coordinated with one another, provided that the general framework from which the procedures flow has been properly thought out. By carrying out what they are told to do without any interpretation and without deviation, the staff members allow the strategic and organizational principles to prove their effectiveness.

Procedural constructs therefore require three fundamental conditions to be satisfied for them to be beneficial or rational. First, they must be stable in time and space. Second, it is essential that the corridors of action are perfectly laid down, being both exhaustive and at the same time specific. Finally, it is presumed that the individuals and the organizational units demonstrate, voluntarily or under compulsion, a great sense of discipline. They apply what is imposed upon them. In a perfect world, the supervisory staff concentrate entirely on verifying that conduct conforms to the norms (Taylor, 1947).

A second approach associates the instillation of foresight within the organization with the building of a moral or cultural community. Strong pressure is exerted through propaganda and sermonizing. The task of top and line management is convince staff and to obtain if not an ideological conversion at least an emotional loyalty. The CEO is also a preacher.

One way of doing this is through so-called company projects. These involve the whole of the staff around shared values. The staff are assumed to take on board the medium-term view of head office. Company-wide meetings make everything official. This propaganda also takes on an informal and everyday guise. For example, an immediate superior uses personal charisma to get direct subordinates to subscribe to some abstract or prescriptive message.

Such an approach is based on the gamble that there is a direct and specific causal relationship between normative references and relational behaviour. When, and only when, A and B have subscribed to the same values, it will then be possible to make them walk in step with one another and so make their choices secure and their actions not unpredictable.

A third approach advocates a method of foresight based on the handling of power games through influence on the preferred functions of each player. Let us imagine that individuals in an organization are characterized by the fact that all of them at their respective levels have a margin of autonomy and they aim to achieve particular targets. The firm is like a political system that is by nature fragmented and disjointed, in which there is no endogenous collective challenge that unites the players to pursue the same goal. It can be managed only through the inclination of the preferences that the staff, acting in a selfish way, seek to satisfy (Simon, 1957). The organizational management that prevails is transactional. No loyalty is expected outside the short-term contracts and transactions. The top creates temporary coalitions, puts the operational units in competition with one another, and satisfies particular issues such as autonomy and prestige, that is, issues that are non-rational from the point of view of strict economic utilitarianism.

Despite the radical oppositions that exist between these three approaches, they do share a point in common. They shrug off the question of knowledge in the conduct of an organized activity. Everything happens as though the players obeyed and accepted the propaganda or satisfied their desire for self-interest and autonomy without integrating the meaning of the actions and the logic of the consequences caused by the choices that they implement at their level.

Now the capacity for foresight is increased, or indeed diminished, depending on whether there are or are not cognitive phenomena shared by the players in an organization. It should be remembered that endogenous language ensures two essential functions: it facilitates the integration of both horizontal and vertical interfaces, it also makes the choices and behaviour of numerous players reliable and predictable.

Placing knowledge in sealed compartments is an acceptable approach in specific economic contexts. A case in point is where a firm operates in a relatively stable environment and adopts a so-called exploitation strategy. Here there is no need for a common language. A cognitive activity such as interpretation is not very important when learning does not provide any advantage relevant for action. Two conditions have to be satisfied: first, there must be routines and these routines must change only slowly and over a long period of time; and second, the staff remain together for a long time, facilitating their socialization and allowing stable cooperation to become established.

In contrast, knowledge becomes a critical factor for survival when the contexts of action are ones of strong uncertainty or even the unknown, and when innovation generated from within is adopted as the strategic stance. In this case the activities of gathering and interpreting information are truly important for the adjustment and regeneration of the action.

On the one hand, the company faces changes in attitudes. Employees may easily leave their job and benefit from a labour market that favours applicants. The customers are much less willing to remain hostage to the products and services offered by the firm; they do not want to put up with restrictive competition. The shareholders become more active and raise their voices. In short, the stakeholders of the firm become more restless and vociferous. The strategy of loyalty is replaced by that of voice and exit.

On the other hand, third party threats become apparent and have vital consequences for the survival of the firm. Alternative technologies emerge. The channels of distribution diversify. Public regulations concerning competition, the certification of products or the protection of the environment are changed. Now the operational units have a major role in capturing and decoding such changes sufficiently quickly, because they are in touch with the front lines on the field of battle.

Foresight is at the heart of the quality of a firm's actions when it moves in a world where knowledge prevails as a collective competence. That assessment is certainly no discovery. It corroborates the experiences of firms faced with hypercompetition. On the other hand, observation shows that the operational implications that are drawn from it generally remain unexploited and leave many general managements in confusion. Intellectual understanding does not necessarily lead to *savoir-faire* and action.

Several points should be noted here. First, firms are under considerable pressure to prioritize short-term financial returns. Second, the capacity for foresight is not something that can be decreed. It requires a relatively long period of time to develop. This period sometimes exceeds the very short life cycle of a general management.

What is more, the process for creating an endogenous language cannot be managed in the same way as one programs the operation of an automatic machine or plots the path of a space probe. A linear or ballistic engineering approach is not possible. Management of the cognitive remains largely an art, not a technology totally controllable by a single person and programmable once and for all from the top. There is at least one reason for this.

An endogenous language is the product of a collective construct that is fashioned in the course of disjointed interactions and partitioned interfaces. General management will never be the sole designer, an all-powerful programmer of a new shared language. The better top managers have the intelligence not to suppose they are absolute masters of the 'clocks' of their company, while at the same time giving priority attention to the cognitive aspect of their organizational model by putting in place conditions favourable to the emergence of shared language.

How is knowledge generated and diffused through an organization? Table 7.1 shows three different approaches that are found in firms: tacit accumulation, discretionary codification and explicit articulation.

Codification	Tacit accumulation	Explicit articulation
Procedures, rules, routines	Interactions with senior staff, experience	Formalised interactions between functional or hierarchical correspondents
Substitutability of people	Closeness and trust between people	Face to face meetings and briefings with explicit discussion
Immediate time horizon	Long time horizon	Short time horizon
Abstract principles	Concrete information	Applied concepts and reasonings
Conformity, discipline	Socialisation, experimentation through trial and error	Structured apprenticeship, quasi-negotiation
Narrow corridors of action	Shared language	Shared knowledge (cognitive structuring of action)
Exogenous language	Endogenous language	Endogenous language
Foresight virtually nil	Foresight contained	Strong foresight

Table 7.1 Process of disseminating knowledge

This table is inspired by the work of Zollo and Winter (1999).

7.4 Discretionary Codification

Discretionary codification relates to a method of organizational management that combines codification and derogation. The hierarchy, starting from head office down to front-line units, specifies narrow and relatively precise codes defining what to do, how and when. In other terms, the top does not just diffuse general principles. It also allocates derogations for these same codes when these are needed or defined as necessary. Codes are understood to be back-ups such as rules, procedures, manuals and the like. Derogations are activities through which a subordinate gets the hierarchy to authorize solutions that do not conform to the current codes.

The two constituents are in fact closely interlinked. Government by the rules is accompanied by arbitrary action. The person who pronounces the rules is often at the same time, directly or indirectly, the one who tolerates and covers up for the exceptions and allows the non-conformity. Thus patterns of action are created that may be characterized in three ways:

- First, they are made commonplace. Everything is taken back to programming and signposted in a uniform and detailed way. The operator is not expected to show any initiative or any duty of interpretation.
- Second, they are specialized. The regular systems of action are assigned according to the narrowness of their area of competency and the boundaries between these systems contain no overlap or redundancy.
- Third, there is a high degree of substitutability among employees. The job takes precedence over the individual. In fact, individuals are disposable if they do not behave in a way that conforms to the injunctions of the hierarchy. For this reason, a high turnover of staff is not seen as having a bad effect on the conduct of the business; it may even become a sign of good management.

The knowledge for action that is diffused appears through very narrowly defined and marked corridors of action. What is more, these corridors reflect solutions from the past or those legitimized through experience. In other words, action consists in calling upon causality schemes between ways and means that reflect plans that have already been thought out in advance by third parties (Heiner, 1983).

The combination of narrowness with instrumental programming makes it problematic to deal with an anomaly, uncertainty or new information. Improvisation is seen as a sin. The cognitive scheme that belongs to the codes as well as the derogations is not interiorized by the player who is subjected to them. The sender authorized to produce codification and discretion, namely top management, divides up the action and thought at the heart of the organization in a permanent way. The result is a reliance on 'good practice': the copying of so-called good practices and the passive imitation of ready-made techniques that have been developed outside the organization; the recruitment of managers with the decisive criterion of choice being that they are functionally efficient (but without considering whether they fit the organizational and cognitive system); taking on consultants to whom the renewal of the codification is entrusted; and other such practices. In short, in such a case, if the knowledge is diffused, it remains by nature exogenous.

7.5 Tacit Accumulation

Another pathway for the dissemination of knowledge is via the process of tacit accumulation. It is found in particular in Type 2 or self-sufficient configurations.

In this case, knowledge is carried or turned to account through the permanence of people at the heart of the organization. Long-serving executives and managers are a visible characteristic of the firm. They are recruited very young and remain in the business for many years, if not for life. Human resources policy gives priority to their social role. This ensures that support for a common vision of a collective future is developed. On the other hand, the firm avoids taking on ad hoc, for specific needs, people who are older. An executive moves around in the firm; he or she occupies several positions in succession and builds a wide circle of personal relationships. At the same time, action is conducted on terms that favour permanent interaction between various individuals, hierarchical ranks or different functions. The organization chart, when there is one, scarcely reveals how choices are made or roles distributed. In other words, the pressure of proximity and continuity in the people represents a key vector for management to ensure that decision making and the units function well. There is no room for individual or eccentric acts.

In this approach, knowledge is transmitted slowly. At the same time it remains implicit and tacit. The behavioural rules of the game as well as the cognitive references remain informal. The way things are done here and now, which is regarded by different people as taken as read so far as acting and deciding are concerned, develops in two ways.

The first takes the form of a progressive learning process. The individual successively holds various positions in different departments. This rotation serves as a source of selective personal experimentation. In return, and at the end of a varied career, the firm recognizes his or her professional maturity and judges him or her to be 'autonomous from now on'. The apprentice can in turn become an expert, and transmit a professionalism that boasts skills that are for the most part hard to explain explicitly and knowledge that is specific and unique to the firm.

The second relates to a phenomenon often cited in anthropology and ethnology. The individual is subjected to formalized and informal processes of feedback or appraisal that are extremely varied in nature and in their contacts. A person's career in the firm takes the form of an initiation that alternates between ritualized bullying and elitist rites of passage. Social distinction counts at least as much as functional performance. To be appraised means to be recognized as an equal by others and to share the characteristics that identify the group. Such an approach assumes that there is in the firm a dynamic for apprenticeship and involvement that is permanent and common to all its members.

The structuring of knowledge therefore is like a sort of black box. The process is fed with concrete information and involvement in action. It is also experienced by the individuals as a sequence of creative frustrations.

Tacit accumulation generates a very particular type of knowledge. In contrast to discretionary codification, it allows improvisation. In fact, it puts together corridors of action that are wider for the individual or for the unit. The limits for action are interiorized and negotiated in an implicit manner among the members of the firm. In this way the basis for an endogenous construct is created so far as foresight is concerned. All individuals reach the stage of intuitively understanding the others, the ends that condition their actions, the processes that they use. Together, they reach the point where they share common references even if these arise from the implicit or the unsaid.

A corollary of this is the increase in the feeling of mutual trust between the members of the organization. For everyone knows that their contacts know what they know. The corridors respect the identity of the collective in which the individuals feel themselves responsible when faced with exterior events. As a consequence, this diffusion process requires time. It also demands close attention and considerable energy from the most senior staff members in the organization.

7.6 Explicit Articulation

A third approach to diffusion of knowledge takes the form of explicit articulation. It is characteristic of the Type 1 or organic organizational configuration. As in the case of tacit accumulation, explicit articulation relies on endogenous shared languages. But it possesses three distinctive traits:

- The diffusion is more compacted and accelerated in time. Instead of taking fifteen or twenty years, it happens in two or three.
- The cognitive references are not transmitted tacitly; they are transferred and stated explicitly.
- Its existence does not depend on staff being permanent and learning through successive experimentation.

Explicit articulation is diffused through interaction procedures that are controlled or systematic. Its specific aim is to bring about the emergence and formalization of continuity by making the interfaces at different levels fit together. It proceeds by the quasi-negotiated building of explicit references. The content of the latter is the result of a co-produced formalization. It is punctuated with revisions that must be justified quite explicitly.

Such a way of proceeding is not generally adopted in an organization as a spontaneous approach or as a natural vector for communication between people. In fact, it makes use of activities of exchange, briefing, working together and education (in the broad sense). The top promotes its policy to the bottom. In this way it commits itself by renouncing part of its discretion. At the same time, it grants cognitive autonomy to the bottom, which is thus able translate the policy formed above through its actions. The top allows the bottom margins for interpretation in the local context, which itself may vary in time and be different in space. In return, the bottom sends to the top information that it has decoded in relation to the policy promoted by the top.

Such production of explicit articulations or chains of causality between the players requires both to spend time on the matter. Tichy gives a convincing example of this (Tichy, 1999). In such as approach, the firm functions according to a cascade of successive articulations like a Russian doll.

There are two styles or attitudes of management that are the complete opposite of this method of functioning. One is charismatic leadership. The leader only communicates with those who share his or her abstract values, that is, values that are not referred to operationally determined dimensions. The second is the holding of large-scale briefings or 'high masses' that involve the whole of the firm upstream and downstream. They certainly create emotional tension, but they do not change much in the cognitive references and behavioural rationality. Neither charisma nor masses induces consequences once the employees return to their daily jobs.

Management by cascade, on the other hand, operates through a series of interactions between two immediately adjacent levels. These interactions are carried out from top management down to the bottom through successive stages. First, between level n (general management) and level $n - 1$ (the first rank of subordinates); then, between this level $n - 1$ and level $n - 2$; then, between $n - 2$ and $n - 3$; and so on through the hierarchy.

Two factors facilitate this process, which is like a set of quasi-negotiations to achieve a quasi-contract. The hierarchical rake or span of control must not be too wide. Eight to a dozen subordinates is an acceptable number. More than this and the interactions are diluted. The hierarchical line must also remain sufficiently short or flat. Piling too many levels on one another makes issues fuzzy and lowers visibility.

The fitting together starts with an explanation and a formalization of reciprocal commitments. The superior explains in detail his or her ideas, values, priorities and motivations, if necessary putting them in writing, and communicates these to subordinates. The explanation is structured around specific references: this hypothesis on consumers, that positioning of the firm in three to five years, or this value to be achieved and the reasons for doing it. In this way, the subordinates find themselves committed morally and cognitively. It becomes difficult for them to run away from the quasi-contract, to avoid it or twist its meanings. In fact, the cards are on the table. The aims of the superior are explained and discussed. As a result the subordinates will not later be able to say that they did not know the aims or that they did not apply to them. For their part, they take three dimensions on board. They must develop solutions and actions that satisfy the superior's objectives. They negotiate the necessary autonomy and resources. They provide the relevant information on the conduct of business and the achievement of the objectives.

To summarize, in order that levels n and $n - 1$ produce shared knowledge in an endogenous way, n needs to communicate quite explicitly to $n - 1$ two facets related to action taking. First, what are the priorities or values that the superior, at level n, takes responsibility for? Second, how do these priorities or values feature in the world of action of level $n - 1$, and what implications do they have for the latter?

The same approach applies to the horizontal interfaces between different departments. Thanks to sequential overlaps, common references are established that are not necessarily the same from one interface to another. They explain the causalities that little by little allow articulations that are both cognitive and relational. The continuity begins from successive fitting together. Gradually, a halo effect produces an endogenous cognitive dynamic.

7.7 The Strength of Cognitive Communities

In practice, firms rarely arise from a pure type of knowledge diffusion. They are often hybrid systems.

This is true of Agro. As an organization it does not follow any one the three approaches described above. More precisely its management style keeps switching from one approach to the other, combining and recombining some of their characteristics. In a way Agro is the reverse of a pure or clear-cut textbook case. It shows that in real life top managements in firms handle their tasks through a series of disjointed actions.

One section of the managers operates in a context where a process of tacit accumulation is clearly dominant. This is especially true of those in charge of the commercial departments. Another section takes the codification approach. The AIG is an example, as the department responsible for the development of active ingredients. To be precise, this codification is more of a false codification to the extent that it does not define the routines clearly. Its cognitive content remains rather weak in the sense that it does not lead to concrete information that is useful for every level. Only the EVA evaluation technique provides something tangible. As for explicit articulation, it is generally missing, even though head office shows vague desires for it to be adopted.

The limitation that confronts the firm arises from the fact that the practice adopted, especially by head office, gives too much prominence to a technique that has been shown earlier to be empirically deceptive. This is the desire to win over the managers as individuals, by appealing only to their emotions. But appealing to the emotions and persuading through personal charisma do not generally prove to be lasting and effective substitutes for cognitive systems. The reason is clear: the cognitive is transmitted in an organization through the range of behaviours and experience, not through the range of attitudes and values. In the firm, and in particular at the heart of general management, little use is made of the feedback from the choices made by individuals when carrying out their tasks, or the policy of sanctions–rewards (moral as well as material) that extends it.

The cross-fertilization of varied and truncated approaches remains weak, because it is little activated. In fact, the types of network that exist in the firm do not encourage it. Knowledge is diffused badly because the networks operate according to very mixed systems. So tacit accumulation occurs within networks that are compartmentalized and where each remains withdrawn into itself. The information that circulates in a network is by nature redundant – it reproduces old and narrow action repertoires that it does not renew with contributions from outside, while at the same time it cannot be accessed by third parties outside the network as presently constituted. This only strengthens the identity of such networks and separates their members from the rest of the organization.

In Agro, knowledge remains stored on the periphery, in the commercial departments, through the sales function. Their immediate interfaces with, for example, marketing in the larger countries is reduced. Power struggles, reciprocal autonomy games or jealousies between corporations conceal breakdowns and discontinuities in the methods of managing the diffusion of knowledge and therefore describing it.

As a consequence, and more generally, for head office to manage an organization cognitively it has to structure the networks in an appropriate way and facilitate their mutual communication. This function belongs to head office. It should hardly ever be subcontracted to a staff unit such as a human resource department. It is not satisfied with either the establishment of information and audiovisual technology or the recruitment of psychologists.

Cognitive management produces languages for action that may be classified on a continuum. At one extreme are the languages that are exogenous in relation to the firm that carries them. They are basically instrumental. They are characterized by the fact that the level of knowledge that they transmit is reduced to a minimum, that is, to narrow pragmatic ways to operate and to act. They are carried by methods of organization management that call upon discretionary codification. The result is a negligible degree of foresight.

At the other extreme lie endogenous languages: that is, cognitive systems collectively set up in the organization. They transmit common knowledge about ends and means that comes from corridors of action that are both wide and well defined, and that foster and maintain permanent interactions among the organization's members. The production of explicit articulations among departments and levels of the firm creates or encourages the emergence of strong cognitive communities. It is associated with a high capacity for foresight about the firm as well as about the market and the outside world in general. As for tacit accumulation, this is situated nearer to explicit articulation than to discretionary codification because it is produced endogenously by the organization. On the other hand, it offers a more limited or contained capacity for foresight.

Cognitive communities are therefore a decisive factor in generating flexibility and managing improvisation when necessary without destroying the policy perspective of the firm.

Improvisation furnishes the organization with new and flexible solutions around a common framework. It moves and models itself to a large extent according to the terrain and the local contexts. For the common framework to exist, it must be nourished and guided by the cognitive maps held by the players. When the internal cognitive processes are weak or discontinuous, the players at grassroots level no longer know how to register their own individual choices in a collective and strategic corridor of action. This either proves too fuzzy or appears too narrow. For their part, top managers do not know how to convey in concrete terms the messages they issue, which have strategic implications, since they have a poor understanding of the specific contexts to which they apply. The company faces a situation of double cognitive uncertainty owing to the lack of overlaps and relays of the successive translations between the top and the bottom of the company. The resulting lack of knowledge of what is happening on the ground further decreases any possibilities for improvisation.

The Type 3, or mercenary organizational model, is in this respect extreme. A firm that positions itself upon the paradigms of exploitation and with a short-term horizon is perfectly satisfied with limited cognitive chains. A shared language is of little use to it. It is quite content with narrow corridors of action and thus with weak capacities for improvisation. Recruiting mercenaries to fill executive posts, accepting a high rate of staff turnover, doing without teams that know the organization and its external context, all are factors that offer some relative advantages, but on one condition: these practices must be compensated for by recourse to routines and the adoption of 'good practice' that is more or less commonplace and uniform. The exogenous nature of the vectors of foresight that mobilize the firm is associated in Type 3 with capacities for improvisation that are reduced to their lowest level.

That being said, the destruction of the existing endogenous cognitions and of the former capacity for improvisation can in certain cases be seen as necessary. Repositioning the firm on the Type 3 model allows a little time for triggering a cultural shock, and in fact destroying at a stroke an asset of traditions and procedures accumulated in the course of its history. The clean sweep brought about by resorting to the exogenous at the level of personnel and knowledge is then associated with a crisis situation. Let us suppose that the social regulation within the organization is weakened and that the cognitive community becomes more loosely coupled. In such a case the achievement of short-term economic results (survival) or a strategic repositioning within a short time (a modification of the threat) imposes refocusing or restructuring which may be dramatic and is managed by the mercenaries. Meanwhile, the abilities to improvise and to create organizational complexity remain as competencies that are absent or neglected.

CHAPTER 8

Cosmophar: Excellence in Tacit Accumulation

The concepts that we have developed in the Agro case study can be validated by studying another example. The Cosmophar company is very different from Agro and its problem areas are different, but we shall see how the languages for action remain a key factor for success in making strategy and organization compatible.

Cosmophar operates in the sector of body care, health and beauty. The company is a world player, active in all the serious markets on the planet. It is also a stock exchange star, even when the market is in deep depression. It represents a special case for several reasons: the quality of its products, its dominant market share and its financial performance, which has been growing steadily for half a century.

There is another reason for taking an interest in Cosmophar. How did this medium-sized family firm succeed in achieving such economic excellence while adopting management practices that are completely heterodox, if not wayward, from the point of view of current management theory (the absence of an organization chart being an obvious example)? How does its management style, which arises from the model of tacit accumulation and which reflects a management model that is at the very least complex, cope with modern times? Is it something outdated that should be abandoned in order to enter the ranks of orthodox management?

8.1 The Keys to Success

The success of Cosmophar is rooted in the company's origins and flows in a continuous way around various paradigms of which four seem essential.

8.1.1 A Shared Destiny

People at Cosmophar give the impression to outsiders that they belong to a community that is driven by some transcendent belief or principle, and that the outside events or situations they face are in any case, if not controllable, at least manageable by them.

A shared threat, or more accurately a transcendent ambition, cements and directs the actions of a hybrid human community. During the years 1950–70 the staff recruited by Cosmophar and with whom the CEO surrounded himself came from very different backgrounds, whether social or scholastic. For example some were completely self-taught. But the differences of origins were erased by a common project about the firm. Young people, fresh from the Second World War, held a shared view of the future. Everything went forward as if they were playing out their personal existence through the growth of their company. They lived their successes as professionals and their self-development as human beings through the success of their team and not through long individual paths from one company to another. For these people the possibilities are immense. They have been through difficult periods. For the rest of their lives the struggle for daily survival will remain a major driving force. Their firm provides not only a job, but a community that is fragile and therefore has to be cautiously handled. Their demands are therefore limited. For everyone the possibility of making their way in life is already of major importance. From such a low starting point the chances of success in terms of self-realization become very high.

These people built themselves and their identity through the company. Cosmophar provided a quasi-total institution of which they felt moral co-owners. It provided both the professional apprenticeship and the conceptual structure. Even in the 1980s, few managers had been trained by business schools. Their skills were structured within and across the firm. Upward mobility derived from the performance of the company. There were shared languages and a common understanding. The facts show that Cosmophar has collectively invented many of the approaches and know-how of modern consumer marketing and branding. The school is not only an inventive organization, it also acts as a community that gives 'meaning' to its members. Once employees interiorize such a 'meaning', there is no longer any doubt about the future or the moral reasons to fight the economic battle that the firm has been patiently winning since its foundation. For Cosmophar is not an ordinary company. It has a particular destiny and mission that is not just producing profits.

This transcendence has enabled the firm to become a world player, accepted and supported by its shareholders. It has established a destiny that is common to shareholders and management alike, with a strong implicit convention with regard to the hierarchy of objectives. Growth is the first objective. Profit, in particular through its distribution, is a method or a condition of support and not the ultimate objective. The result is a distribution of revenues in which the collective plays an essential role.

8.1.2 An Internal Renewal

Cosmophar also adopts a process of regeneration by endogenous means. The centre encourages managers to pay close attention to the evolution of society and the market. More precisely, it does not give priority to quantitative and routinized approaches that can be bought from market research companies. On the contrary it favours and helps build a strong intuitive capacity inside the firm, at all levels and in all functions, aiming to be the first in the industry to feel and interpret emerging trends of consumption and of fashion. Real customers are considered as more relevant than statistics in this perspective. It is this ability to understand the clients, to grasp their needs even while they are latent, to understand properly the role of those who promote a product, and of those who influence the end customer, that allows the company to build real value to the original consumer and to create many new types of market. Sales forces raise strategic opportunities and action hypotheses about new markets and products. Marketing experts evaluate the potential of new products. Head office manages collective commitments for success in action.

Priority is given to innovation, adjustment and a permanent process of renewal. Cosmophar has never had a real scientific breakthrough, but it has been innovative. While the company has failed to produce new molecules by scientifically developing what existed on the market, it has known better than any of its competitors how to bring new products and services with added value to the market on a permanent basis. These are adapted to needs that are identified as they emerge.

The growth of the firm has largely been accomplished, from inside, in an endogenous way, with a strong contribution from all the departments, from R&D to commerce and logistics. The company, furthermore, has rewarded most of the staff, executives as well as workers, who have helped it become what it is, with money but also with pride and respect. Individuals have been offered career opportunities and challenges which they could hardly dare think of outside the firm. All the new territories that the firm has conquered, and all the new frontiers that it decided to occupy, were taken by the same population.

8.1.3 An Organization Adapted to Strategic Aims

Cosmophar also shows excellence in building and refining a suitable organizational model and human system.

Every strategy that does not take sufficient account of the history and origins of the organizational systems runs, *de facto*, the risk of remaining an intellectual exercise. It will be rejected at all levels. Head office is quite sensitive to possible contradictions between the strategic aims and what the organizational system is capable of managing. The striking quality of Cosmophar is probably its capacity to create and achieve an exceptional fit between the paradigms for success and its organizational system.

For this reason the firm has internal frontiers that are fuzzy and permeable. It shows a complete and durable avoidance of any instances of strongholds of compartmentalization or autonomous territory. There are three contributory factors: the existence of common languages and references that traverse the network horizontally and vertically, the rapid rotation of staff from one job to another (facilitated by the shared languages and by the network effects), systematically allowing people to bypass formal channels so long as they do it for the good of the firm. In addition to this, the emphasis on innovation prevents the creation of strongly exogenous locations, such as might occupy purely scientific departments whose reference point would be external and not within the firm. Finally, the fuzzy frontiers allow any conflicting or contradictory information to be transmitted and decisions to be implemented rapidly.

Another characteristic of this cohesiveness lies in the systematic construction of corridors of action that are long, negotiable and able to accommodate broad spectrums of intention. Shared languages and a common destiny are the strongest factors that allocate wide areas of autonomy to each employee. The corridors of action are widened, and if necessary modifiable depending on circumstances. This is only possible if the ownership and understanding of the strategic aims are so diffused that the responses are generally compatible. Moreover, the level of informality and the fuzziness of the frontiers make conformity quickly verifiable.

At the same time, reference and knowledge groups develop over time and these form the basis of language sharing and trust. In general, if the people who enter this firm do not leave quickly after a short probationary period, they stay a long time, do not leave of their own accord and are not asked to leave. Such conditions allow a collective feeling to develop, and strengthen the sharing of risks and benefits in the widest sense. But loyalty and trust do not imply the absence of sanction. The right to experiment and make mistakes exists, but subject to the condition that the risk is reasonable and above all that people learn from it: that is, the same type of error is not allowed to recur.

Cosmophar operates a strict policy of limiting the interchangeability of personnel. While the firm offers a common destiny founded on mutual learning, it will never give rein to any initiative that, through inattention or opportunism, would favour the appearance of a different organizational model, such as a provisional grouping of interchangeable individuals. The firm is able to command the loyalty and long-term commitment of the talented managers and employees it recruits and raises. It rewards them well. In exchange they become citizens of a community that makes considerable demands. But at the same time the firm manages its human resources in a remarkable way. The collective pressure upon the individual may be strong but everyone is empowered and pushed to keep his or her specific individual identity. 'Cosmopharians' exist but the individual remains.

8.1.4 Cognitive Assets

Fourth, and finally, Cosmophar builds and benefits from a system of action that is fed by shared knowledge.

The common cognitive matrix and the strong or lasting overlaps that it creates for collective action are brought into play in two ways. Horizontally, between the various functions, the firm encourages and develops in its executives a formal and informal knowledge of the business conducted by their contacts or their interfaces up and downstream. Vertically, or in the hierarchical plane, given that the majority of managers start their careers in a succession of junior posts in two or three different functions, the social rotation thus managed sharpens an awareness of what is concrete in each task and prepares areas of common understanding. Indeed, it is quite probable that top management has personal experience of what an interlocutor from below is reporting; management knows what the junior level is talking about.

From this there flow strong networks that link departments with one another and transcend the hierarchical levels. There is no need for a formal organization chart or job definitions. The cognitive assets are sufficient to ensure communication, cooperation and coordination.

8.2 New Challenges in a Global Economy

The organizational and cognitive set-up that has just been presented has produced an extremely successful firm that has not become furred up over a long period of time. The shared knowledge and strong socialization might have led to a perverse endogenous result, that is, to a permanent rigidity in the firm. This has not happened because a combination of ambition, shared destiny in a challenging world and very strong leadership has avoided divisiveness and power-based oligarchies. However, circumstances and contexts have changed. They reinforce the need for conflicting hybridization and encourage the firm to renew itself even quicker. The challenge today is to evolve both in organizational systems and in its chosen cognitive mode without losing those aspects that have worked as the engines of growth and the roots of its identity. Three major issues must be addressed by the firm.

8.2.1 A Narrower Room for Manoeuvre

Cosmophar is faced with the demands of globalization and hypercompetition. The fact that the world has become global is not news. However, it is necessary to get to grips with the meaning of this word 'global'. Being global does not mean selling everywhere, it means carrying on a complex business activity everywhere, having dealings in the majority of countries in the world where all products and all functions are present. In other words, a firm such as Cosmophar faces increasing complexity and manages more unknowns to the extent that the markets, the people and the cultures differ all around the globe.

Hypercompetition for its part increases the pressure on the firm, especially when it is involved in transactions far from its usual European base and in competition with firms that are better established in places such as Asia or Africa. In addition, it limits the possibility of long-term adjustment. This imposes on the firm rapid changes that are not compatible with the shared references and informal training it has been used to.

In addition to this, financial markets are increasingly demanding and more exacting. Like its competitors, Cosmophar has to submit to the requirement of quarterly, twice-yearly and yearly reporting for the financial markets. Any suggestion of anxiety about the future, any gamble that seems in any way risky, would immediately meet with sanctions that are often quite disproportionate to the possible dangers. Long-term strategy and intangible or adventurous ideas have no place here, although this does not seem to prevent speculative forays.

Cosmophar also faces the changes brought by new generations with their own attitudes and culture and who do not share the pioneers' experience.

Managers of the post-war generation, who often had had neither the time nor the opportunity to receive a formal education, are being replaced by those who have entered business life after gaining often quite advanced qualifications from university. These managers have built up their skills sequentially and not all at once as happened with the earlier generation. When they join the firm they already possess, or think they possess, the conceptual knowledge that has been portrayed to them as universal in the books they have read. Their references were acquired before they arrived in the firm. They immediately make use of this as exogenous, especially when they move rapidly from firm to firm. This phenomenon is often dominant when a firm recruits a lot of MBAs.

Engineers or an arts graduates who bring preconceived ideas to the firm will learn what matters or the references needed for making business in the firm or through its mediation. As a result, their openness and capacity to absorb endogenously are increased. They lose the systematic response of 'I know', and show more humility in not basing their conceptual constructs on one particular reality.

MBAs may dream of arriving at the top of the ladder faster than others. It is built into their expectations to make it quickly. The long process followed by the previous generation, which meant that in every case each person found his or her own route, suits them less well. Being full of academic knowledge, they tend to behave as experts, applying to each situation solutions learned elsewhere. This phenomenon is even more marked because of the rapidity with which the students are rotated among different firms. They lack sufficient time to develop an endogenous understanding in each one. The capacity for learning and for sharing understanding is therefore limited or even smothered at birth. The future is lived in an individual way and in the main exogenously in relation to each company.

For Cosmophar, all these changes constitute an immense challenge in as much as they may cast doubt on its ability to manage an organizational hybrid. The firm was in fact already managing a hybrid, but with sufficient margins for action and time to be able in due course to make compatible demands that were sometimes contradictory. These margins have become narrowed, possibly through institutionalization and the pressure of demands.

The first challenge for its management is to control the conflict between an ambition to exploit and a requirement to regenerate. The previous management had given priority in both words and deed to regeneration. Nowadays, the pressure of the financial markets reduces the company's freedom to act. It becomes increasingly difficult to manage the attention and energy directed to exploitation and regeneration unobtrusively or in a discretionary manner. The danger lies in the temptation to simplify and let a new broom sweep through, reversing the order of strategic priorities. To manage this hybrid and to pilot the conflict between these paradigms of action requires the re-creation of a system of organization that can adapt to this.

8.2.2 Complexity and Efficiency

The second challenge is concerned with control, conformity, effectiveness and the corridors for action.

Exploitation demands increased operational effectiveness; for example, manufacturing costs, transaction costs and complexity costs. But organizational complexity, the acceptance of trial and error costs and of tests and errors, and duplication through redundancy are, at least in part, the price to be paid for a close understanding of what happens at the ground level, a creative organization and a permanent flow of innovation and adjustment. The hybrid favours tinkering about. In its turn, tinkering and improvising lead to the blurring of boundaries, then to short-term and less defined control, even to a lack of clarity. The bad news is that none of these favours an organizational configuration that leads to efficient exploitation.

The problem is all the more delicate in that Cosmophar will in future have to manage a stronger geographical and cultural distance between head office and business units. As long as the activity was concentrated in what was essentially European space, the centre had almost no periphery. The various locations across Europe were in quite close and easy contact. Players did not have to climb over high cognitive and temporal barriers. But the firm is now global, which means that its operations and offices in Asia and in America are rather far-flung, with large staffs of newcomers. As the exchange of information has stretched, a form of differentiation between centre and periphery, between head office and local subsidiaries has occurred, despite the fact that the common process of apprenticeship remains the same between individuals and between the units.

In a cognitive configuration that made use of organizational technologies, such as codes, procedures and routines, and gave priorities to functions such as control, the dialogue between periphery and centre could apparently be easier. People who can be substituted one for another live in the corridors of everyday actions. Cosmophar's difficult challenge lies in the need to marry together globalization with a system of tacit accumulation of knowledge in which mutual knowledge is based on an increasingly complex content of the tacit and a weaker appeal of common emotions.

8.2.3 Speed and Socialization

The third challenge lies in the need to reconcile speed of action with the tacit accumulation of knowledge.

Alongside a system of tacit accumulation, hypercompetition demands strong and long-term interactions between the new and the old, the seniors and the juniors, and what is nourished by experience on the ground. It is these interactions and experiences that allow the building of networks of confidence, socialization and solidarity, through which concrete information is produced and diffused and knowledge is shared. This process needs continuity and time, preconditions which hypercompetition finds hard to tolerate.

The demands of efficiency, the lack of time, the insufficient availability of the former experienced staff, the level of training of the new, all require that a new way of doing things should be considered. This latter would take into account the requirements of control while preserving the opportunities of transmitting the endogenous know-how. There is in fact a great distance between, on the one hand, the analytical knowledge recognized by the management professionals and the business schools and, on the other hand, the know-how composed of intangible references and tricks of the trade that enables a company to be innovative or quick in its responses, thanks to the mutual understanding in action that links all those involved.

For Cosmophar, finding a solution that marries the strategic with the organizational certainly provides a challenge. Unless it is to become a firm like all the rest and expose itself to the logic of best practice, the updating of its organizational complexity offers the best prospect of building decisive competitive assets. The solution will only be found within the company. If the model of tacit accumulation fails to work, Cosmophar could either adopt an explicit articulation approach, which requires a major revolution of its internal management style and its cognitions, or it might slowly enter a process of increasing codification, which would make it identical to all its competitors and therefore much more vulnerable.

CHAPTER 9

Where Management and Strategy Strengthen One Another

At first sight, new is bad. For the management of a firm the economic battle demands everything and its opposite. Thus at the same time it must extract short-term value and invest for the medium term. No strategic and organizational model allows a company to satisfy at the same time endogenous exploitation and regeneration. Simplicity is as destructive as bureaucracy. Except in business school classrooms, pure models of organization and clear-cut linear ambitions do not often achieve success.

The good news is that complexity works. It is still possible to lead organizations that are complex or hybrid. The management of contradictions is even very efficient. In any circumstance one fundamental condition should be taken into account: it has to occur through the enrichment of the cognitive assets or action language shared by the members of a goal-oriented organization. There is in fact a sounding board that allows management to meet this demand.

9.1 Four Fundamental Guidelines for Managing Complexity

The combat platoon or army commando is often mentioned as the archetype of what a simple organization should look like. The lieutenant in charge lives in very close contact with his men and sets an example by being first in the assault. Polyvalence, flexibility and a high group morale pave the way for excellence. The headquarters defines some mid-term goals and provides an empowerment blueprint to short-term achievers. Basically, action is induced by what happens on the front line.

Bureaucracy serves to illustrate what firms should never be: complicated organizations. In order to bypass the routines and the power games, the hierarchy must show a sharp sense of political tactics and informal inventiveness. The top leaders resembles assembler–integrators. They are at the same time the strategists or architects in charge of a general concept, and site supervisors managing the details on the ground. Or, to change the metaphor, consider the conductor who holds the orchestra together by improvising arrangements without losing as it were the leitmotif of the score.

How is it possible for managers to make major contributions that enrich the cognitive potential of the firm and mobilize it to deal with contradictory policy and management demands? A repertoire of managerial skills exists for that purpose. Composed of four principal actions, it also involves four distinct competencies:

- redrawing the internal frontiers
- destroying the citadels
- fixing the horizons
- disseminating awareness of threats.

9.1.1 Drawing up the Boundaries

Part of the management of the contradictions, and therefore of the complexity, occurs through control of the boundaries. Drawing up the boundaries between jurisdictions leads to configuring the rules at the heart of the organization. An organizational jurisdiction is here understood as investing an operator with both a legitimacy and an obligation in dealing with a functional domain or a limited geographical area. It is at the same time inclusive and exclusive in the sense that it separates two or more operators from one another.

An organization draws a certain advantage from having within it boundaries that demarcate territories within which certain tasks, but not all, are accomplished, and define zones for action, particularly with a view to an evaluation in relation to the results obtained. Size in particular is significant. When a company becomes bigger, specialization becomes functional. Whenever a company follows an exploitation-strategic route, stable, clean and clear-cut boundaries facilitate the distribution of tasks and the measuring of results. The division of work through the procedural process allows costs to be reduced, overlaps and redundancies to be eliminated, and stabilizes quality (Emery and Trist, 1965).

However, there is a price to pay for this type of configuration. Effectively, it tends to generate areas of autonomy. Apathy and egocentrism are exacerbated. People in their own area of jurisdiction withdraw into their own domain, avoid involvement with the business of others and develop peer group patriotism (Crozier, 1963). Separate areas of jurisdiction destroy solidarity, champion localism and impoverish the ability to share common knowledge. Setting boundaries strengthens externalization and rigidity. This destroys the organizational ability to regenerate surpluses and competitive advantages in an endogenous manner. Securing future rents is more difficult and costly. Without a high level of relational cooperation and without sharing common language, the process will never produce good results.

It is therefore one of the responsibilities of management to find a happy medium. When the lines of sharing are defined and drawn up, it is important that the boundaries remain sufficiently porous and the associated jurisdictions sufficiently fuzzy to allow areas to emerge that encourage collective action at the heart of the firm. What is more, the boundaries cannot remain fixed on principle, not for too long. The system of separation must be flexible in order to take account of different challenges that the firm faces and, if necessary, to allow room for growth in the importance of the non-traded sphere of activities and transactions. The boundary that is perhaps the most essential is the one that marks out the traded interfaces or territories and the non-traded ones.

A possible misunderstanding should be explained. The fact that some territories or interfaces are traded does not mean that they must be outsourced beyond the firm. Firms embrace and shelter both traded and untraded areas. Moreover, this confusion makes for tense relationships and sometimes pollutes the dialogue between the R&D department and the other parts of the firm. So long as research is integrated and fits into the cognitive world shared with the rest of the firm, R&D remains an endogenous activity that uses market data received from the operational units in contact with the market to establish its choices and decide its focus of attention. The fact that it is not subjected to the same measurement and evaluation criteria as the other units is something that they find more understandable and acceptable. On the other hand, from the moment that the research becomes purely scientific and concentrates on invention or breakthrough, it escapes from the demands of the market. It immediately becomes an exogenous element, as if it were located outside the firm, like a university research centre to which the firm had subcontracted a particular project, working to a well-defined specification.

The drawing up of the boundaries is in no sense a war game where experts in producing organization charts come together in a war room. It should not be predicated on some principle of formal elegance. The drawing up of the boundaries must be done by the managers in contact with events, not by service departments or consultants. The result does not necessarily have to be fixed forever in written documents. It can perfectly well be amended temporarily and on an ad hoc basis, in order to deal with a particular situation in the space of a moment. This pragmatic flexibility allows compromises to be found when the situation demands an exception without the rule otherwise being changed. It is justified by the gamble that is taken in modifying a pattern that is judged to be obsolete, in order to produce one that is in line with strategic ambitions for the present and for the future. In this sense, the type of boundary – its outline and its relative permeability – or the domain of jurisdiction that a unit is assigned reflects a theory of action for a strategic ambition that the firm adopts for its future. Organizational properties and strategic ambitions have to be compatible in some way.

9.1.2 Destroying the Citadels

A second class of managerial action that allows organizational complexity to be dealt with has the characteristic of what might be called the art and technique of destroying citadels or internal monopolies that have become dysfunctional.

A citadel appears as a monopoly within the organization. Excessive isolation and inward withdrawal shown by a unit are made possible by the fact that the unit occupies a key position in the firm and there is no alternative route allowing it to be bypassed. In other words, a unit controls a key to uncertainty for third parties, if not the whole firm, which allows it to dictate to third parties the conditions for dialogue, the terms of exchange. It gets back from its partners much more than it delivers to them. In other terms it enjoys a position of power. It closes itself off from the world that surrounds it, starting with those units that are the most dependent on it. It develops its own routines, perceptions and interests up to the level of absolute criteria. It dictates its own rules for the cooperation game. It conserves and solidifies.

Reconciling exploitation and regeneration, doing its best to set up provisional trade-offs, cannot remain the task of general management alone. It must be taken on board, relayed and assured through the daily actions of the whole staff, by everyone and at all levels.

In an ideal setting, all individuals in their own way reconcile specialization with opening up. The sales network sells the portfolio of products assigned to it. From the perspective of exploitation neither their production nor their future are its problem. From the viewpoint of regeneration, it is expected that salespeople, apart from collecting information on everything to do with existing products, their use and their customers, should also observe new trends that might be germinating, figure out the development of customer tastes and types of distribution with a broader perspective than that tied to their current portfolio. The sales department is not a fortress belonging only to the salespeople who occupy it, a kind of ghetto for relationships with customers. It is a place of interaction with the market for the future downstream, and with marketing and research upstream.

Knocking down the citadel walls requires extremely close vigilance and sensitivity in action. The best approach is to anticipate their possible appearance and act in a preventive way. That said, the hierarchy does not always know about them. Nevertheless, even if the cost of late or drastic intervention is high, it is justified.

In fact, citadel effects are collectively devastating for an endogenous regeneration. They lead to power rents. They contribute to the break up of cognitive continuity.

At the same time, it would be a mistake to assess the nuisance caused by such a unit without considering the strategic route that top management has chosen with respect to regeneration. Let us here assume that regeneration makes use of an exogenous process, through buying a start-up company, or new income is entrusted to the whims of invention, that is, subcontracted to the non-traded market. In this case, head office may tolerate the fact that, for a more or less lengthy period, citadels raise their drawbridges and focus solely on exploitation. At the same time, by doing so, it only postpones the day of reckoning. Once the new rent or competitive advantage has been exploited, the management will have to sweep away the citadel. Other collateral damage will also occur. Because of the absence of sharing and continuity, other units in the meantime will have also abandoned the game of opening-up and sharing a common language for action. They will have raised their own drawbridges, with the result that they too will have to be prised open and their walls destroyed.

Ghetto thinking is dangerously and rapidly contagious, if a general management turns a blind eye and fails to deal with it quickly. The citadel effect is not a moral problem, the stigmatization of the behaviour of freeloaders who are happy to leave to others the responsibility for ensuring the firm's future survival and success. It is like a cancer whose metastases weaken the collective fabric and the capacity for complexity, and which in the end kill not only the inhabitants of the citadel but also those of all the surrounding territories.

9.1.3 Fixing the Horizons

A third action concerns the fixing of horizons. In this case management entails controlling complexity by establishing definitions and deadlines in time and space in relation to which the firm operates as an organization. Managers are controllers of the clocks, adapting schedules and the allocated time periods according to the ambitions and constraints that they impose on themselves.

The scale and content of activities or interactions that are run by administrative criteria inside the firm vary over time. The same goes for the time and space of the traded elements, of the exchanges that are settled under quasi-market conditions. It is therefore difficult to imagine or accept that the administrative or bureaucratic sphere has no limit, so that a unit assigned to invention, for example, remains non-trading for the whole of its existence. Long time horizons are not insignificant dimensions for establishing a translation of strategic ambitions and for promoting collective learning and creativity.

On the other hand, infinite horizons, ambitions without time and space limits, are dysfunctional. In fact, both time and space horizons provide the legitimacy and keys for head office and the operational units to govern situations of dynamic conflict. They set the deadlines, they spell out the obligations to find solutions, while encouraging broad and involved participation from the players. The conflict processes become dynamic and even functional. Norms set moral duties and limits about how far one is allowed to go in not communicating to others or not caring about collective implications. The centre of the firm, using the monopoly of formal authority, formulates discretionary orders that are legitimate. The civilization of conflict is a major mechanism of management in the hands of any head office.

The general management of a firm controls the game, its process and content, by defining its time scale and by prescribing its boundaries. For the rest, it largely leaves the players to their exchanges and their confrontations. The hybrid character of the process of exploitation–regeneration allows the establishment of flexible arbitration and methods of allocating resources that belong to the art of fine-tuning. It is precisely head office's capacity for mastering this art that governs whether or not compromises turn out to be acceptable.

Quasi-marketized approaches to organizational management do not mean the decline of principles such as domination and authority. The reverse is true. Administrative or bureaucratic models show persistently more tolerance toward behaviours that soften hierarchic pressure and discard action constraints. Planning and programming techniques used in this perspective are rather sophisticated paper work, laying down precise deadlines for each unit. But in fact head office has no real muscle in terms of power to get them implemented. In quasi-market types of organization, head office is less a memorandum producer and more a clock manager. Performance-based appraisal of action raises individualism, while setting references such as shared time horizons may enhance behavioural and cognitive abilities to cooperate and act as a team. The maximum of pressure is therefore put on the staff, as individuals as well as a community.

9.1.4 The Role of Threats

A fourth and final key for the management of complexity is provided by recourse to threats.

The endogenous coupling of exploitation and regeneration requires a permanent culture of commitment to be interiorized by the staff and the parts of the organization. Nothing is taken as read or for granted. Success means that one must do even better. This prompts not arrogance but modesty.

Two conditions are vital for this culture. The commitment must be shared upstream and downstream and from top to bottom, which implies that it is generalized. In addition, it feeds on the perception and expression of threats. Their management assumes that, in order to be credible, such threats have to be not only perceptible but also reasonable. Threats that make no sense have no consequences, except for those who emit them. They lose credibility.

The context of hypercompetition gives a good illustration of the disadvantages that arrogance and a feeling or superiority bring with them for firms and their managements. Keeping the operational units at a distance – that is, sending them a message that they are inferior – and allowing so-called high flying young managers to believe that they are superior simply by virtue of their qualifications and their rank, are two among a long list of examples of the way that ambition becomes dulled and success devalued in the social body of the firm.

A consciousness of fragility and vulnerability implies that a sentiment of threat is present. Recourse to the collective is therefore accepted as necessary and taking the path of effort is seen as inevitable. Sociology and history are full of examples of firms that, having economic rents that they prefer to buy rather than produce themselves, end up by declining and becoming marginalized. Similarly, so long as an organization externalizes its operational costs and gets paid by third parties (the customer or the state), so long as staff and managers have the feeling of being protected from any danger, the door is open to the encouragement of an outbreak of immobility, complacency and rejection of the new. One of the lessons of hypercompetition is precisely that in the interests of its survival the firm should challenge its competitive advantages even though they may appear to be at the peak of their capacity to supply monopolistic rent.

One feature of threats deserves close attention: their audibility.

In an exogenous strategy of regeneration, the threat may be individual, targeted at a unit or a person, and internal, for example through competition between units or people. Regeneration occurs through crisis, a major organizational change or a policy redefinition happening every five or ten years. In such a case no learning is required since the renewal is imported in the form of complete kits from outside. No threat of a collective nature is ever audible as such to the staff and business units in an organizational model that favours individualism. The collective dimension, the fact that the organizational community as such is in jeopardy, remains an issue or a stake that concerns general management or the single proprietor. To a certain extent, the main perceived and audible threats are internal, starting with one's closest neighbour in the firm.

In an endogenous process, the nature of an audible threat is necessarily collective and external. The firm progresses via incremental and successive breakthroughs accompanied by periods of learning that extend over long periods. Beyond what is individual, the effective threat is directed towards the collective so that each person understands that his or her future is linked to the common effort.

9.2 Management, Firms and Competition

Opting for decentralization does not reduce the function of a general management. If the tasks are transferred to the business units, if the staff of head office is reduced, decentralization coincides with a remarkable increase in the responsibilities of managers. A glance at the points made earlier in this chapter should convince the reader of this.

Taking ownership of the cognitive is not in itself a new idea. At most one might think that the somewhat hysterical pressure of the past few years that has made short-term performance attractive has obscured the fact that this ownership has been current for a long time. Moreover, firms in the past practised cognitive management without knowing it or without being aware of doing so, particularly through tacit accumulation. The difficulty in making explicit what one does can be accounted for by the cultural growth of so-called scientific management models, by the pretentiousness of gurus and academics who offer simple, all-purpose solutions. It is also true that hybridization and compromise are difficult acts and skills to visualize.

Cognitive management allows one to re-examine the question of general management in firms. It is not simply a hierarchical artefact. The authority of the top sometimes seems like a framework with no content, especially when firms adopt radical principles of decentralization according to a binary system such as the head office–business units structure. Experience shows that this appearance is far from the truth. A headquarters is much more than the highest floor of a pyramid, one among many layers of a whole. It is a centre, which implies that it has a monopoly on something crucial and that a periphery exists which depends upon its domination. Cognitive management validates another aspect of general management's legitimacy: an institutional facet. How does one describe a centre?

- First, head office defines the agenda for the organization. In other words, it sets out preferences, solves problems, and fixes the priorities and methods of doing things.
- Second, head office represents authority. It constructs asymmetrical interactions and statuses in terms of hierarchical relationships, establishes the content of legitimacy and mobilizes the forms of control.
- Third, head office also has a monopoly: it is the only centre. No other part may act as such.
- Fourth, as the centre, it institutionalizes and dominates a periphery normatively and cognitively. Within an organization an empirically identifiable zone called the centre creates and structures a set of units and staff that may be called the periphery. Head office incorporates them into a collective framework that transcends and transforms their concrete and particular existence (Shils, 1975). The centre is a consensus source that is relatively consensual. For this reason it carries collectively shared values while also producing systems for interpreting the outside world and action. It therefore provides a major source of institutionalization and allocation of direction.
- The centre moreover integrates heterogeneities and pacifies conflicts. It ensures a civilization function – commonalities – and produces foresight – stability and trust. It controls the how-to approach and handles order and action. It includes and excludes people, know-how, events, and other elements.

Such a reminder may seem useless since it appears so obvious, and anachronistic since it appears to swim against the tide of current management language. According to many seasoned writers and practitioners, firms are supposed to enter a new era called post-bureaucratic or post-modernist; soft domination techniques offer substitutes for old command and control processes, and networks perform better than hierarchies. Is it reasonable to think that the functions listed earlier, which present a robot portrait of an all-knowing centre, oppressive and heavy, are compatible with the imperatives of flexibility, simplicity and decentralization? Does there still need to be a centre when firms increasingly incorporate their activities and their personnel through transactional or quasi-market mechanisms?

Despite the shrinking of hierarchical lines, despite the adoption of economic criteria for judging performance, and despite the need to have an ear to the ground, the function of the centre is not on its way out. Quite the contrary, its future remains assured, even if there are weaknesses, and new methods of practice are appearing that are concerned with it.

These weaknesses appear in different ways. Executive teams are experiencing a quite dramatic growth in the turnover of their members. Many are fired and others experience burn-out pathologies. It is not enough for teams to raise the profile of their members, even by attracting managers from more elitist educational backgrounds. Head office is isolated from the rest of the organization. The setting of directions and resolving of conflicts are entrusted to external consultants and to magic procedures. These however only make more obscure the ambitions proclaimed by head office, and reinforce the sense of arbitrariness that those at the bottom feel about these choices, despite the fact that hyper competition requires the centre to become accountable more than ever for the content of the cognitive systems mobilized by the operational units.

One excuse often given by top managers is that there is not enough time for them to address such issues. In their opinion, languages for action are constructs produced by human collectives that reflect the heritage of the past. They therefore appear as fixed objects whose content in the short term it is hardly possible to change.

Such a view is more an easy excuse than a correct empirical statement. On the contrary, under certain conditions cognitive systems can be amended or reoriented through voluntary choices and concrete actions generated by head office. So far as the cognitive management of organizations is concerned, there is definitely a competence that is an essential ingredient of competitive ability. This competence flows largely from a position adopted by the centre, namely that of ensuring the interface between the environment and the frontier of the firm. Its mission is to make two distinct systems compatible: the market and the organization. Intellectually, the fact seems to be accepted. In reality, there is much greater confusion in the matter.

It is sometimes recommended that, in any case, whether the chosen strategic positioning be exploitation or innovation, recourse to methods of internal management that are inspired by the market should take precedence from the point of view of survival and effectiveness. We can see this view at work in the various procedures and techniques that support the relationships between the downstream departments and those upstream in open and competitive transactions concerning internal pricing structures or the choice of suppliers. It is also supported by those who liken the head office to a shareholder managing a portfolio of independent investments, with each subsidiary or strategic business unit representing a line of this portfolio. A third example is the set of procedures that essentially appraise if not remunerate executives according to short-term financial performance criteria. The firm is seen as a quasi-market that could be governed like the market.

By reducing the firm to the market, that is, confusing the interior with the exterior, such an approach makes a mistake. It pours scorn on Darwinism, that is, on what constitutes the dynamic of selecting the best or the most capable. There are in fact two perspectives of the processes of selection through competition, visions that are radically different. One is neo-liberal; the other relates to the community.

From the neo-liberal standpoint, the market is seen as a place for the confrontation of individual players. This individual confronts those individuals. The evolution process selects the best, the most capable or the most suitable, having regard for the environment in which they are situated.

As a result, the firm as such occupies a transitory status as soon as it comes to explaining the action and anticipating the dynamic of the economic competition. It is in the final analysis reduced to a temporary collection of resources (financial, human, etc.). Such resources are subjected to the same type of competition at their heart as that which is current on the outside. If the environment is carried along by a strong dynamic of change, the life of the firm is akin to what might describe as a biological system. It consists of breaks and discontinuities; it is punctuated with explosions and partial reconstructions. Evolution is marked by imposed mergers, bankruptcies, take-over bids, brutal changes of management, and the like. In short, only two strategic factors count: on the one hand, the volume of financial resources possessed by the competitors, and on the other hand, the capacity for acquisition that these funds provide them with.

The organizational configuration referred to earlier as the mercenary model, which belongs to the exploitation paradigms, implies that there is a market Darwinism that might be found within the firm. It postulates the supremacy of the individual human capital juxtaposed to the collective organizational capital. It relates to the dominance of the exogenous over the endogenous.

As a consequence it is based on two rejections. On the one hand it refuses to allow complexities to exist, because any complexity would by nature cause inefficiency and a loss of profit. On the other hand it is hostile towards the value of testing processes of trial and error, because methods that are fed by the duplication and overlap of organizational situations, even by surplus of resources, would themselves prejudice effectiveness. In addition, it advocates the shrinkage of the non-traded or bureaucratically run sphere of interaction and interdependence which, in essence, cannot be governed by the mechanisms of the market.

The consequence of this approach is clear. Management is reduced to the art of shortening the cognitive links, using rules and putting the emphasis on control. In short, it reduces the objectives of collective activity to a juxtaposition of individual objectives that are disjointed, quantifiable, financial and short term.

Comparing the processes of growth and the generation of rents in firms provides an example of this type of approach. A competitive advantage or a monopolistic rent is a consequence of an asset, whether it be human, physical, tangible or intangible, that for a variable amount of time shelters the firm from the competition. These rents may be created in an endogenous or an exogenous way. Endogenous creation suggests a process of test, trial and error and the accumulation of knowledge, requiring continuity and cooperation. The exogenous appropriation of rents that are largely from the domain of the tangible is by contrast based on a process of rupture, possibly of symbolic or social violence, because the new rent, not being the outcome of the culture of the firm, can find itself incompatible with this cultural background.

A communitarian reading of economic competition, for its part, shows up the fact that the struggle for survival between firms brings into conflict not only individual players but also collective players, or more specifically organizations. It is as though two worlds fashioned in a different way were co-existing. The competition would be the specific and fundamental fact on the outside of the organization, that is, the market. Solidarity and cooperation would rule the interior of the firm, namely the organization. Internal aggressiveness would therefore be focused on the exterior. The market would represent an exogenous type of phenomenon. For its part, the firm's response to the market would be the result of an endogenous process.

This type of approach ties in with the now classic analyses in the field (Coase, 1937; Arrow, 1974; Williamson, 1975). The limits to the dynamic of the market suggest that the organization methods of firms are based on hierarchies and on communities. In fact the price mechanism has serious deficiencies. Such is the case in a situation of uncertainty, when ignorance of the future reaches a high level, when the preferences of the decision makers are ambiguous, when external events affect incomplete contracts, or again when information is inadequate, implying heavy transaction costs and permanent negotiation. Arrow makes the point of emphasizing that, in the traditional market scheme, there is little need for information. The individual must know what he or she wants. The employee has to satisfy a selfish constraint, which is to get an income, without having to consider the social consequences of his or her own choices. Now, from the point of view of efficiency and justice, something more than the market is needed in order to control the allocation of resources. This is also the implication of Nash's theory of the equilibrium of joint benefits (Nash, 1950). The maximization of joint benefits and attempts to beat the market mechanism call for a method of sharing that is not resolved through a simple market mechanism (hence the role of threats or the existence of lateral payments).

9.3 Some Brief Theoretical Implications

By emphasizing the organizational character of the firm in this way it is at the same time possible to become aware of the economic status held by a language for action. Managing a firm like a cognitive community helps to ensure the link between, on the one hand, the competition or the strategy in the market and, on the other hand, the conduct of the members of the firm or the management of their internal interdependencies. In the medium term, the challenge facing head office is to get away from any passively made choices and those imposed from outside the firm. The key to survival is to question permanently the basis for success and the foundations of compatibility with the environment. While the firm is itself subjected to this questioning, the latter can also be applied proactively through the exercise of anticipation.

Theories of endogenous growth developed by the economic sciences have meant a major break with a number of theories of equilibrium. In fact, they have irreversibly challenged the belief in the advantages of decreasing marginal productivity and constantly increasing output. This criticism is based on the observation that the accumulation of knowledge and know-how that goes on in a human collective is not subject to the law of decreasing marginal productivity and consequently the gap between firms, regions or countries can increase, not decrease.

Another major scientific discovery in this regard is that the more a cognitive system is enriched, the more its capacity to manage complexity is improved and the more trust becomes a decisive ingredient in the relationships and interfaces between the members that go to make it up. 'What appeals to the imagination is the internal organization' (Coase, 1937).

The differentiation and its renewal that the centre seeks to encourage in the market are not easily obtained on a permanent basis through solutions coming from outside and imported as they stand into the heart of the firm. The latent process of copying that forms part of seeking out the best third party practice, apart from posing problems of cultural integration that in themselves are not easy to manage, drives firms to converge on similar procedures and products. Such is the case of recourse to free-rider behaviour and the practice of hostile raids on other firms. The result is that this limits the possibilities for real differentiation between them.

For a head office, acting differently from competitors means that it accepts *ipso facto* that it must build and manage organizational, and therefore cognitive, complexity at the heart of its company. While the complexity is indisputably a source of costs, it is also the most fruitful vector for generating and making available to the firm intangible capacities that competitors find it difficult to identify and replicate. In this sense, organizational complexity is the foundation of the solidity and permanence of competitive advantages. Cognitive and organizational predation are averted.

In such a case, the actual learning is a social and active process at the heart of organization; it is not individual and passive. The most important asset, which forms the added value of management, lies neither in explicit rules and formal procedures nor in financial incentives or psychological inducements addressed to people individually. Organizational complexity creates rents and competitive advantages because the firm possesses a capacity for cooperating in the face of the uncertain and therefore innovating at the right time. But this capacity remains largely tacit and implicit. It acts as the nourishing soup for intuition, judgement, expertise, common sense: all the activities and know-how that a cognitive community uses when confronting the apparent chaos of everyday work.

While shared languages, common codes or common knowledge appear to be essential solutions for the management of complexity and uncertainty and for obtaining and transmitting relevant information, they do in turn pose two problems: the time necessary for common learning and the mutual trust without which the learning cannot develop.

Trust provides an indispensable ingredient for the endogenous. It permits a reduction in the costs associated with internal coordination and vertical integration: agency costs, influence and persuasion costs. Trust finally allows the development of the capacity to reconcile two methods of management that *a priori* are not very compatible, such as a very close integration of the firm with its suppliers and the adoption of a quasi-market approach within the firm (Fukuyama, 1995). It also facilitates conciliation, something never assured but always essential, and for which head office must take responsibility between the short term and the medium term, between exploitation and innovation, and between the competitive advantages of today and the monopolistic rents of tomorrow.

Complexity, trust and imagination are hard to manage through a market system; they relate to administrative approaches. But the non-traded approach consists of quite specific dimensions that are not easily formalized and are not generally recognized as rational or capable of being reduced to techniques for management manuals. It is made up of history, tradition, common experience, the implicit and the unspoken. In a certain sense, it is something priceless. Continuity, identity, loyalty – everything that goes to make innovation and flexibility, which in other terms allows economies in the costs of internal and external transactions – can only be located outside the sphere of the traded. How the boundaries between market and hierarchy logics of action are drawn and define what the territory is furnished with, from that moment becomes an essential act and competency.

However, adopting a non-traded logic of action and interaction does not mean that the organization isolates itself or even refuses to have a relationship with the market. It means something quite different. The procedure involves standing back from the traded logic of action for a reasonably long time. This establishes a distance from the markets as they operate at a given moment, in the knowledge that they are economic spaces that evolve and that anticipation of the market leads one not to accept short-term signals and requirements as the sole empirical truth criterion.

At the same time, the administrative logic of action and interaction must be linked to the ultimate changes of this market, to the weak signals that can only be perceived through contact with the ground and cannot reach the top management of firms unless there is shared cognition. It must consequently be strongly connected to the developments that, as things go along, structure the economic stability. In no sense does the non-traded status constitute a guaranteed income or a perpetual protection that would allow the organizational units and staff who benefit from it to feel free from any constraint at all.

How to Observe and Analyse Action Languages

Languages for action as cognitive frameworks are not as such immediately visible and identifiable in an organization. To identify their existence and content specific events have to be studied and data have to be collected. Languages surround the actions and non-actions at the heart of the firm. They express themselves through their effects on the content of the decisions and choices made daily by the individuals, groups and departments in the setting where their tasks are carried out. This implies to a large extent the adoption of an inductive analytic approach.

Languages for action are not mere words, rhetorical artefacts or discourses. In other terms they cannot be detected by just listening to verbal expressions, for instance, to what individuals say about what is or should be done how, when and why. Most of the time what people say, as recorded by interviewers, does not describe in an accurate or unbiased way the actual behaviours adopted in specific contexts or situations. Cross-checking, which could imply interviewing other actors who take part in the same events, shadowing or observing behaviours as they happen on the spot, or going back to written sources such as files, is always necessary.

What people say about organizational matters nevertheless makes sense. In other terms, words about behaviours and narrations of decisions have to be taken seriously. People as such do not lie or talk randomly. They have good reasons to express what they do and why they do it. They also talk about other persons in the organization, and the relationships they experience, in a specific way. Instead of simply describing, they use a register of expressions that are emotional, loaded with judgements and feelings, such as 'I like my boss – she is a nice person', or 'It is not so easy to do that task'. Verbal descriptions also are a rather good proxy for studying norms and cultural schemes in an organization. But to track cognitive constructs in acts requires something different.

Concrete behaviours are linked to cognitive references in an indirect or rather implicit way. What the players say about why and how they do what they do is one thing, and why and how they really think and reason about what they do may be something else, depending on the circumstances. The relationship between cognitive languages and behaviours is not necessarily direct or causal. Hence the prudence shown by observers when they are exposed to the rationale that a player puts forward. We can assume it is convenient to relax somewhat the premise of internal coherence between what is done and why it is done; sometimes action content and action elaboration do not fit together. On the other hand, if each of these two phenomena produces consequences for the firm, it is a foregone conclusion that actions generally, with a few exceptions, produce chain effects that are more immediately of consequence for the firm.

For analytic purposes, we may consider decisions, acts and choices in their behavioural substance as implementing ways of reasoning, knowing and interpreting. The players who make the choices (or the context in which it occurs) are considered to carry them, whether or not they are conscious of this and whether or not they intend to.

It can be assumed that these cognitive systems are not due to chance, as if drawn from a lottery. They can be linked to several factors: instrumental procedures, norms decreed by professional bodies (chartered accountants, management controllers), and the distinctive characteristics of cultural communities, among others. They can also be produced and modified by day-to-day processes of organizational operation and by relational dynamics of networking or socialization in the firm.

They are understandable as theories in use that the decision maker employs in a broadly implicit way, along the lines of 'that can be taken as read, no need to spell it out or to justify it'. It is also accepted that, in a precise context, there are alternatives available that the player may forget.

The work of the analyst is to reconstruct their dimensions, particularly but not exclusively from the following angles:

■ The vision of the world that the players carry with them, the signals and types of parameter that they consider relevant and worthy of attention.
■ The criteria that form the basis of the choices that the players make.
■ The causality relationships that link one parameter to another.
■ The representations of the world and of the action in this world that they imply.
■ The status that the players attribute implicitly and in reality to relevant phenomena for the future of the firm.

A good way for the analyst or observer to characterize the methods of reasoning and the cognitive references that the players implement is to reveal the consequences that such languages have for the organization to which they belong, and in particular for its positioning *vis-à-vis* the market, the competition and customers. The cognitive systems also draw up as many specific models that are both economic and organizational.

The most fruitful angle for reconstructing such interpretation systems in use is provided by situations of interdependence that are as much vertical (the hierarchy of authority) as transversal (between upstream and downstream in the firm). One very simple but fruitful way is to watch them when languages for action emerge, when they are enacted empirically, more precisely in relation to items or issues that matter for the actors and for the performance of the firm. It is revealing, for example, to observe transactions between two business units or to study the allocation of financial resources or grants made by the headquarters to business units.

Thus, in the case of the Agro company discussed earlier in the book, an approach comprising two different facets was set up to observe items and events that lie at the heart of the organization, just as in experimental physics a body is bombarded from different angles in order to study its core properties.

On the one hand, the organization was studied from a vertical perspective. This considered the authority relationships and the way asymmetric interdependence is handled between the centre and the periphery as they connect through management's decisions throughout a chain of seven hierarchical grades, from the CEO of the company to the middle managers working in contact with the external environment. An issue that was constructive for the firm and significant for the various grades under observation was chosen. This concerned the decisional acts involved in the renewal of the product ranges.

On the other hand, a horizontal study was made of the interactions and exchanges between downstream and upstream. This shed more light on the transversal interfaces, from research departments to sales networks. In this case, the issue under inquiry related to the development process for three new molecules, from their discovery up to their placement on the market by the company. Here again, the objective is to observe minutely the behaviours that are adopted daily in the conduct of operations to implement the positioning of the firm in the marketplace.

Finding a location for systems of shared understanding involves the observation of realities that are more or less common to the various players. Are there parameters and criteria that have a collective status, that are shared by all members and parts of the organization, and others that are not?

Evidence of common knowledge or shared languages for action relates to the finding of similar kinds of corridors of action in use by more than one actor or unit. A corridor of action becomes apparent through the fact that the participants know what they must do when faced with certain situations, and they adopt an identical understanding of each other's capacities and limitations. For example, A will know what the limits are to the options that B can exercise. Correspondingly, B will know the same with regard to A. In other words, A and B have no illusions about the space and time for action. Empirically speaking this is usually manifest by the fact that partners in interfaces and interdependencies express feelings of mutual trust. This verbal trust may be ascertained and analytically grounded by observing a number of events and ways of managing interdependence: methods of coordination and cooperation, handling of differences of interests, and so on. It also ensures the creation of a world and sense of transparency. Trust and transparency appear to the eye as sequenced phenomena, not as polite discussions held in front of third parties. They are forged in stages, through trial and error. They may therefore be seen at work daily. They also refer to the fields of action, that is, to the processes of negotiation between players that ensure that their field of action and dependence *vis-à-vis* third parties becomes acceptable for each of them.

A programme turns this analytical framework into a set of information that needs to be assembled from observation:

- *The elements on which head office relies in order to build its relationship with the operational units and service departments*. In particular, the key points it brings to bear on this, the ways in which it obtains the diffused information, the intermediaries and support that it activates (networks, etc.), its recourse to shared identity constructs.
- *The way in which the units share information between themselves and head office*. In particular, the methods of communication used, the types of cooperation or non-cooperation that exist, the handling of events considered to be key moments, together with their meaning and their method of construction, the circles of trust that go to make it up.
- *The capacity of head office to have its language or cognitive framework understood by the units*. In particular, the processes and vehicles used, the types of adoption by the units, their method of selection and interpretation, as well as head office's treatment of the unexpected, the unforeseen, and of exceptional or abnormal situations.
- The monitoring of the evolution and change development of the socio-economic environment (market, competition, societal transformations) by head office and by the units. Notably with regard to the transverse

aspects that have a collective impact on the firm. In particular, the events that engage attention, their consequences for established routines, the factors that make understanding credible, the areas of ignorance that may exist.

■ *The evaluation of the performance of units by head office*. In particular, through the identification of the criteria used, their origin and their definition, their method of application, their consequences, their link with the policy announced by head office.

The technique of in-depth interviewing provided a privileged source of information gathering. Thus at Agro, 19 people were questioned, of whom eight were seen twice or even three times. The fact of seeing certain managerial executives twice, as much in head office as in their units, allowed questions to be focused much more closely on particular phenomena and to test the validity of some of our interpretations. Two dimensions of understanding were particularly enhanced on these occasions: first, how situations of choice that connect systems of action, interests and potentially contradictory interdependencies are dealt with, and second, identifying the areas of crossbred and mutual knowledge, areas that are the source of situations and schemas of spontaneous trust.

In addition, an abundance of written documentary material was collected with the aim of validating the sequence of events (notably through the positions adopted by the various players and the agreements or decisions taken) and establishing the impact of the references adopted for the action. This written material was especially significant in following the developmental processes of new molecules from the phase of fundamental research right up to commercialization, such processes extending over periods as long as six to eight years.

Distribution of Functions Between Head Office and Units within Agro

Head office	Supreme decisions
(Cost centre)	Strategy Choice of performance indicators Systems of audit and control Appointment of heads of commercial subsidiaries
Service units for the operational units	**Benchmarked services**
Cost(s) centres negotiated annually and possibility of outsourcing	Innovation Finance Legal affairs Human resources
Operational units, country unit and Active Ingredients Group	**Supreme decisions**
(Units subject to EVA)	National development Technical positioning by country Marketing positioning by country Investments by country (under 1 million euros) Interfaces with certification departments Formulation of active ingredients Human resources by country Commercial policy Interfaces with customers Promotion and publicity

Simplified Organisation Chart of AIG

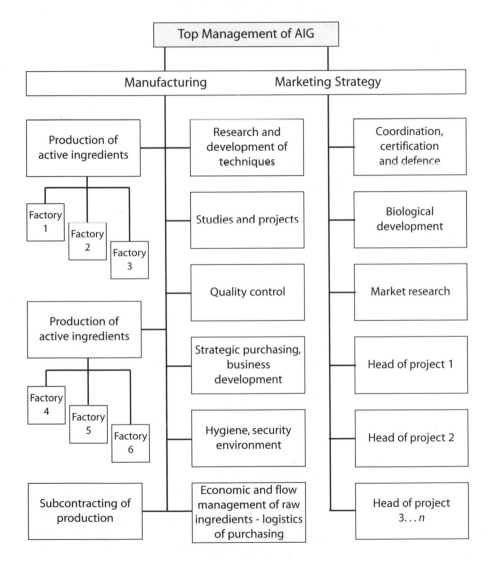

The AIG is a unit of the Agro company that is managed jointly by two people. They are responsible for a single trading account. The AIG reports to general management. The unit head who looks after the manufacturing side reports to the assistant director general who is responsible for the whole of the manufacturing sector of the firm. The other head, who looks after marketing and strategy, reports to an assistant director general responsible for these functions in all sectors and, apart from active ingredients, for all the activities of all the units. The AIG employs about 75 managers and executives.

BIBLIOGRAPHY

Aldrich, H. (1999) *Organizations Evolving*. London: Sage.

Arrow K.J. (1974) *The Limits of Organization*. New York: W. W. Norton.

Baumard P. (1994) *Tacit Knowledge in Organizations*. London: Sage.

Becker H.S. (1982) *Art Worlds*. Berkeley, Calif.: University of California Press.

Beuzit P. (1999) *La Recherche au Coeur de la Stratégie de la Firme: L'Exemple de Renault*. Paris: École de Paris.

Blumer H. (1969) *Symbolic Interactionism*. Berkeley, Calif.: University of California Press.

Burgelman R.A. (1991) Intraorganizational ecology of strategy making and organizational adaptation. Theory and field research 1. Stanford Graduate School of Business, Research Paper 1122.

Burt R. (1992) *Structural Holes: The Social Structure of Competition*. Cambridge, Mass.: Harvard University Press.

Burt R., R. Hogarth and C. Michaud (2000) The social capital of French and American managers. *Organization Science* (2): 123–47.

Coase R.H. (1937) The nature of the firm. *Economica* (4): 306–405.

Cohen M., J. March and J. Olsen (1972) A garbage can model of organizational choice. *Administrative Science Quarterly* 17 (1): 1–25.

Courpasson D. (1999) *L'Action Contrainte*. Paris: Presses Universitaires de France.

Crozier M. (1963) *The Bureaucratic Phenomenon*. Chicago, Ill.: University of Chicago Press.

Crozier M. and E. Friedberg (1977) *L'Acteur et le Système*. Paris: Le Seuil (translated (1980) as *The Actor and the System*, Chicago, Ill.: University of Chicago Press.)

Daft R.L. and K. Weick (1984) Toward a model of organizations as interpretive systems. *Academy of Management Review* (9): 43–66.

D'Aveni R. (1994) *Hypercompetition*. Glencoe: Free Press.

Drucker P.F. (1994) The theory of business. *Harvard Business Review* (5): 95–104.

Duhaime I.D. and C.R. Schwenk (1985) Conjectures on cognitive simplification in acquisition and divestment decision making. *Academy of Management Review* (10): 287–95.

Dupuy F. (1999) *The Customer's Victory*. London: Sage.

Dupuy F. and Thoenig J.C. (1986) *La Loi du Marché*. Paris: L'Harmattan.

Dutton J.E. and J.E. Jackson (1987) Categorizing strategic issues: links to organizational action. *Academy of Management Review* (12): 76–90.

Eden C. and J.C. Spender (eds) (1998) *Managerial and Organizational Cognition*. London: Sage.

Emery F.E. and E.L. Trist (1965) The causal texture of organizational environments. *Human Relations*, (18): 21–31.

Fukuyama F. (1995) *Trust: The Social Virtues and the Creation of Prosperity*. London: Hamish Hamilton.

Gioia D.A. and J.B. Thomas (1996) Identity, image, and issue interpretation: sense-making during strategic change in academia. *Administrative Science Quarterly* (41): 370–403.

Goshal S., C. Bartlett and P. Moran (1999) A new manifest for management. *Sloan Management Review* (3): 9–20.

Hannan M. and J. Freeman (1989) *Organizational Ecology*. Cambridge, Mass.: Harvard University Press.

Heiner R. (1983) The origin of predictable behavior. *American Economic Review* (8): 560–95.

Hogarth R., J.L. Mery and C. Michaud (1980) Decision behavior in urban development: a methodological approach and substantive consideration. *Acta Psychologica* (45): 95–117.

Jacobs J. (1969) *The Economy of Cities*. New York: Random House.

Kim C. and R. Mauborgne (1999) Strategy value innovation and the knowledge economy. *Sloan Management Review* (3): 41–53.

Landau M. (1969) Redundancy, rationality, and the problem of duplication and overlap. *Public Administration Review* (29): 346–58.

Mason R.D. and I.I. Mitroff (1981) *Challenging Strategic Planning Assumptions*. New York: Wiley.

Meindl J.R., C. Stubbart and J.F. Porac (eds) (1996) *Cognitions Within and Between Organizations*. London: Sage.

Michaud C. (1994) Potentialités de changement et de développement des entreprises du canton de Neuchâtel. *Études sur les core competences*. Conseil Suisse de la Science, Berne.

Moss Kanter R. (1997) *When Giants Learn to Dance*. Cambridge, Mass.: Harvard University Press.

Nash J.F. Jr. (1950) The bargaining problem. *Econometrica* (18): 155–62.

Nelson R. and S. Winter (1982) *An Evolutionary Theory of Economic Change*. Cambridge, Mass.: Harvard University Press.

Paradeise C. (1998) Pilotage institutionnel et argumentation: le cas du département SHS du CNRS. In A. Borzeix *et al.* (eds), *Sociologie et Connaissance: Nouvelles Approches Cognitives*, pp. 205–28. Paris: CNRS Éditions

Peters T.J. and R.H. Waterman Jr.. (1982) *In Search of Excellence*. New York: Harper and Row.

Pfeffer J. (1981) Management as symbolic action: the creation and maintenance of organizational paradigms. *Research in Organizational Behaviour* (3): 1–52.

Piore M.J. and C. Sabel (1984) *The Second Industrial Divide: Possibilities for Prosperity*. New York: Basic Books.

Powell W.W. (1987) Hybrid organizational arrangements: new forms or transitional development? *California Management Review* (1): 67–87.

Prahalad C.K. and R.A. Bettis (1986) The dominant logic: a new linkage between diversity and performance. *Strategic Management Journal* (6): 484–501.

Raghavendra R.P. (1995) Efficient markets in the presence of an 'irrational' investor: the case of the INSEAD ball ticket market. Fontainebleau: INSEAD Working Paper 95/66/FIN/EPS.

Salais R. and M. Storper (1993) *Les Mondes de Production: Enquête sur l'Identité Économique de la France*. Paris: Éditions de l'EHESS.

Salancik G.R. and J.R. Meindl (1984) Corporate attribution as strategic illusion of management control. *Administrative Science Quarterly* (24): 238–54.

Schumpeter J. (1942) *Capitalism, Socialism and Democracy*. New York: Harper.

Schumpeter J. (1967) *History of Economic Analysis*. London: George Allen and Unwin.

Schwenk C. (1988) The cognitive perspective on strategic decision-making. *Journal of Management Studies* (25), 41–55.

Shils E. (1975) *Center and Periphery*. Chicago, Ill.: University of Chicago Press.

Simon H. (1957*)* *Administrative Behaviour*. New York: Free Press.

Staw B.M., P.I. McKechnie and S.M. Duffer (1983) The justification of organizational performance. *Administrative Science Quarterly* (28): 582–600.

Taylor F. (1947) *Scientific Management*. New York: Harper.

Thoenig J.C. (1998) How far is a sociology of organizations still needed? *Organization Studies* (2): 307–20.

Thom R. (1991) *Prédire n'est pas Expliquer*. Paris: Eshel.

Thomas J.B. and R.R. McDaniel Jr. (1990) Interpreting strategic issues: effects of strategy and top management team information processing structure. *Academy of Management Journal* (33): 286–306.

Tichy N. (1999) The teachable point of view: a primer. *Harvard Business Review* (3): 82–3.

Vincent J.D. (1996) *La Chair et le Diable*. Paris: Odile Jacob.

Williamson O. (1975) *Markets and Hierarchy: An Analysis and Anti-trust Implications*. New York: Free Press.

Zajac E.J. and M.M. Bazerman (1991) Blind spots in industry and competitor analysis: implications of interfirm (mis)perceptions for strategic decisions. *Academy of Management Review* (16): 37–56.

Zollo M. and S.G. Winter (1999) From organizational routines to dynamic capabilities. Fontainebleau: INSEAD Working Paper 99/48/SM.

INDEX